Making Babies, Making Families

Other Works by Mary Lyndon Shanley

Feminism, Marriage, and the Law in Victorian England

Feminist Interpretations and Political Theory
(edited with Carole Pateman)

Reconstructing Political Theory
(edited with Uma Narayan)

Mary Lyndon Shanley

Making Babies, Making Families

What Matters Most in an Age of Reproductive Technologies, Surrogacy, Adoption, and Same-Sex and Unwed Parents

BEACON PRESS | *Boston*

Beacon Press
25 Beacon Street
Boston, Massachusetts 02108-2892
www.beacon.org

Beacon Press books
are published under the auspices of
the Unitarian Universalist Association of Congregations.

06 05 04 03 02 01   8 7 6 5 4 3 2 1

This book is printed on acid-free paper that meets the uncoated
paper ANSI/NISO specifications for permanence as revised in 1992.

Composition by Wilsted & Taylor Publishing Services

LIBRARY OF CONGRESS CATALOGING-IN-PUBLICATION DATA
Shanley, Mary Lyndon.
Making babies, making families : what matters most in an age of
reproductive technologies, surrogacy, adoption, and same-sex and unwed
parents / Mary Lyndon Shanley.
p.   cm.
Includes bibliographical references.
ISBN 0-8070-4408-3 (hardcover : alk. paper)
1. Family—United States.   2. Family policy—United States.   3.
Domestic relations—United States.   4. Parents—Legal status, laws,
etc.—United States.   5. Human reproductive technology—Law and
legislation—United States.   6. Adoption—Law and legislation—United
States.   I. Title.
HQ536 .S4816 2001
306.85'0973—dc21   00-012727

For Fred
and for our children,
Katherine and Anthony

Contents

Preface

*I*n the summer of 1998 my family and I traveled to Bogotá, Colombia, on a trip that was vitally important for all of us. We went to visit the adoption agencies in which my children had spent the first weeks of their lives, and to see something of the city and country of their birth. Kate was then seventeen, Anthony fourteen. Our decision to make the trip had been set in motion by Kate's desire to know more of the circumstances of her birth mother's decision to place her for adoption. Anthony, for his part, expressed a desire to learn the hour of his birth, letting that lacuna in the records we had stand in for all the other unknown details of his early life story.

The trip we four made together was significant to each of us individually, and to our life together as a family. To make the journey seemed to all of us inevitable and compelling. Returning with our children to the place we had adopted them, and having the pleasure of seeing again and talking with the social workers who had interviewed us and entrusted these children to our care, was a way for Fred and me to share with our children some aspect of our experiences of years ago. To be with them as they experienced the complex emotions that accompanied their own encounters with their beginnings allowed us to understand some emotions of loss and regret that are nearly impossible for a child to speak to a parent. The opportunity to share these moments of recognizing the complexity of our family bonds, which encompass original families whom we will probably never meet, was a tremendous gift to me.

My experiences attempting to have children and then adopting led me to think hard about the nature of the desire to be a parent, and about the ways in which both procreation and raising a child are part of many people's understanding of the good life. We live in a time in which the ways of bringing children into a family have expanded greatly. Since the 1960s adoption across racial lines has become more common (although in the United States it disproportionately involves the adoption by white parents of black children and children from Asia and Latin America). So has "open adoption," in which the birth parents and the adopting parents meet one another. New reproductive technologies have made it possible to use eggs, as well as sperm, from someone else, which, along with in vitro fertilization, has made it possible for couples to conceive who previously would have been unable to do so. Single women and lesbians can also now conceive using donated sperm, and single and gay men can use donated eggs that a woman (called a "surrogate mother") can gestate for them.

The centrality of parenting in my own life's goals has made me eager in my work as a political theorist to clarify principles that can help people to construct families ethically. My first book examined nineteenth-century reforms of marriage law, and I now wanted to think about what principles should govern the ways people bring children into a family, and competing visions of how we should support family life. Although sometimes a difficult case has led to the articulation of new legal rules, there has not been much discussion about whether there are common ethical principles that apply to all the various ways of bringing children into a family through adoption or the use of reproductive technologies. But both new technologies and social practices have sparked a bevy of difficult and controversial questions: What defines a parent? Is race relevant to family ties? How many parents can a child have? Do parents need to be of different sexes? Is it genetic material alone or the labor of parenting that gives anyone a claim to legal parenthood?

In attempting to answer these questions, I have resisted the dichotomy between "tradition" and "individual choice" that runs through many discussions of family policy. That division pits those who argue that there is a single legitimate form of family, rooted in "nature" or long-standing traditions of American society, against those who assert that there is no single desirable form of family and that people should be free to form families however they choose. I insist that it is possible for law and social policy to promote liberty and choice while at the same time advancing equality, recognizing and protecting family relationships, and providing care to those who need it. How best to achieve these goals is not self-evident, but I provide examples of ways of moving toward a society committed to such a vision.

I hope with this book to further the vitally important public discussion of policies and laws that affect the ways in which people make babies and make families, topics touching not only the most personal and private aspects of people's lives, but values central to public life as well. Different perspectives and complex narratives characterize every one of the issues I examine in this book; I make no claim to have the final word on how we should think about and regulate these practices. In the chapters that follow, I draw both on my family experiences as daughter and sister, wife and mother, and on my training as a political theorist to propose ethical principles to guide family law and policy. While people such as doctors who work with biotechnology or lawyers who practice in family court may have particular perspectives on these issues, every person who reflects about her or his experience of family life has a vital contribution to make to the discussion. Only by listening to people with many different kinds of experiences and points of view—including those who are often marginalized or ignored, such as unwed mothers or people in poverty—can we move toward a widely accepted ethics, both public and private, governing the ways people make babies and make families. I hope my reflections will move as many readers as possible to join in the conversation.

Reinventing the Family

*T*he traditional fabric of family law is unraveling. We are living in an historical moment in which understandings about what constitutes a family, what family members owe one another, and how long family relationships endure are undergoing rapid transformation. The title of this book, *Making Babies, Making Families*, draws attention to the fact that the seeming stability of family boundaries established by the natural tie of heterosexual attraction, coital procreation, and biologically based family genealogies has been challenged. There are growing numbers of families in which the adult partners are of the same sex, children have been created from donated genetic material, adoptive and birth parents know one another and are both present in a child's life, households of "step-siblings" and "half-siblings" create "blended families," or adults raise children as single parents. To some people the degree of variation in family forms and the amount of personal choice in making babies and making families seems to invite liberation and fulfillment; to others it seems to create practical confusion and moral chaos.

The cultural and legal definition of family now under siege has predominated in the Western world since the sixteenth century. Not only was the family considered to be a natural, hierarchical, private association made up of a heterosexual couple and their biological children, but it was "naturally" headed by a male: the husband had authority over his wife, and the father had more authority than the mother over their children. This tradition assigned men and women very different roles: men were breadwinners, women were caregivers and nurturers. In some times and places, the law reflected the assumption that members of a family would be of the same race; some American states prohibited marriage between persons of different races, and interracial adoption was almost unheard of until the late 1960s.

Starting in the mid-nineteenth century, both legislation and court decisions began rejecting these premises, positing more equality between husband and wife, allowing that marriage might be dissolved by divorce, striking down antimiscegenation laws, creating the means for legal as well as informal adoption, requiring parents to send their children to school and inoculate them against certain diseases, and subjecting families to state scrutiny in cases of suspected neglect or abuse. But with all of these political modifications of the "natural" family order, no comprehensive new understanding of family relationships has taken its place. Rather, the old order has been pushed and pulled into new shapes by a host of economic, technological, and ideological forces.[1]

In the decades after World War II, the combination of need produced by falling real wages and the desire of many women to engage in paid work changed the middle-class pattern of male breadwinners and female homemakers drastically. The percentage of married women in the labor force, which had been 4.6 percent in 1890, increased to 24.8 percent in 1950, and to 58.6 percent in 1991. The speed at which this increase took place is astounding; from 1950 to 1991 there was a gain of 33.8 percentage points, and the number of employed wives more than doubled.[2] Statistics concerning families with children were equally striking. In 1950, 60 percent of American households had male breadwinners and full-time female homemakers, regardless of whether children were present. By the 1990s, the figure was reversed, and more than 60 percent of married women with children under the age of eighteen were in the labor force.[3]

Single-parent families also increased, in part due to divorce, in part due to a rise in never-married parents. The increase in the divorce rate was steady from the 1860s (when the first statistics were collected) until the 1980s. In 1983 the divorce rate was eighteen times higher than it had been in 1860, and almost two and a half times what it had been in 1940. In the 1990s, the likelihood of a first marriage ending in divorce was above 50 percent.[4] Single-parent households headed by a woman were more likely to be poor than were single-parent households headed by a man, and if the woman was black the chances of her children living in poverty increased.[5] In 1997 changes in the welfare laws allowed states to require recipients of Aid for Families with Dependent Children (AFDC) (90 percent of whom were women) to take a job after six months and placed a lifetime limit of five years on receiving welfare benefits, regardless of whether there were children in the home. Economic and social factors alike made the full-time stay-at-home mother a statistical minority by the last years of the twentieth century.

At the same time, ideological pressures were reinforcing the impact of economic change on the family. The women's movement, followed by the gay and lesbian movement, articulated more egalitarian ideas concerning men's and women's roles in society. Feminist theory asserted that women should be able to assume the responsibilities of work, professional authority, and political activity previously regarded as the prerogatives of men. Feminists also challenged male authority in the household, as women insisted that their voices be heard in everything from family finances to the division of household labor to the frequency of sexual relations. While many feminists insisted that women's equality was not inconsistent with family stability, the very idea of equality put in question traditional family models based on clearly differentiated sex roles and "separate spheres" for men and women.

Changes in medicine and reproductive technology affected sexual behavior and family formation in numerous ways. The development of "the pill" altered sexual behavior both within and outside marriage by making it easier to avoid unwanted pregnancies and to plan the timing of children. In vitro fertilization made it possible for some previously infertile couples to have genetically related children. This and other reproductive technologies made possible "collaborative procreation" among people who did not engage in sexual activity with one another: alternative insemination by donor and ova extraction and transfer allowed heterosexual couples who could not conceive using their own genetic material to have children, and was also used by some single persons and same-sex couples. Through "contract pregnancy" or "surrogate motherhood," couples or individuals could contract with a woman to gestate a fetus conceived using alternative insemination or in vitro fertilization, relinquishing the child after birth.

With these extraordinarily changed possibilities for family formation, myriad ethical and legal dilemmas have presented themselves to a baffled society. When genetic parents (those who provide the sperm and the egg), gestational mother, and social and psychological parents (those who raise the child) are not the same, who should be declared the legal parent(s) of a child? Should people other than the legal parents have rights to access or visitation after adoption or after assisted conception or gestation? Should children (or the adults they become) have the right to obtain information about their progenitors?

While long-standing practices of informal and formal adoption have placed children to be brought up by people other than their biological parents in the United States, the relatively new practices of formal open adoption and transracial adoption have raised questions concerning the importance to be given to the genetic tie. Should children maintain contact with birth parents on the one hand and with racial and ethnic groups on the other? States are divided about whether to allow the law to recognize two sets of parents: the adoptive parents, who have custody, and the birth parents, who have some visitation rights. Public opinion and public law are also divided over the desirability of race-matching in adoption. In the United States, federal law requires that Native American children be placed with Native American parents whenever possible but prohibits the use of race in the placement of other children, raising all kinds of questions about the relevance of genetic bonds to our understanding of race as well as of family formation.

Other issues about the recognition to be given to the genetic tie concern the question of what parental claims, if any, a man who is not married to a child's mother should have. This question has been raised starkly in cases in which biological fathers have sought to void an adoption and gain custody after the birth mother, without informing the father of his paternity, relinquished the child for adoption. In another case, a man who had fathered a child and lived for a while with the child and her mother, despite the fact that the mother was legally married to someone else, sought to establish legal paternity so that he could petition for visitation with the child. In some of these cases courts held that the biological tie provided grounds to assert legal paternity, while in other cases courts held that being the biological progenitor of a child did not necessarily create standing to seek legal recognition of paternity. The general public as well as the courts were deeply divided over the questions of what resolution was proper, and why.

The fact that people now *plan* and agree in advance to make babies who will not be raised by one or both of their genetic parents has given rise to other controversies. Should there be an open market in human sperm and eggs, or should such sales be prohibited or regulated? If regulated, in what ways and on what grounds? Should the law recognize contracts for human procreation? What should a court do if someone changes her or his mind and wants to annul or modify a contract concerning procreation? For example, does a woman who agrees to bear a child for someone else but changes her mind during pregnancy have any right to be named the child's parent or to get visitation rights? Does it matter whether or not the child was conceived with her egg? If a child is born with disabilities is the contract affected? When same-sex couples who had a child together using donated sperm or eggs (and, in the case of gay men, "gestational services") separate, does the nonbiological parent have the same right to custody as the biological or genetic parent? Does a lesbian partner of a biological mother who has shared all the care of a child they planned for together have a right to sue for visitation after the couple separates? Does a man who has donated sperm to a lesbian couple and who is known to their child as her biological father have a right to seek legal recognition of his paternity in order to seek visitation when the mothers have decided they do not want the child to see him anymore?

Some people cling to tradition to ward off the uncertainty these changes have generated. I prefer to try to devise new expectations and rules grounded in familiar ethical principles. I ally myself with those who struggle to devise principles and rules that allow new measures of equality between men and women in families, new possibilities for people previously unable to create families, and new protections for children in all kinds of families. Like some theorists who have worked to construct rules based on values prior law ignored, and some who have sought to connect the principle of individual freedom with the values of intimate association, I suggest changes in the ways we think about and regulate family life that reflect the tremendous complexity in the relationships that bring adults and children together in families. But accepting change does not mean that "anything goes." New practices that allow people previously unable to create families to do so require that law and social policy pay careful attention to achieving equality between men and women; protecting family relationships, especially those involving children; and taking care of vulnerable family members.

Dilemmas abound in the efforts to reshape family law in accord with each of these ideals, and theorists differ in the weight they give to the principles at stake and in the conclusions they reach.

One strain of thought grows out of that aspect of the liberal tradition that recognizes liberty, consent, and choice as fundamental values to our political and legal system. These values place the self-governing individual at the center of social concern, and historically they have inspired important developments in laws relating to the family. Prohibitions against interracial marriage were struck down when the Supreme Court held that marriage is a fundamental right that the state can abridge only for a compelling interest. The Court also declared first that married couples and then that individuals have the right to decide whether or not to use birth control. Once people do have children, the Court had already decided, they have a right to make certain decisions about educating their children free from state interference. Unmarried as well as married fathers have a right to custody of their children if they have had a significant relationship with them.

Dealing with current dilemmas, theorists making personal liberty their highest principle would craft new law allowing people in most instances to be their own lawmakers—to decide for themselves how to create families and conduct family life. For example, they argue that the right to privacy that underlies people's right to prevent conception or to end a pregnancy should also guarantee people's right to use reproductive technologies without state regulation or restriction. They favor letting people who engage in collaborative procreation make their own agreements about allowing the biological or genetic parents access to the child. In adoption, they would allow birth parents and adoptive parents to agree to whatever degree of openness or secrecy they see fit. Similarly, they would allow heterosexual, gay and lesbian, and single persons to contract for gametes (that is, eggs or sperm) and gestational services, and to reach their own agreements, before the child is conceived, about the degree of contact, if any, there will be between the donor(s), the child, and the custodial parents.

As I explain in the chapters that follow, I have serious reservations about relying on the principle of individual liberty as the primary or unqualified foundation of family law. The liberatory potential of the freedom to make choices in this vital aspect of social life depends on what choices are available and to whom. In a society already deeply structured by sex, race, and class, announcing that people have a "right to reproduce" may mean that some people get the right to take advantage of others' vulnerabilities. There is, moreover, a danger that the rhetoric of liberty and choice will result in various aspects of family formation being taken over by market mechanisms. Competitive pricing of gametes, for instance, according to the donor's characteristics such as academic performance, athletic ability, and racial features is a deeply troubling move toward the commodification of genetic material and the children it produces.

My approach is to balance rights of personal choice with concern for relationship and association as crucial elements of individual and social well-being. New law, I believe, should insist that people assume the responsibilities of supporting and caring for family members, particularly children. The primary relationship of parent and child is one of stewardship, and stewardship means that parental authority must be grounded in the assumption of responsibilities that are not subject to parental will or negotiation alone. Moreover, public policy should create conditions under which people are best able to make deep commitments of emotional and material support to one another. The assumption of responsibilities should not be left solely to individual volition, and the fulfillment of those responsibilities should not depend solely on individual resources.

One of the difficulties with insisting that intrinsic obligations set limits on how adults may choose to establish and order their family life, however, is that society has traditionally assigned the tasks of caregiving to women, and this has created significant economic and political inequality between women and men. Since the Industrial Revolution, the demands of caring for children and a household were usually met by wives' unpaid labor or by female servants. Because caregiving was what women did, and was seen as part of the private realm, it did not appear as an object of political discussion. It is clear, however, that women cannot be entirely responsible for the family's "home life" and also participate meaningfully in the public realm. If the requirements of care are to be met, men will have to take more direct responsibility for childcare and domestic tasks, as some men have begun to in the past few decades.[6] If men and women are to enjoy equal liberty, and also are to sustain relationships of care, their roles within both the family and civil society will have to change, and extensive new social practices supported by law will be necessary. In short, liberty must be limited by the demands of equality, relationship, and care.

I try to address many, although not all, of these issues in the chapters that follow by looking at a series of questions involving family policy and law that have troubled legislatures and courts in recent years. In Chapter 1, I show that the controversies that have arisen in the past several decades over transracial adoption and open adoption reflect significant developments in thinking about families and how they are formed. Unlike earlier adoption practices that tried to make adoptive families resemble a biologically related family as closely as possible and made a "clean break" between the family of origin and the adoptive family, both transracial adoption and open adoption suggest that adoptive families may have a form of their own that does not mimic the biological nuclear family. In Chapter 2, I argue that the decision to relinquish a child for adoption belongs to biological parents who have provided care to a child, not simply to people related to the child biologically. Does the fact that the mother and not the father carries the fetus through pregnancy give the mother greater parental rights than the father at the time of birth? When couples are married the law says that the couple's commitment to one another in marriage makes them equal partners in parenting. But what about unmarried parents? Does sexual difference affect their parental rights? Should it do so? I examine this issue using the controversy over whether an un-wed father should have the right to veto the mother's decision to place their child for adoption. I defend the priority of responsibility and care over biology for grounding parental rights, and suggest ways in which men could demonstrate their intention to care for their off-spring even before the child is born.

Chapters 3, 4, and 5 move from a consideration of adoption, which involves thinking about parental ties to existing children, to assisted procreation, in which adults plan in advance of conception to have the genetic and/or biological parents be different than the social and psy-chological parents who have legal custody of the child brought into being. In Chapter 3, I consider the ideas reflected in the current prac-tice of using other people's eggs or sperm to produce a child "of one's own." I focus on two salient features of gamete transfer in the contem-porary United States: the anonymity of donor and recipient, and the unregulated market. I argue that doing away with anonymity would be desirable in gamete transfer as well as in adoption, and that society should oppose a market in human gametes just as it currently does a market in children. I continue to examine new procreative services in Chapter 4, where I discuss the issues raised by contract pregnancy (surrogate motherhood). I argue against enforcing pregnancy con-tracts. I also argue that because of the ways in which race and class, as well as sexual difference, affect these practices, paying a surrogate for gestation should be prohibited. Chapter 5 brings many of these issues together as I consider lesbian couples' use of donated genetic material (gay men must acquire both ova and gestational services) to have chil-dren. I argue that the biological mother who bears a child after alter-native insemination should have no greater claims to parental rights than her lesbian partner. I examine the controversy over whether the sperm donor, if he is known to and involved with the child, should have any legal status or rights. These families return us to the question of how far new family forms should be allowed to depart from the model of the biologically related family. In the epilogue I argue that the erosion of the notion that there is only one kind of family does not entail the end of family values or of ethical reasoning about family ties. The pluralization of family forms requires us to articulate new principles to insure the well-being of families and all their members, principles that must place gender equality and children's well-being at their center.

It is clear that we live in a time of transition from a patriarchal familial and social order to a new order whose values are matters of debate and whose final contours it is impossible to predict. Living through a transition and trying to formulate principles to guide family policy and law are difficult tasks. The assumption of natural hierarchy and a male-headed family can no longer serve as a normative foundation for family law. I find it impossible to lament the demise of a social and legal order permeated by sexual inequality. I also find it impossible to embrace a voluntaristic or contractual foundation for family policy and law. The primary focus of any normative theory of the family cannot be on adults' volition, but on children's needs and the right of every child to be parented. Law and public policy must recognize that children have a right to be cared for, and to have specific persons responsible for their upbringing. They must recognize that caregiving is an obligation of men and women alike. Law and public policy must also realize that society has a responsibility to make sure that adults who are responsible for children have access to the means and services that will enable them to fulfill their tasks adequately. The responsibility of meeting children's need for care is not a private responsibility alone, but one of society—that is, of government. The dilemmas that arise for feminism and law involve the necessity to balance the demands of liberty, equality, relationship, and care, values that endure even as people engage in new practices in making babies and making families.

CHAPTER 1

Transracial and Open Adoption: New Forms of Family Relationships

*T*hinking about adoption is a good place to begin rethinking the ethics that should guide family formation and the relationships among family members. The dominant cultural image of family in the United States is that of a heterosexual couple, their offspring, and relatives by blood or marriage—aunts, uncles, nieces, nephews, grandparents and grandchildren. Even now when tradition is giving way to a variety of family forms, traditional discourse suggests that family ties are created "by nature." Adoption complicates this picture by allowing the severing of family ties given by nature, and the voluntary assumption of parental rights and responsibilities for children by adults who are not their biological parents. Adoption concerns both ending an existing set of family relationships or potential relationships, and establishing new ones.

Although most people regard adoption as an important way to make certain that children are well cared for, strong disagreement exists over two issues: whether children should be placed across ethnic or racial lines, and whether adoption records should be open and parties to an adoption should be able to know one another's identities or even meet. Should a Catholic child be placed only with Catholic parents, a Muslim child only with Muslim parents; should a black child be placed only with black parents, a Filipino child only with Filipino parents? Should adoptees have access to their original birth certificates, and should birth parents be able to know who adopted their children? Should the infant available for adoption be understood as an individual who can be moved without constraint from one family to another, or as someone with ties to persons outside the adoptive family—genetic kin or a racial group—that deserve some kind of social and legal recognition?[1]

Traditional policy and practice have assumed that adoptive families should resemble as closely as possible biological families, and that infants relinquished for adoption (older children are regarded differently) should be regarded as freestanding individuals with no relevant links to either their birth parents or the racial, ethnic, or religious groups to which their birth parents belong. These policies formed adoptive families to be "as if" families, that is, families in which children to all appearances might have been born to the adoptive parents. Typically, children were placed with adoptive parents with the same racial features. Birth records were sealed, and the birth parents disappeared from the child's life. The result was to ratify a family based on biological ties to both parents as the desirable norm.

Recent pressures from several sources, however, have posed serious challenges to the "as if" model of the adoptive family. In transracial adoptions the parents' and child's differences in physical appearance publicly announce that they are not biologically related. Proponents of transracial adoption argue that an infant awaiting adoption should be placed without regard to race so that neither the child nor the adoptive parents will experience discrimination.[2] Opponents of transracial placement insist that being a member of a racial minority gives the child an interest in being raised by others of that minority, and gives the group an interest in raising the child.[3] The movements for unsealed adoption records and for open adoption are another challenge to the tradition of the "as if" adoptive family. Unsealed records make original birth information available to adult adoptees, and open adoption brings birth parents and adoptive parents into contact, sometimes even before the child is born. Proponents of secrecy in adoption tend to regard the infant as an individual and worry that unsealed records and open adoption place too much emphasis on biological relationships, and may impede the forging of strong bonds in the adoptive family.[4] People who advocate doing away with secrecy argue that knowledge of the genetic link between biological parents and child is part of the identity of each of them and should not be permanently hidden or inaccessible.[5] Those who favor either transracial adoption or open adoption assert that there is no overriding need to make all aspects of an adoptive family conform exactly to those of families formed biologically.

The debates on these topics have for the most part taken place quite separately. People discussing whether or not adoption records should be accessible by the adult adoptee have by and large not talked about ethnic identity and minority group rights. People discussing whether or not children should be placed for adoption across racial lines have rarely focused on the issue of sealed records. I bring these discussions into dialogue with one another because together they illuminate the values expressed—and the values excluded—when policy is based on the presumption that there is only one normative model of family. The debates over transracial and open adoption are part of a more general recognition that there are a number of kinds of families in which parents (or one parent) and child are not genetically related, including blended families, heterosexual families that use donated eggs or sperm, and gay and lesbian families. Juxtaposing these discussions also brings to light, and suggests ways to ameliorate, the effects of gender and racial hierarchy that have marked aspects of adoption and the use of reproductive technologies alike.

Transracial adoption pits values of integration or assimilation against multiculturalism, and individuality against racial-ethnic community.[6] Disputes about secrecy, for their part, pit values of privacy against those of knowledge and freedom of information. All of these values are fundamental to pluralist democracy in the United States. The complex moral and policy issues involved in open and transracial adoption are, in Janet Farrell Smith's words, "not resolvable without remainder." That is, in situations involving "a complex set of conflicting practical demands, each tied to a set of apparently morally reasonable supports, taking up one of these positions will not nullify moral demands of the alternatives not taken."[7] But in the real world where all of us must act, we cannot avoid judgments and policy choices that will favor one side or the other: the law will either prohibit or allow the disclosure of identifying information about the parties to an adoption; and the law will either prohibit or allow the placement of children across racial lines.

My own thinking is that both unsealed records and transracial adoption allow greater room for expression of the values of liberty, equality, relationship, and care in the functioning of families than did the older approach. In developing new family policies, it is crucial to place children at the center of analysis, and to remember that children's need for care requires social policy that supports parents in their caregiving efforts.[8] By challenging the dominance of the norm of the biological family, transracial adoption and unsealed records represent an opening for a plurality of forms that I see as necessary for a more humane family policy. Developing an ethical basis for family law and policy requires carefully weighing multiple values and interests, not adhering to a single principle alone; that balancing guides this discussion of adoption and of the topics that follow.

Traditional Adoption Policy and Practice

While new reproductive technologies have made the separation of genetic and social parenthood seem like a relatively recent development, legal convention, and not biology alone, has always determined who would enjoy status as a legal parent. As Thomas Hobbes pointed out, while maternity could be observed at the time of birth, knowledge of paternity depended on the not always reliable word of the mother. Bastardy laws proclaimed that biological fathers would be recognized as legal fathers only if they were married to the mother of their child. Not all women who gave birth were regarded as the legal mothers of their offspring: slave mothers (along with slave fathers) did not have parental rights.

The creation of legal adoption in the mid-nineteenth century was a radical innovation because it dissolved the "natural" (blood) ties that bound families together and replaced them with "artificial" (legal) ties of kinship.[9] In the American understanding of kinship, recounted by anthropologist David Schneider, "family" means biological parents and their children, and "[t]he relationship which is 'real' or 'true' or 'blood' or 'by birth' can never be severed, whatever its legal position. Legal rights may be lost, but the blood relationship cannot be lost. It is culturally defined as being an objective fact of nature, of fundamental significance and capable of having profound effects, and its nature cannot be terminated or changed."[10] Although children were sometimes adopted by members of their extended family, the primary model of formal adoption was "stranger adoption." Statutes allowing legal adoption undermined the traditional understanding of the indestructible and involuntary nature of family bonds by severing the legal tie between original parents and their offspring and creating a new legal tie by convention and choice.

Despite the fact that adoptive families were created "artificially" by a legal procedure, however, from the mid-nineteenth to the mid-twentieth century most adoptive families gave the *appearance* of having resulted from sexual relations between the parents. Parents were of the age to have borne the child, and of the same race and often the same religion as the biological parents. The dissolution of the child's legal ties to its original parents made it possible for the adoptive family to simulate a biological family, "reflecting the deeply embedded notion in the ideology of American kinship that the only 'real' relation is a blood relation and, by extension, the only experience of authentic identity is bestowed by blood ties."[11]

Adoption law assumed that the family of which the child would become a member would have a particular configuration. There would be two (and only two) parents, of different sexes, and of the same race as the child. The sealing of adoption records reflected the legal assumption that parenthood is an exclusive status that can belong only to two persons at a time with respect to any one child. Underlying the policy of placing children with adoptive parents of the same race was the social fact that interracial marriage has been the exception rather than the rule in the United States (only in 1967 did the Supreme Court rule that state prohibitions on interracial marriage violated the Constitution). Adoption laws and policies were designed to make adoptive families imitate what was seen as a norm given by nature.

The creation of an "as-if" adoptive family incorporated a model of the individual and social ties consonant with the assumptions of liberal individualism and liberal political theory. Infant adoption, in particular, seemed to rest on the notion that at least for a brief period of time after birth, the child could be regarded as an individual who could be moved from one family to another and expected to take on an identity shaped by the roles, status, and obligations that membership in the new family entailed. Legal discourse about adoption focused on the right of a child to a permanent home, and the obligation of the state to protect children by placing them with adults who were financially and emotionally capable of providing care. The intermediary role performed by the adoption agency, which accepted the child from the birth parents and then placed her with adoptive parents, reflected the fact that for a moment the child was a ward of the state not bound to any other specific persons, an individual awaiting the creation of lasting family ties by an adoption decree.

Society dealt with unmarried motherhood differently depending on the race of the mother. Prior to World War II, adoption was not common among whites in the United States.[12] During the first two decades of the twentieth century, a woman who bore a child outside of marriage was considered a "fallen woman," shamefully weak or immoral. A child born out of wedlock was stigmatized, labeled "illegitimate" and a "child of sin," and considered likely to grow up to be a delinquent. Society expected the mother to raise the child herself as punishment for her transgression and as a "lesson" to other women who might be tempted to engage in illicit (that is unmarried) sex. In the 1930s, extramarital pregnancy continued to be socially condemned, but the advice about what to do changed. An unmarried white woman was now counseled to hide her pregnancy, give the child up for adoption, and never see the child again. It was hoped that by keeping the adoption secret she could "get on with her life" by marrying and eventually bearing "legitimate" children.

In the United States, blacks' experiences and attitudes toward adoption have typically been different from whites'. Both during and after slavery, black children who were orphaned or separated from their parents were often taken in by other families. There is a long history of informal adoption in black communities with roots in some West African cultural practices.[13] By contrast, to formally relinquish a child for adoption because of an unwed pregnancy was rare. Because of the rape and sexual exploitation of black women by their white masters during slavery, black communities have tended not to stigmatize black children born out of wedlock.[14] Many black infants were raised by members of their mother's extended family, often without being legally adopted. Raising such a child was regarded not only as caring for an individual child, but as contributing to the well-being of the black community. Black women who bore children out of wedlock were labeled by white society as loose or immoral, and they were not offered the services of maternity homes and adoption agencies to help them in their pregnancies and with the placement of their children. In addition, many black families could not meet some of the criteria agencies used (for example, stipulating family income or number of bedrooms in the house) to select adoptive homes.

After World War II, the stigma and embarrassment about sexual or reproductive inadequacy still haunted infertile couples, while the stigma attached to out of wedlock pregnancy for the white mother became more complex. Some social workers (influenced by psychoanalytic theory and by the scarcity of newborn white infants to adopt) began to shift their view of the unwed mother from someone morally deficient and incorrigible to someone caught in the throes of a psychological conflict that led her (unconsciously) to seek to bear a child.[15] By and large the stigma that had been attached to white children born out of wedlock disappeared, and they began to be regarded as innocent and desirable. This acceptance did not extend to the black mother or infant, however.

> Public and private agencies and government policies viewed both black and white women as breeders, but with a major and consequential distinction. The former were viewed as socially unproductive breeders, constrainable only by punitive, legal sanctions. . . . White unwed mothers in contrast were viewed as socially productive breeders whose babies, unfortunately conceived out of wedlock, could offer infertile couples their only chance to construct proper families.[16]

Race significantly influenced the status of birth mothers and the estimation of their mothering capabilities.

These factors contributed to a change in adoption practices meant to make it easier both to relinquish and to adopt white infants. During the 1940s many jurisdictions began to seal adoption records, making it impossible for *anyone* to discover the identity of the biological parents of an adopted child.[17] E. Wayne Carp has argued that what he calls the move from confidentiality (records closed to all but "the parties of interest," i.e. birth parents, adoptive parents, and child) to secrecy (records inaccessible to everyone except by a court order) was in response to a complex set of factors, including the adoptive parents' fear that the birth parents might reappear, unwed mothers' desire to avoid social condemnation, and social workers' efforts to "increase their own influence and power, and bolster social work professionalism."[18] Adoptive parents pushed for secrecy to avoid the stigma of infertility and the possibility that the birth parents might reappear. Unwed mothers sought secrecy in order to be spared social condemnation. Seeking to avoid an investigation of their life circumstances and the six-month wait for a placement that were often standard in state agencies, unwed mothers turned to private, unlicensed adoption agencies that promised them privacy. As a result, state agencies changed their procedures and urged legislatures to mandate that adoption records be sealed.

The sealed records' concealment of the child's biological parents smoothed the way for the construction of an "as-if" biological family by adoptive parents "who, by physical appearance and age could have conceived the infant."[19] Various secretive practices developed that promoted the construction of the "as if" family. Unwed white pregnant women would often leave home, telling friends and neighbors that they were traveling or visiting relatives, and stay in homes for unwed mothers during their pregnancies. Upon the birth of the child, the birth mother signed a document in which she irrevocably severed her rights and responsibilities to the child. The adoption agency took custody of the child and attempted to match the characteristics of the adoptive and original parents. Statutes and court decisions "used tests of adoptive parental fitness, and strict eligibility standards to make the artificial family approximate the legal ideal of a proper natural one in age, race, affection, and legal authority."[20] When the adoption became final, usually after a probationary period of six months to a year, the court sealed the original birth certificate and adoption records and entered into the public record a new birth certificate, which contained only the names of the adoptive parents. The sealed records could be opened only by court order after a showing of "good cause." (In some states, a petitioner could establish good cause by demonstrating medical necessity; in others, a strongly felt psychological need to discover one's genetic identity came to constitute cause.) The general exclusion of single persons and of gay and lesbian couples from the pool of adoptive parents also made the adoptive family resemble a biological family.

These practices in both U.S. and international adoptions have become known as the "clean break" approach to adoption, in which the integration of a child into an adoptive family "is premised on the complete severance of ties with the biological family." In an intercountry adoption, the clean break model also involves the child's assumption of a new "national identity—as 'Swedish' or 'American' rather than 'South Korean,' 'Colombian,' or 'Chinese.'"[21] Paradoxically, as Barbara Yngvesson notes, the clean break model, which incorporates an individualistic view of the child who can be moved from one family to another across all kinds of cultural and geopolitical lines, also implies that the ties between child and birth parent are so strong that unless the child becomes "parentless" (for example by being legally abandoned), new ties cannot be created.[22]

Many factors, both sociological and ideological, have in recent years challenged the idea that an adoptive family has to simulate a biological family, or that an infant voluntarily relinquished for adoption is a "parentless" child. One consequence of the relatively low number of white babies available for adoption, due in part to contraception and abortion, and in part to the decreasing stigmatization of unwed motherhood, has been the increasing openness of many people's efforts to find healthy infants through ads or public notices seeking women interested in placing their babies for adoption. Single persons and gay and lesbian couples have found ways to adopt children. Some people have adopted across racial lines, making the constructed nature of at least some adoptive families readily visible. Some people have entered into open adoptions, in which members of both the family of origin and the adoptive family are known to everyone involved.

The variety of new forms of families being created through open and transracial adoptions, then, has thrown into question the traditional assumptions about adoption. In the case of nonsecret or open

adoption, the birth parents' and the child's right to know one another's identities is at issue; in transracial adoption, both the child's
right to a particular cultural identity and the group's right to raise "its
own" are at issue. I bring the policy debates over secrecy vs. nonsecrecy and same-race vs. transracial adoption together here because
both raise the question of whether or to what extent the law should
treat an infant available for adoption as an autonomous individual in
need of a family, or as an individual in part defined by relationships to
persons or groups beyond the adoptive family.

The "As If" Adoptive Family:
Nonsecrecy and Open Adoption

Both open adoption and transracial adoption challenge the notion
that adoptive families should mirror the nuclear family composed of
a heterosexual couple and their biological offspring. David Schneider
has pointed out how strongly the possibility of having biological offspring a couple could raise together influenced the American understandings both of "family" and of legitimate sexual relations.

> Sexual intercourse between persons who are not married is fornication and
> improper; between persons who are married but not to each other is adultery
> and is wrong; between blood relatives is incest and is prohibited; between per-
> sons of the same sex is homosexuality and is wrong; with animals is sodomy
> and is prohibited; with one's self is masturbation and wrong; and with parts
> of the body other than the genitalia themselves is wrong. All of these are de-
> fined as "unnatural sex acts" and are morally, and in some cases, legally,
> wrong in American culture.[23]

Schneider might have noted that intercourse across racial lines was
also prohibited by both cultural and legal rules, on the grounds that it
was "unnatural" and an offense to both custom and morality. Interracial marriage was a crime in some states until the Supreme Court
struck down antimiscegenation statutes in *Loving v. Virginia* in 1967.
As late as 1984, Florida argued before the Supreme Court that a divorced white woman should be denied custody of her white child because the mother's new marriage to a black man would create social
difficulties for the child as she grew up. The Court rebuffed Florida's
reasoning, saying that "The question . . . is whether the reality of pri-

vate biases and the possible injury they might inflict are permissible considerations for removal of an infant child from the custody of its natural mother. . . . The Constitution cannot control such prejudices [against interracial marriage], but neither can it tolerate them."[24] Even as the Court rejected any legal validity to the notion that families had to be racially homogeneous, it acknowledged the power of such an idea in Americans' imaginations and social practice.

The primacy of blood ties in many Americans' understanding of family deeply affected the practice of secrecy in adoption. Initially, adoption records were kept confidential in order to protect the privacy of all parties, particularly the birth mother, from outsiders; confidentiality was not meant to block the exchange of nonidentifying information among parties to the adoption. Carol Sanger has pointed out the stigma attached to *all* birth mothers, married and unmarried alike, who decided not to raise their children or who were forced by circumstance or social pressure not to do so.[25] The shame attached to unmarried women bearing children did great harm to individual women and children and played a large role in the subordination of women as a group. Women were often "ruined" by an act from which men might walk away unscathed. Fear of such dire social consequences increased the pressure on women to marry and surrounded premarital sexual activity with fear and anxiety. The practice of hiding one's pregnancy and childbirth in order to resume a "normal" life was the best many women could do in the face of these social pressures, but the toll such secrecy exacted was tremendous.

Open adoption developed in response to the realization of white birth mothers that "the agencies needed them, rather than birth mothers needing the agencies," and it has received considerable support from the adoptees' rights movement. This movement is made up of adult adoptees and others who contend that to be denied access to knowledge of one's genetic history may impede the development of a person's identity and sense of self-worth. In a typical formulation, Vermont state senator Richard Sears (Democrat—Bennington), who was adopted as a child, argued in favor of a proposed statute to open Vermont's adoption records that adoptees "are the only people in the nation who are denied the basic right of knowing who they are."[26]

Most people take knowledge of their genetic origins for granted; members of the adoptees' rights movement maintain that access to such information is a basic civil and human right.

Notwithstanding the development of the practice of open adoption and pressure from various quarters to abandon sealed records, not everyone agrees that *all* adult adoptees should have access to their adoption records. In their eyes, the right of the birth parents to anonymity is very strong and may override the adoptee's right to know the identity of his or her birth parents, particularly if the birth records were sealed at the time of the adoption. State laws vary quite a bit in their provisions for disclosure and secrecy.[27] Some advocates of secrecy worry that if birth parents cannot be guaranteed confidentiality, some birth mothers will choose to terminate the pregnancy or retain custody. Even birth parents who might go through with adoption will face the dilemma of acknowledging the pregnancy and adoption to a future spouse and children, and some may live in dread of being contacted by the grown child later in life.

It seems to me, however, that except in cases in which knowledge that she had once borne and relinquished a child would put a woman in grave danger, the adult adoptee's right to know his or her specific history overrides the birth parents' right to privacy (particularly eighteen years after the birth). The original parents are under no obligation to meet their offspring, much less develop a social relationship (although they may do so if they all agree to); indeed, original parents may get legal protection from attempts at contact that are harassing or threatening.[28] The adoptee does not have a right to an actual social relationship with the original parents; but adult adoptees should not be deprived of the information they need to construct a coherent story of origin, an explanation of how they came into the world.

We think of ourselves as temporal beings, as coming out of a past and being formed by what has gone before us, and of having a connection with the future. We are shaped by and shape the world through physical procreation, works of craftsmanship and art, friendships, material bequests and spiritual legacies, and in many other ways. Our sense of history and continuity, extending back into the past and forward into the future, is part of what gives meaning to our existence and our works. It is this experience of oneself as a being in time that underpins a person's right to specific knowledge of his or her origins.

Although some people contend that nonsecrecy and open adoption idealize the blood tie by continuing the contact between birth parents and child, I think these practices would undercut the blood-based understanding of family bonds by giving custodial authority to adoptive parents *even though* the identity of the birth parents was known. Unlike the secrecy that implies that new family ties can be forged only if the original family is rendered invisible and inaccessible, nonsecrecy and open adoption suggest that a child can have multiple sources of family identity and multiple mothers and fathers. The identity of the child is constructed neither exclusively by the original family nor exclusively by the adoptive family, but by the child's knowledge of or contact with both of these families.

As Barbara Yngvesson has shown, for a child to occupy space between two families, however, a radical transformation in the understanding of "family" must take place. This is because the traditional understanding of the family "as constituted by shared biological heritage, by the 'mystical commonality' of mother and child, and as whole rather than split (it excludes difference, it is complete in itself)—is fundamental to the tension surrounding the place, and lack of place, of the birth mother in the adoptive family." The practice of secrecy, Yngvesson notes, reflects the belief that the adoptive family could mirror the unity and inevitability of the biological family only if the birth mother were rendered invisible. "Only by outlawing her (splitting her off) through various forms of legal and social closure—sealed records, rewritten birth certificates, the silences that meet revelations that one is a birth mother or that one is a child with 'two mothers'—can the adoptive family *become* a family, 'as if' it were biological, and the adoptive mother become 'real.'"[29] For the adoptive mother to become "real" the birth mother had to become a nonmother; and for the birth mother to "get on with her life" she had to leave her pregnancy and child behind her as if they had never been.

Nonsecrecy, whether achieved by unsealed records or open adoption, recognizes children as distinct individuals yet also acknowledges the significance to them of how they came to be. The adopted child has two sets of parents; the birth parents do not need to be obscured for the other parents (or parent) to assume their role in the child's life. In making the identities of birth parents either known or ascertainable at a later date, nonsecrecy has marked a departure from the traditional practice of creating an "as if" family. Yet while nonsecrecy and open adoption recognize both the child's individuality and relationship with the family of origin, discussions of nonsecrecy have rarely addressed the issue of the child belonging to a distinct *group* of origin. That question, however, has sparked a heated controversy about transracial adoption, a practice that also challenges the "as if" adoptive family.

Transracial Adoption

The public debate over whether children, particularly black and Native American children, should be adopted by people of other races has brought a whole raft of distinct considerations to the question of whether the "as if" adoptive family should be the norm. To what extent should the freedom to adopt or to be adopted be constrained by the requirement that the race of the child and that of the adoptive parents match? Underlying that question are assumptions about individualism and group identity. Should children available for adoption be placed as quickly as possible with a suitable family regardless of race, or should they be treated as members of a racial group and matched with parents of that race? And who should have a say concerning whether or not race should play any part in placing a child: the birth parents, the adoptive parents, the adoption agency, the child's racial community of origin, or, in the case of Native American children, the tribe?

The controversy over transracial adoption has its roots in both sociological and ideological legacies of the Civil Rights movement. Although both advocates and opponents of transracial adoption oppose the legacy of racial discrimination and seek greater social opportunity and justice for people of color, they differ markedly in their judgments about what strategies are likely to create a society free from the scourge of racism. Over the past three decades the debate has gone through a number of phases, which together illuminate these strategies.

Before the 1960s, there were very few transracial adoptions. Racial prejudice and segregation meant that interracial families were stigmatized, even though many American families were of mixed white, black, Native American, or Hispanic ancestry. The "normal" family, whether biological or adoptive, was racially homogeneous in appearance. The Civil Rights movement of the 1950s and 1960s, however, led some whites to adopt black children as a way of manifesting their belief that love could occur across racial lines and as a way of providing for children otherwise likely to grow up in poverty. By the early 1970s the Child Welfare League, which had long opposed adoption across racial lines, reversed its position and endorsed transracial adoption. By 1972, approximately 20,000 black children had been adopted by white parents, and the number of Native American children adopted by white parents also increased markedly.[30]

Adoption of black and Native American children by whites did not sit well with all advocates of civil rights, however. In 1972, the National Association of Black Social Workers (NABSW) went on record opposing transracial adoption. They contended that transracial adoption was a form of cultural genocide, and that black children could develop neither "Black pride and a Black identity" nor the practical "survival skills" necessary to live in a society infused with racism unless they were raised in black families.[31] In 1985 William Merritt reiterated the NABSW position: "We view the placement of Black children in white homes as a hostile act against our community. It is a blatant form of race and cultural genocide."[32] In the face of this opposition, adoption of black children by whites fell off immediately and continued to decline.

Similarly, in the 1970s, many Native Americans began to see transracial adoption as a threat to the preservation and cultural integrity of Indian tribes. In states with large Indian populations, studies revealed that perhaps as many as 25 to 35 percent of all Indian children were removed from their homes by the state and placed in adoptive homes, foster homes, and institutions like the boarding homes run by the Bureau of Indian Affairs; the vast majority of such placements were in non-Indian homes.[33] Indian rights advocates urged Congress to adopt the Indian Child Welfare Act of 1978 (ICWA), which declared it to be "the policy of this Nation to protect the best interests of Indian children and to promote the stability and security of Indian tribes and families by the establishment of minimum Federal standards for the removal of Indian children from their families."[34] The ICWA stipulated that when an adoption concerned the child of a member of a recognized Indian tribe, the tribe should have jurisdiction over the adoption; if the matter remained in the hands of the state courts, the court should first try to place the child with a member of the child's extended family, then with a member of the tribe, then with another Indian family, and only as a last resort with non-Indians.

This approach of accepting transracial placement only when placement with parents of the same race proved impossible appealed to James Bowen; in a 1987 law review article, he recommended that Congress pass an Afro-American Child Welfare Act modeled on the ICWA.[35] Bowen's proposed act would have established an Afro-American Child Welfare Commission to review all cases in which the removal of black children from their biological parents was contemplated, and it required such measures as mandatory appointment of counsel and state payment of attorney's fees if the parents were indigent. Bowen also proposed giving subsidies to adults who had informally adopted children (usually members of the extended family) and "a procedure to flush out potential non-related same-race adoptive parents in case no relative comes forward."[36] Bowen's suggestions for recruiting minority adoptive parents and scrutinizing the criteria used in decisions to remove children from their homes were picked up by many workers in the field. His proposal that transracial adoption be prohibited unless no adoptive parents of the same race could be found for a child was not acted upon, however, and Congress has since forbidden the use of race in the adoption of non-Indian children.

Federal law thus currently treats the role that race may play in the placement of Native American and black children very differently. While the ICWA required that tribal membership be taken into account in placing Indian children, the Multiethnic Placement Act of 1994 (MEPA) required adoption agencies to ignore race in foster and adoptive placement of non-Indian children. Indeed, Congress has strengthened that prohibition in recent years. In 1994, MEPA stipulated that while adoption agencies receiving federal funds might take into account the "racial background of the child and the capacity of the ... adoptive parents to meet the needs of a child of this background" as one of a number of factors in making an adoptive placement, these considerations could not preclude or even greatly delay permanent placement.[37] Despite this tone of compromise, MEPA offended some activists on both sides of the transracial adoption controversy. Because it did not *require* an effort at same-race placement, MEPA failed to satisfy proponents of race-matching; because it did not *prohibit* race-matching altogether, it failed to satisfy proponents of race-blind placement. Those opposed to race-matching got their wish in 1996, when Congress incorporated the Adoption Anti-Discrimination Bill into the Small Business Job Protection Act. Better known as the Interethnic Placement Act (IEPA), that law denied federal funds to any state or private agency that used race as a criterion for the placement of a child.[38] The IEPA explicitly exempted proceedings involving Indian children covered by the ICWA.[39]

In prohibiting the use of race as a factor in the adoption of non-Indian children, Congress was responding to the kinds of arguments put forward in Elizabeth Bartholet's 1991 article, "Where Do Black Children Belong?"[40] That article, which took issue with the practice of making transracial placements only after attempts at in-race placement had failed, set the terms in which transracial adoption would be debated throughout the 1990s. The article began with an account of Bartholet's experience as she began her quest, as a single, divorced white woman, to adopt a child: "When I first walked into the world of adoption, I was stunned at the dominant role race played. ... It was central to many people's thinking about parenting. And it was a central organizing principle for the agencies which had been delegated authority to construct adoptive families."[41] Bartholet, who had worked in the Civil Rights movement, was disturbed by the role race played not only in the policies of adoption agencies but also in the attitudes of potential adoptive parents. "The large majority of the people actively looking to adopt in this country are white and for the most part they want white children, at least initially." The shortage of healthy children to adopt is in reality a shortage of white children and of infants—there are many older children of color available for adoption. "The familiar refrain that there are no children available for adoption is a reflection of the racial policies of many adoption agencies and the racial preferences of many adoptive parents."[42] There are many older children available in foster care: "The proportion of [children of color] in foster care is three times greater than in the nation's population. . . . More than half of the children waiting for adoption nationally are children of color, and this population is rapidly increasing in most states."[43]

Bartholet argued that adoption agencies should change their policies not only to allow white parents to adopt black children, but also to encourage transracial adoptions by counseling potential adoptive parents. Many people who might not initially think of adopting a child of a different race or an older child might be receptive to the idea if asked to consider doing so. She argued that the preference for same-race placement violates the principle of antidiscrimination, harms children waiting to be adopted by delaying their permanent placement (and thereby sometimes preventing it altogether because older children are harder to place), and harms prospective adoptive parents by depriving them of the chance to nurture and love a child.

Although Bartholet was mainly concerned with the adoption of older children in foster care, many of whom had become available for adoption when the state terminated the parental rights of their parents, she and other opponents of race-matching did not limit their opposition to such cases. Even when efforts at race-matching would not delay the placement (for example, of an infant voluntarily relinquished at birth), she thought that a preference for racial homogeneity in the family was offensive; arguments that families should be racially homogeneous reflected an "inappropriate separatist agenda."[44] Randall Kennedy struck a similar note, contending that "Racial matching is a disastrous social policy both in how it affects children and in what it signals about our current attitudes regarding racial distinctions." In his eyes, "Racial matching reinforces racialism. . . . It buttresses the notion that people of different racial backgrounds are different in some moral, unbridgeable, permanent sense." Most important, racial matching in adoption or marriage "belies the belief that love and understanding are boundless and instead instructs us that our affections are and should be bounded by the color line regardless of our efforts."[45] Hawley Fogg-Davis concurred: a race-neutral adoption system would "send a powerful message to all

Americans that racial ascription should not be a barrier to the intimate association of family life."[46] Public policy allowing agencies to restrict placement across racial lines would reflect misguided biologism and would fail to affirm the human capacity to love beyond racial boundaries. By contrast, lifting those restrictions would deal a blow to the model of the "as if" adoptive family.

Opponents of race-matching put forward various proposals to guarantee race neutrality in adoption. Bartholet and Kennedy lobbied during the debates on both the MEPA and IEPA to prohibit any effort at race-matching when there are qualified adoptive parents of any race who want to adopt the child. Guaranteeing adoption choice was in their eyes the way to make sure that the child's equal protection right to expeditious permanent placement was not violated. Richard Banks and Hawley Fogg-Davis went even further, arguing that not only should adoption agencies be prohibited from race-matching, but that prospective adoptive parents should not be permitted to signify what race child they wanted, or what race(s) they wished to exclude from consideration. Banks proposed that agencies that receive any government funding should not be allowed to classify or list children by race, a practice he called "facilitative accommodation."[47] Once agencies ceased to maintain lists of children "sorted" by race, prospective adoptive parents would have to consider each child as an individual. In addition, eliminating the adopter's choice would compel prospective parents to envision themselves as members of a multiracial family.

Fogg-Davis similarly supported a prohibition on listing children by race. For one thing, she considered it inappropriate for an adoption agency to decide to which racial group any particular child belongs. Although people in the United States are "born into racial categories," we must not elide "the role of agency in the identity development of individuals living in a social system of racial classification."[48] Particularly for a mixed-race or a transracially adopted child, racial identity is not a "given" but is arrived at by what Fogg-Davis termed "racial navigation." Racial identity is influenced but not determined either by one's biological parents or by the groups to which one's parents belong; it is always in part to be negotiated or navigated by the individual herself or himself.[49] In both Banks's and Fogg-Davis's view, "Adoption is about matching a parent to a child, not a parent to a race."[50]

In these debates, individual rights are pitted against group rights; a self with a fluid and "negotiable" racial identity is contrasted to a self with a fixed and inherited racial identity; ideals of integration and the "melting pot" are set against ideals of ethnic nationalism and cultural difference. Advocates of transracial adoption frame the issue as one of antidiscrimination, focusing on the rights of the waiting child (or parents) to equal protection. In Randall Kennedy's terms, "There was a time when forward-looking people would have thought it praiseworthy for prospective adoptive parents to have said to a state welfare agency, 'we are willing to raise a parentless child regardless of the child's race.'" Race-matching, even the version authorized by the MEPA, by contrast, "denigrates such people, portraying them as a mere fallback for parentless children of a different race than they."[51] It is telling that Kennedy spoke of a "parentless" child, drawing attention to the need of the child already in state custody to find a permanent adoptive home. The need to place "parentless" children directs the attention of those thinking about adoption policy forward from the present into the future, not back into the past.

Underlying the dispute over race-matching are also differing views about a person's links to his or her racial group of origin. As Twila Perry noted, proponents of transracial adoption tended to adhere to a highly individualistic model of liberal theory, while proponents of race-matching, like herself, tended to be more communitarian and group-oriented in outlook.[52] The insistence on seeing black children awaiting adoption strictly as individuals disconnected from blacks as a group is, as critics of race-blind placement asserted, double-edged. While the assignment of rights by race can constitute invidious and unconstitutional discrimination, people in the contemporary United States neither perceive nor treat one another as raceless. Throughout their lives black children's position in and experience of society will be linked to the position of blacks in general. Critics of race-neutral adoption policy argued that federal law dictating that black children must be placed without regard to race might perpetuate notions about the inadequacy of black families and black parenting that are harmful to these children and other blacks.

A policy of nondiscrimination may also divert attention from the social problems, including racism, that lead so many minority children to be in the adoption and foster care system. When proponents of race-neutral placement insist that what parentless black children need is "not 'white,' 'black,' 'yellow,' 'brown,' or 'red' parents but loving parents,"[53] they focus on the individual child rather than the systemic social forces that put birth parents under such strain that they relinquish the child for adoption. The disproportionate number of black children awaiting adoption is "an indicator of a web of racial disadvantage in American society: the fact that blacks are more likely to be poor than whites, that poor blacks are more likely than poor whites to have their parental rights terminated by a court, that white women who give birth to biracial babies may be motivated by racist social pressure to surrender their children for adoption." Transracial adoption may gradually diminish social attitudes that insist upon racial uniformity in intimate and family relationships. But transracial adoption does not attack the "web of racial injustice that makes so many black children available for adoption in the first place."[54]

Transracial adoption thus poses a dilemma for advocates of racial equality and nonsubordination. Multiracial families give testimony to the ability of people to love and take responsibility for one another across racial lines. First-person accounts of transracial adoptees attest to their love for their parents, although some suggest that the dynamics of race in this society may create difficulties for parent and child alike.[55] Despite their love for their children, when white parents adopt children of color, they may reinforce white privilege and a sense of entitlement to whatever they desire, and contribute to the denigration of blacks and Native Americans as parents. While this dilemma cannot be entirely done away with, certain changes in the discourse and practice of adoption might undercut some of the dynamics of white privilege. As both transracial adoption and nonsecrecy have begun to undermine the hold of the "as if" adoptive family (and hence of the racially homogeneous family) on our social imagination, so they might also undermine the notion that the child available for adoption is a "parentless" child. These changes are linked; the virtual disappearance of the family of origin in the construction of the "as if" adoptive family suggested that the child available for adoption was unencumbered, a person without ties to parents, simply awaiting placement with new parents to begin a new life. Under the traditional model, the child was treated as figuratively "abandoned" and so without roots. It is possible, however, to change practice and discourse so that they do not suggest that adoption entails a clean break from the original parents, following their abandonment of the child, but instead suggest that many parent(s) relinquish their children because they can't give them the care they need. This change would counteract the disparagement of people, primarily women, who place their children for adoption, and in particular would give dignity and voice to women of color.

The "Parentless" Child

While there have always been a significant number of adoptions, whether formal or informal, in which children were placed with family members or friends who maintained ties with the original parents, the traditional model for legal adoption was "stranger adoption." Under this model, social practice and law made a clean break between the family of origin and the child, and then placed the now "parentless" child in an adoptive family. In domestic adoptions, the clean break was facilitated by sealing adoption records. In international adoptions, United States law required that in order for a foreign-born child with two surviving parents to qualify for "orphan" status—which is necessary for adoption in the United States—the child must be legally "abandoned" by both parents. These measures were designed to prevent kidnapping and involuntary relinquishment, but they also constructed the child as "a kind of open cultural space (little, cute, girl) which simply needed to be filled with love."[56] In both domestic and international adoptions, the child was often represented as a foundling, a generic child without traceable roots in a specific past, even though in most voluntary adoptions the birth parents planned to relinquish the child, whether to an agency, doctor, or lawyer.

The legal and cultural construction of the child available for adoption as a "parentless" child affected the way people viewed not only the child, but also the adoptive parents and the original parents. The adoptive parents were often portrayed as rescuers, while the original parents were imagined as people who had "abandoned" their child. By and large, society did not judge those who relinquished a child for adoption kindly or compassionately. The widely accepted procedure of confidentiality and issuance of a new birth certificate "lock[ed] into place the notion that relinquishing one's child need[ed] to be hidden" and "sustain[ed] the view that the separation itself was inherently bad."[57]

The understanding of the adoptable child as a parentless child and the practices that contributed to it started to change, however, when some states began mandating unsealed records and permitting open adoption. These changes, as Sanger noted, occurred partly in response to birth mothers' realization that they controlled "a desirable commodity in short supply" and so could "think through the terms under which they might be willing to part with it."[58] This exercise of agency or decision-making authority by the birth mother or birth parents altered the depiction of the child available for adoption as "parentless" or "abandoned." In open adoption the birth mother changed from supplicant to partner in making a decision about the placement of her child; the terms of adoption, once thought to be absolute, became negotiable to some extent; the original parents remained a presence in the life of their child.

With open adoption, even though a definitive transfer of custody took place, the child and the birth parents did not disappear entirely from the other's life. As Barbara Yngvesson and Maureen Mahoney persuasively contend, the child could be understood as an individual who, though separated from his or her family of origin and joined permanently to another family, was also partially constituted by his or her origins, which did not need to be concealed for the new bonds to be deep and truly familial. The original parents (often only the birth mother) could be understood as individuals for whom the fact of having begotten the child could not be obliterated.[59]

In an essay recounting her experience as a birth mother when a college student, Maureen Sweeney stated that she now wished to "develop adoption into an empowering option for pregnant women who feel that they cannot raise the child they are carrying."[60] Sweeney was not arguing for open adoption per se, but for the development of a "new paradigm" of adoption based on the experiences and observations of many people that adoption is not a temporally singular "event," not something that people experience and then "get over," but rather an ongoing reality in the lives of birth parents, adoptive parents, and adoptee. Sweeney's analysis paid particular attention to the ways in which society could view birth mothers as taking steps to provide care for their children, both in relinquishing parental rights and by their willingness to be known by and accessible to their offspring. Relinquishing a child for adoption, then, would be seen not as an act of abandonment (although this is not to deny that some parents do abandon their children) but as a responsible act for the good of the child, arising from "an ethic of care for and responsibility to all those whose lives are indelibly changed by the adoption experience."[61] The birth mother would be seen as taking steps to make sure others would take care of the child in the future.

The consideration of the birth parents' concern for the child is largely absent from arguments on *both* sides in the transracial adoption debate. Given the terms in which that argument has been framed, this is understandable. Those who have asserted that adoption agencies should not be able to place children according to race do not want to allow birth parents to insist on same-race placement. Those who have favored race-matching do not want to allow anyone, even birth parents, to select adoptive parents of a different race. Given the focus on the racial composition of the adoptive family, the disputants rarely have asked whether the birth parents—in particular the birth mother —should have a say in where her child is to be placed.

On the few occasions when someone has raised the question of whether birth parents should have a say about the race of adoptive parents, the answer has almost universally been that they (or she) should not. For example, Donna J. Goldsmith argued against giving the birth mother any opportunity to influence the placement of her offspring under the ICWA: "The concept that a mother has the right to remove her child from its extended family and community, thereby depriving the child of its heritage . . . is foreign to American Indian cultures."[62] Evelyn Blanchard gave similar testimony before Congress in 1988:

> Indian people have two relationship systems. They have a biological relational system, and they have a clan or band relational system. It is the convergence, if you will, of these two systems in tribal society that creates the fabric of tribal life. And each of us as an Indian person has a very specific place in the fabric. Those responsibilities are our rights, individual rights. And even our mother has no right to deny us those rights.[63]

There is, of course, no legally recognized body like a tribe that might be given authority to place children of other ethnic groups. When James Bowen faced the question of how the group of origin could have weight in the placement of black children, he proposed that the law give "any blood relative" of a child awaiting adoption the right to petition the court regarding custody of the child and order the court to give preference to the wishes of the extended family.[64]

Twila Perry did pay attention to the birth mother, arguing that race-blind placement could reinforce the subordination of racial minorities, particularly minority women. Responding directly to Bartholet's "Where Do Black Children Belong?" in an article she published just about the time Congress adopted MEPA, Perry explained that, contrary to Bartholet and MEPA, she preferred placing black children with black adoptive parents when possible. Her preference did not stem from concern about the survival of the group, since black survival is not really threatened by transracial adoption; the psychological well-being of children adopted by parents of another race, since many of these children seem to be very well-adjusted as children and as adults; or the transmission of cultural values, since the acquisition of a culture is distinct from membership in a particular race. Rather, Perry objected that the *discourse* about transracial adoption did nothing to challenge, and even reinforced, notions of white superiority and black inferiority that help perpetuate social inequality. Discourse about the benefits to a black child of being adopted by whites suggested that white women were superior mothers. To say "we will place this child without regard to color" simply because there is a white adult or family who wants the child, seems to give whites the power to decide whether and when to "disconnect" the child from the black community.[65] Indeed, in practice, "transracial adoption" has referred only to the adoption of black children by white families, not to a true colorblind system in which all children are assigned to prospective adoptive parents without regard to race.[66] Perry did not propose such a colorblind system; instead, she advocated attempting to match parents and child by race first, then turning to transracial placement if necessary.

Lying behind Perry's opposition to color-blind adoption was the realization that all too often society portrays black women as "inadequate to the task of mothering Black children, while white women are seen as competent to raise children of any race."[67] Viewing transracial adoption as a way to help black children can mask the ways in which the rhetoric, and possibly the practice, can perpetuate the notion that black women's bodies, and their offspring, can be appropriated or put to use by others. Similarly, Dorothy Roberts demonstrated that the denigration of black motherhood has a long history, stretching from slavery, to the exclusion of most black women from "mothers' pensions" in the 1920s and 1930s, to criticism of black matriarchy in the Moynihan Report, to excoriation of the "welfare queen" in the 1990s. Roberts warned that the abandonment of race-matching in adoption could contribute not only to the desirable goal of defying racist assumptions that would limit love by race, but also to the continuation of "a system designed to provide childless white couples with babies and with the type of babies they prefer." While transracial adoption can and does help specific black children and defies segregationist practices, "[i]t does nothing to diminish the devaluation of Black childbearing."[68] Required race-matching acknowledges black families' child-rearing abilities, but undercuts efforts to form families across racial lines.

I am uneasy with arguments both for and against race-matching that do not make the birth parents' wishes concerning the race of the adoptive parents part of the placement decision. Arguments for race-matching run up against the fact that in other contexts liberal theory and law abjure the notion of assigning identity or rights by blood. Painful as it may be for others, when someone changes nationality, converts to a new religion, or forges a racial identity different from that of her relatives, a liberal society allows, and should allow, such self-definition. Indeed, I find it important to the legitimacy of the ICWA that the parents' tribal membership, not simply their race, creates the grounds for transferring jurisdiction to tribal courts. As long as people can exit from the tribe, the parents' tribal membership is in some ways a stand-in for their understanding of their identity. Until children grow up to decide such matters for themselves, their parents' declaration of self-understanding and intent may properly be taken as a proxy for their own. Parents have this authority not because they "own" their children, but because someone must speak for the child, and liberty is best protected if parents, not the state or other individuals or groups, assume this responsibility. If parents are tribal members, it is proper that the tribal courts have jurisdiction in matters concerning custody of their children. What about situations in which adoption cases involving Native American children are heard by state courts? I am not convinced that these courts should be bound to place the child with Native American adoptive parents regardless of the declared wishes of the birth parents (often the birth mother). The child available for adoption cannot be treated simply as someone so "embedded" in a racial group that the group can claim the child regardless of the mother's wishes; I am loath to take away agency and voice from a woman in difficult circumstances, and I would side with her even in the face of tribal opposition.[69]

I also find suggestions that birth parents should not be able to request same-race placements disturbing. Parents with vibrant ties to a group may express their hope that their children be placed where they will have the opportunity to forge similar ties. Richard Banks argued that because white privilege confers so much power, he finds parental choice by minority-race parents more acceptable than by white parents.[70] Giving choice to black birth parents would undermine racism regardless of whether they sought same-race or different-race placement: black birth parents' choice of same-race placement would empower blacks as a group, and their choice of transracial placement would create multiracial families. White birth parents' choice of same-race placement, however, would replicate rather than challenge racial hierarchy, and whites would be unlikely to choose to place their child with parents of a racial minority group. These considerations are strong arguments for a racially differentiated policy. But the Equal Protection Clause of the Constitution prohibits laws that on their face treat individuals of different races differently. Giving the state the power to exclude expressions of parental choice by white but not by black birth parents raises such difficult equal protection issues, and would in practice do so little to dismantle existing racial hierarchies, that I reject it.

I propose reframing the issue of where to place the Native American or African-American child from one that pits equal individual rights (of the adoptive parents or the child) against group rights, to one that reinserts the birth parents, particularly the birth mother, into the discussion. The relative invisibility of the birth parents—usually, in fact, a single mother—in the debates about transracial adoption reveals the way in which gender and race combine to marginalize birth mothers who are members of a racial minority or mothers of biracial children. One would think that the birth parents, as the concrete link between the child and the racial group claiming an interest in or jurisdiction over the child's placement, would be the appropriate persons to present their understanding of their own and the child's racial identity, but neither ICWA nor MEPA gives birth parents much voice. Unfortunately, the dismissal of the birth mother's views and wishes reinforces presumptions about the irrelevance or the irresponsibility of women who relinquish their children for adoption.

Antiracists' reservations about transracial adoption by whites often stemmed not from an objection to mixed-race families themselves, but from an awareness of the historical and contemporary struggles of black women to keep custody of their children, to protect them from harm, and to raise them to healthy adulthood in a racist society. Framing the debate on transracial adoption as one involving the possible conflict between individual and group rights (or between liberal and communitarian values) does not capture the complex dynamics of sexual and racial subordination involved in minority women's efforts to control their reproductive and family lives.[71] Listening to birth parents' views concerning the placement of their children would make it harder both for individuals of the dominant race and for a minority group to lay claim to a child by ignoring or defying the parents' (or mother's) wishes.

Listening to birth mothers cannot, of course, unravel the web of social and economic injustice—including poverty, lack of access to birth control, and stigmatization of unwed motherhood—that leads women both in the United States and abroad to relinquish their children for adoption. But registering a birth mother's views at least makes it harder to regard her simply as the supplier of a resource (babies) for others (adoptive parents). The child available for adoption cannot be dealt with simply as an unencumbered individual without ties to specific others, but must simultaneously be seen as someone with a unique story of origin. Again, this recognition that a child needs to be viewed both as an individual and as a person constituted by various relationships offers an alternative to the norm of the "as if" adoptive family and the image of the "parentless" child. Adoption discourse and practice that recognize the possibility of a variety of family forms, and the multiple relationships that shape adoptee, birth parents, and adoptive parents alike, will make life better not only for families touched by adoption but also for other families that do not conform to the traditional model of the two-parent heterosexual family in which the social and biological parents are one and the same.

Reflections on Policy

The debates over nonsecrecy and transracial adoption not only illustrate the philosophical dilemma of whether (or when) to regard the infant available for adoption as an individual or a person embedded in relationships with others, but also the ways in which traditional discourses concerning birth mothers and their infants contribute to the hold of patriarchal norms in law and social policy. Under the norms that guided traditional "clean break" adoptions, the eclipse of the birth mother allowed the infant and adoptive parents to build their relationship as if starting from scratch. Advocates of nonsecrecy who oppose the sealing of birth records, by contrast, challenge the "as if" family. They attest to the fact that a family does not have to shut out all adults except the legal parents in order to be "real," stable, and enduring. In independent open adoptions in which both birth and adoptive parents choose "people who are 'like' themselves or an idealized image of who they might be," this matching may "perpetuate the notion that a real family is one that mimics biologically based 'likeness,'" at the same time that the openness works to undermine the hold of the "as if" family on people's imaginations.[72] Thus, although open adoption may encourage nonessentialist thinking that does not equate motherhood with a biological relationship and in this way contribute to a pluralization of family forms, it may also encourage people to try to form a family with people like themselves and in that way to mirror the biological family.

Many advocates of transracial adoption, for their part, in focusing on the right of the child awaiting adoption to be placed in a permanent family, draw attention away from the birth parent(s). The birth parents have relinquished their parental rights, severing their ties to the child and the child's ties to a specific family and history. The adoptable child is generalized, a being innocent and deserving of love; the child is like all other children, and his or her race is irrelevant. For opponents of transracial adoption, however, the child's ties to the group of origin, and hence his or her race, are relevant. For these advocates of same-race placement, focusing on the group draws attention away from the birth parent(s).

Brought into dialogue with one another, these discussions of non-secret and transracial adoption highlight the ways that gender, race, and class are implicated in adoption policy. All adoptions challenge the gender norm, which has defined the capacity to bear a child as a woman's preeminent characteristic. Adoption says that a woman may decide not to raise a child she has borne, and a woman who has not borne a child may decide to be a mother. In severing the connection between childbearing and childrearing, adoption suggests both that a woman does not require a male partner in order to become a mother, and that men as well as women can do the "hands on" work of parenting.

Finding ways to acknowledge adoption as a cooperative endeavor may be particularly difficult when the adoptive families occupy quite different positions in the social, racial, and economic hierarchies of their society (including global society in the case of international adoption) than the birth mothers (or parents) do. As Yngvesson's reflections on the experiences of adoptive families in both the United States and Sweden suggest, in nonsecret adoptions, when parents are aware that their child may someday meet his or her birth parent(s), they must do more than accept the "motherless" child, the abandoned innocent. They must receive the child in his or her specificity and acknowledge his or her social history. They not only must love their child, but also make room in their lives for those things that "belong to" their child, although the extent of such sharing will vary greatly.[73] To engage in nonsecret or open adoption should involve not only love for and acceptance of the child, but acknowledgment of the original parent(s).

If public policy encouraged soliciting the views of birth parents and allowing adult adoptees access to their birth records, some of the objections to transracial adoption voiced by Twila Perry, Ruth-Arlene Howe, Dorothy Roberts, and others might be mitigated. A prospective adopter's preference for a child of the same race (or of a different race) is not in and of itself a bad thing; adoptive parents have very different desires and capabilities, and live in communities with widely differing social networks and resources. Diverse circumstances seem to warrant diverse arrangements. What is objectionable is a discourse that obscures the class, gender, and race inequalities that put some parents at such a dire disadvantage and contribute to their inability to raise their children. Were the birth parent(s) to have a say in the placement of the child, to know that the adoptee might contact them when he or she reached age eighteen, and possibly to exchange letters and photographs with the adoptive parents during the child's minority, transracial placements would be less likely to suggest that (white) adoptive parents can appropriate the children of women of color when it suits their purposes.

I would like to see these salutary aspects of independent and open adoption incorporated into adoptions arranged by agencies, and I favor agency oversight of adoptions. Agency adoption suggests that providing physical and psychological nurturance to children is a social and public responsibility, not simply a matter to be arranged between individuals. Placing a public agency between the original family and the adoptive family reflects the notion that the original parent(s) entrust the child to the public (to the state as *parens patriae*), and that the public (in the form of the agency and its rules) accepts responsibility for the welfare of the child. Another family then assumes *specific* responsibility for the child. The practices of independent adoption, particularly some of the advertising, focus on the satisfaction of adults' desires along with the child's interests; agency adoption introduces explicit attention to the public interest in, and responsibility for, children. Developing policies to guide agency adoptions requires us to articulate what principles we think should govern the formation of families in which the social and biological parents are different people. The public discussion of family policy, as well as the symbolic value of the community assuming responsibility for children, are strong reasons to favor agency adoption.

As adoption practice moves toward greater "openness," and the exchange of specific information about the adopted child, general awareness of the coercive effects of some situations in which a woman may "choose" to relinquish her child for adoption will probably increase. One kind of coercion stems from social customs and mores that make bearing a child out of wedlock a cause of stigma and "social death" for a woman. Another stems from economic conditions that put some people in circumstances where they cannot provide a child with food, clothing, and shelter (much less adequate education). There can be no greater indictment of structurally produced inequalities than that they cause some people to have to give up their children. The suggestion by some members of Congress during the debates on the 1996 Personal Responsibility Act (welfare reform) that children of some welfare recipients be removed from their mothers' custody and placed in orphanages was an appalling lapse in moral reasoning and an abdication of social responsibility for children.[74]

Transforming the model of the "as if" adoptive family created by the incorporation of the "parentless" child entails seismic shifts in the ways we view both women and children. The birth mother remains knowable; the child is treated both as an individual and as someone with ties to people outside the adoptive family. Keeping these two aspects of the child's identity in mind emphasizes the fact that the child is no one's possession. "There is a deep and profound sense that we do not own our children. All children can escape the confines of what we would make of them."[75] That parenthood is not a proprietary relationship is true of *all* families, but is easier to see when two sets of parents must cooperate (even if only in the moments of relinquishing and assuming custody) to provide for a child's needs.

By challenging the construction of the "as if" adoptive family, and raising questions about whether the child (particularly the infant) available for adoption should be considered "parentless" or "abandoned," nonsecret and transracial adoption make apparent what discourse and public policy should recognize, that not every child has two, and only two, "parents." Nonsecret and transracial adoption make it clear that parenthood and race are not strictly biological or naturally given categories, and they make the constructed nature of the adoptive family evident. Similarly, open adoption undermines the stereotype of the irresponsible birth mother.

The undermining of the traditional patriarchal family suggests the possibility of a new era of greater sexual equality both within the family and the larger society. As the following chapters show, however, it is difficult both to understand what equality requires, and to get people to enact the measures necessary to achieve equality. Equality between men and women in family life requires attention both to the fact that women (and not men) bear children, and to the social context in which procreation and caregiving take place. Race and class profoundly affect people's opportunities for family life. This discussion of adoption policy reminds us that the responsibility to ensure both that all children are cared for, and that all adults have an equal opportunity to form and to raise families, is not one that falls on individuals alone, but on society as a whole in enacting policy and law.

CHAPTER 2

Fathers' Rights, Mothers' Wrongs, and Children's Needs: Unwed Fathers and the Perpetuation of Patriarchy

*I*n the early 1990s, the cases of "Baby Jessica" and "Baby Richard," young children who had been placed at birth with families who hoped to adopt them, but whose biological fathers subsequently challenged the adoptions, riveted national attention. Pictures of the children playing happily with their adoptive parents, and weeping when they were separated from the only family they had known, disturbed everyone who saw them, although not everyone agreed about what the courts should have decided.

The case of "Baby Jessica" pitted the biological parents, Cara Clausen and Daniel Schmidt of Iowa, against the adoptive parents, Roberta and Jan DeBoer of Michigan.[1] When Jessica was born, Cara Clausen was unmarried, and she gave her irrevocable consent to the child's adoption two days after the birth. The man she named as the child's father on the birth certificate did the same. Within weeks, however, Clausen regretted her decision, and she informed Daniel Schmidt, not the man whose name appeared on the birth certificate, that he was the baby's father. Schmidt responded by filing a petition to establish paternity and initiating legal action to block the adoption. Schmidt contended that a biological father has a right to custody of his child unless it is shown that he is "unfit" to be a parent. After some two years of litigation, Michigan declared it did not have jurisdiction in the matter. Iowa then proceeded to enforce its decree that Schmidt's parental rights had never properly been terminated and the child had to be returned to his physical custody.

In the case of "Baby Richard," Daniella Janikova became pregnant by Otakar Kirchner in June 1990 and began living with him in his Chicago apartment that fall.[2] In January 1991, Kirchner traveled to Czechoslovakia (where both he and Janikova were born and had lived as children) for two weeks to vacation and to visit his ill grandmother. While he was away, Janikova received a phone call from Kirchner's aunt saying that he had married a woman in Czechoslovakia. Distraught, Janikova moved out of the apartment, entered a shelter for battered women for several weeks, and then moved to her uncle's house in the suburbs. Upon Kirchner's return, he contacted Janikova at her uncle's house and asked her to return to live with him, but she refused. On March 16, 1991, Janikova gave birth to Baby Richard in a suburban hospital rather than in the one she and Kirchner had previously contacted in the city. On March 20, the same day that Janikova executed her consent to the adoption, Kirchner contacted her uncle, who told him, on her instructions, that the baby had died three days after birth. Kirchner claimed that although Janikova and her relatives repeatedly told him the baby was dead, he did not believe them and attempted to establish contact with the mother and ascertain the whereabouts of his son.

Fifty-seven days after the child's birth, on Mother's Day, Janikova told Kirchner that the baby had been placed for adoption. He immediately filed an appearance contesting the baby's adoption. The trial court applied Illinois law and ruled that Kirchner was an unfit parent because he had not shown a reasonable degree of interest in the child within the first thirty days of the child's life, and the appellate court affirmed, holding that his efforts were insufficient because he did not contact a lawyer or any state agency.[3] Kirchner again appealed, and the Illinois Supreme Court reversed on June 16, 1994, holding that given Janikova's efforts to deceive Kirchner about the baby, the actions he took were sufficient to establish his claim, and the child was to be placed in his custody.[4] By then, Richard was three years old and had been living with the couple who hoped to adopt him since shortly after his birth.

Much of the public discussion centered around the question of what weight should be given in such cases to the child's emotional attachment to his or her "psychological parents." When a young child has formed strong bonds with the adults caring for him, should he remain in their custody even if others (usually birth parents) have a valid legal claim? Many child psychologists believe that the harm inflicted on a child such as Baby Richard or Baby Jessica by removing him or her from the care of the psychological parents should override any other considerations in making decisions about custody. Others have pointed out, however, that if courts always grant custody to psychological parents, adults will be tempted to keep a child in their care as long as possible regardless of the initial legal merits of their case, so that the passage of time will give them a claim as de facto parents. To protect a child from the trauma of being removed from the adults to whom he has become attached, the state must devise procedures to prevent the possibility of such delays.

At present, legal thinking is quite unsettled.[5] Many courts apply the traditional rule that in deciding whether an unwed father has parental rights they must consider the "best interest" of the child in making any decision about custody. Supporters of biological fathers' rights, by contrast, argue that when the biological mother does not wish to retain custody, the biological father's claim automatically takes precedence over that of a "stranger" who hopes to adopt.[6] Proponents of an unwed mother's right to decide to place her child for adoption, for their part, have argued that since it is the woman who carries and gives birth to the baby, the decision should be hers to make, without interference by the father. According to this view, neither the biological mother nor the state has an obligation to seek the biological father's consent to the adoption decision, or even to inform him of his paternity.[7] The debate among advocates of these perspectives raises the difficult issue of what, indeed, should be the grounding of *anyone's* claim to parental rights. Resolving this question is of practical importance; the less clear the law, the greater the number of disputes and the longer it will take to resolve them.

In my view, the "best interest," "fathers' rights," and "maternal autonomy" standards are all unsatisfactory for resolving custodial claims of unwed biological parents. I am persuaded by considerations advanced by advocates in both the maternal and paternal rights camps that the best interest standard is not appropriate for cases in which newborns are surrendered by their mothers for adoption. It is unsuitable in part because that standard does not adequately recognize the claims of biological paternity, and in part because it is difficult to guard against the biases of individual judges about what a child's best interest might be (a suburban two-parent middle-class family, for instance). A fathers' rights policy grounded in the gender-neutral principle that unwed fathers should have the same rights as unwed mothers in adoption decisions does not sufficiently acknowledge the asymmetry created by men's and women's different biological roles in procreation, particularly women's experience of pregnancy. Nor does it take sufficient account of the sex-based inequality inherent in contemporary economic and social structures. By contrast, many arguments in favor of the mother's right to decide on the custody of her child expose the ways in which gender-neutral rules applied to situations of social and economic inequality in practice perpetuate male privilege. These insights might suggest that one good way to compensate for the present social and economic inequalities would be to give women decision-making authority about reproductive matters until present social and economic inequalities based on sex diminish. This policy, however, would run the risk of reinforcing the gender stereotype that only women, not men, are the natural and proper nurturers of children. Law and social policy in the area of parental rights must walk a very fine line between treating men and women identically on the one hand, thereby encouraging a false gender-neutrality, and treating men and women differently and thereby reinforcing gender stereotypes on the other.

Thinking about what gives someone the right to participate in the decision to place a child for adoption involves thinking about what makes anyone a "parent." Genetic or biological relationship alone is not adequate grounding for legal parenthood. Determining what weight to give biological and genetic ties is important not only in cases involving claims of unwed fathers and mothers when they disagree over the decision to place their child for adoption, but also when surrogate mothers or known sperm donors seek parental rights (as I discuss in Chapters 4 and 5).

Any practice giving an unwed parent a say as to whether her or his child should be placed for adoption must recognize the importance of biological ties; the child's need for and right to emotional and physical care; women's and men's right to equal treatment; and adoptees' right to information about their biological parents and genetic origins. In the case of a newborn, these considerations suggest that in order to have any claim, the biological father must take concrete steps to demonstrate his commitment to the child before the biological mother relinquishes the child for adoption. In reaching their decision, courts must have the authority to judge both his efforts to take responsibility for the child and the mother's objections to his claim. Developing practices and policies that reflect these factors again requires balancing respect for the autonomy that allows individuals to act and to create new families and new family forms, and recognition of the web of sexual, biological, and social relationships that link the original parents to one another and each of them to the child.

In this chapter I continue to explore the question of what kinds of family relationships the law should recognize and protect by examining the issues raised when an unwed biological father tries to veto the unwed mother's adoption decision. As long as biological parents do not live together and jointly raise their offspring—whether because they never married, or have divorced or separated—some of them will argue about custody. Some disagreements could be resolved more quickly if the law were clearer about when, and why, an unwed biological father has a right to step in and preclude an adoption initiated by the biological mother or the state. To be effective and persuasive, the principles in these instances should be consonant with those used to decide other kinds of disputes about who has parental status. Were the law clearer, resolution would come more quickly, and we might avoid tragedies like those of Baby Jessica and Baby Richard in the future.

Historical Background

Despite the stigma that long attended unwed motherhood that I looked at in the last chapter, for a long time unwed mothers, and not fathers, were regarded by the law as the only legally recognized or custodial parent of their children. This was true of the common law (law growing out of judges' decisions) and statutory law (laws passed by legislatures) well into the twentieth century. Gradually, both some statutory changes and developments in constitutional law gave unwed fathers some parental rights. Several Supreme Court cases in the latter half of the twentieth century addressed the question of whether the law should recognize greater rights for unwed fathers, and in doing so opened up the question of what makes *anyone* a legal parent.

The common law, which largely regulated legal aspects of family relationships in America well into the nineteenth century, was profoundly patriarchal; legal definitions of who is a father and the extent of paternal responsibilities governed not only a man's relationships with his children but also with women both inside and outside his family. Under the common law a man had complete custodial authority over any children born of his wife, even if they were sired by another man, yet he had no legal relationship at all to children he sired out of wedlock. The child of his wife took his surname, the nonmarital child did not. The marital child had a right to financial support from him, the nonmarital child did not. The marital child had the right to inherit from him if he died without a will, the nonmarital child did not.[8]

The husband's authority over the marital child was an extension of his authority over his wife. Under the common law doctrine of coverture, a wife's legal agency was subsumed in that of her husband during marriage. A wife could not enter into contracts, sue or be sued, or engage in other legal transactions without being joined by her husband. He owned outright her moveable property and had control of (although he could not alienate) her real estate. Torts she committed in his presence were chargeable to him, not to her. A married woman also had no right to refuse her husband sexually; marital rape was not recognized as an offense. So complete was the husband's custodial authority that during his lifetime he had the power to convey his parental rights to a third person without the mother's consent, and he could name someone other than the mother to be the child's guardian after his death.[9]

Thus, under the common law, a man's legal relationship to his offspring was governed by his relationship to their mother. If the woman was his wife, a child was "his," so much so that he exercised exclusive custodial authority. If the mother was not his wife, however, the child was "*fillius nulli*," the child of no one. Obviously, these rules affected both lineage and property. They allowed a man to lay claim to legitimate heirs (for without marriage, who would know for certain who the father of a child might be?) and to avoid squandering his estate supporting other children. While the father was shielded from financial responsibility for his "spurious" offspring, a woman who bore children outside of marriage was "ruined"; unmarried mothers' desperate attempts at suicide and infanticide dot the pages of social histories and nineteenth-century novels. To keep children off public support, Poor Laws assigned mothers financial responsibility for their offspring and gave them custodial rights as long as they could support them. A woman's responsibility for her nonmarital children punished her for sex outside of marriage and pushed women to join themselves to men through marriage.

It is no wonder that women's rights advocates from the mid-nineteenth century on protested against the patriarchal assumptions and the sexual double-standard implicit in this configuration of rules governing marital and nonmarital progeny. During the nineteenth century, in part due to women's rights advocacy, legislatures began to replace common law rules with statutes that granted wives equal custodial rights with their husbands. By the early twentieth century, judges deciding divorce cases began to prefer mothers as custodians of marital children of "tender years" (usually under seven or ten years of age).[10] Eventually the standard of the "best interest of the child"—which did not automatically prefer either spouse and which purported to recognize the needs of the child as paramount—replaced any presumption explicitly favoring the custodial claim of either married parent when they divorced.

With respect to nonmarital children the law changed more slowly, and the impetus came mainly from children's rights advocates who wanted to get rid of the legal disabilities of "illegitimacy," such as the inability to collect survivors' benefits, receive child support, and inherit from the father.[11] The Civil Rights movement also spurred reformers to get rid of all legal disabilities based on birth, not only those of race. Thus the common law protections of fathers against the claims of nonmarital children and their mothers have been largely dissolved, and paternal responsibility for children born outside marriage established. But getting rid of the common law disabilities suffered by "illegitimate" children was not the same thing as granting unwed fathers the right to custody of their children. Impetus to recognize such a right stemmed from the reconsideration of gender roles sparked by women's changing participation in the paid labor force and by the intellectual ferment of the women's movement. Some advocates of unwed biological fathers' rights asserted, however, that the ability to raise one's biological child is a fundamental good, and that even though this interest was not recognized by the common law, it is protected by the United States Constitution.

Those who argue that under the Constitution men and women must have equal rights to claim custody of their nonmarital offspring, and so to have a say in the decision to place a child for adoption, look to a series of decisions handed down by the United States Supreme Court since 1972: *Stanley v. Illinois, Quilloin v. Wolcott, Caban v. Mohammed, Lehr v. Robertson,* and *Michael H. v. Gerald D.*[12] These decisions have established that at least in instances when an unmarried biological father has established a relationship with his child by an unmarried woman, the father's right to continue the relationship may be constitutionally protected. Although these decisions do not by any means resolve all the dilemmas surrounding the custody of infants born to unmarried biological parents, they provide a useful starting point for thinking about them.

The Court first considered the custodial rights of unmarried biological fathers in 1972 in *Stanley v. Illinois.* Mr. Stanley had lived with his three biological children and their mother, to whom he was not married, intermittently for eighteen years. When the mother died, Illinois declared the children wards of the state and placed them with court-appointed guardians. This was done without a hearing as to Stanley's fitness as a parent. Stanley protested, arguing that Illinois law denied him equal protection of the laws, since neither unwed mothers, nor married fathers or mothers, could be deprived of custody of their children unless they were shown to be unfit. Illinois argued that Stanley's fitness or unfitness was irrelevant, because an unwed father was not a "parent" whose existing relationship with his children must be considered; an unwed father was presumed unfit because he had not married the mother. The Supreme Court rejected Illinois' argument, stating that "[t]he private interest here, that of a man in the children he has sired and raised, undeniably warrants deference and, absent a powerful countervailing interest, protection."[13] Failure to provide a hearing on parental fitness for an unwed father violated both the due process and the equal protection clauses of the Fourteenth Amendment.

In cases after *Stanley* the Court drew distinctions between biological fathers who, like Stanley, had been involved in raising their biological children, and those who had not assumed day-to-day practical responsibility for them. In *Quilloin*, Leon Quilloin sought to prevent the adoption of his eleven-year-old biological child by the child's stepfather, Mr. Wolcott. The Court upheld a Georgia statute that stipulated that a biological mother alone could consent to the adoption of her child; the consent of the unwed biological father was required only if he had legitimated the child by marrying the mother or establishing legal paternity. The Court said that no due process violation occurred if the contact between the biological father and child had been only sporadic. The Court said that if the biological father had never sought custody and the adoption gave legal recognition to the actual living situation of the child, there was no constitutional requirement that the state obtain the biological father's consent to the adoption.

The next year, hearkening back to *Stanley,* the Court said in *Caban* that a New York statute that required unwed biological mothers, but not biological fathers, to consent to the adoption of their children was unconstitutional when an unwed biological father's relationship to his child was "fully comparable" to that of the mother. The case arose when the mother's new husband, Mr. Caban, sought to adopt her children. Like Stanley, Caban had previously lived with the children and their mother for several years. He argued that the law which required only the biological mother's consent to adoption violated the equal protection clause. Caban also claimed that biological fathers had a due process right or liberty interest "to maintain a parental relationship with their children absent a finding they are unfit as parents."[14] New York argued that the distinction between biological mother and biological father was justified because of the fundamental difference between the maternal and paternal relationship. The Supreme Court agreed with Caban, holding that "maternal and paternal roles are not invariably different in importance," but it explicitly declined to offer an opinion about whether a distinction such as New York had made would be valid with regard to newborn adoptions.[15]

Lehr v. Robertson also concerned a biological father's effort to block the adoption of his child by her stepfather, but, unlike Mr. Stanley and Mr. Caban, and like Mr. Quilloin, Jonathan Lehr had had almost no contact with his biological daughter, Jessica. Lehr claimed, however, that he had a liberty interest in an actual or potential relationship with Jessica, and that the state's failure to provide him notice of her pending adoption violated due process. He also asserted that the gender-based New York statute violated equal protection because it required the consent of the biological mother, but not the biological father, for an adoption. Holding that Lehr had not made sufficient contact with the child to establish a paternal right, the Supreme Court declared that an unwed biological father's rights are a function of the actual responsibilities he shoulders. The majority held that the biological connection alone is not sufficient to *guarantee* an unwed father a voice in the adoption decision, although it affords him an *opportunity* to be heard: the "biological connection . . . offers the natural father an opportunity that no other male possesses to develop a relationship with his offspring. If he grasps that opportunity and accepts some measure of responsibility for the child's future, he may enjoy the blessings of the parent-child relationship." But if he fails to grasp the opportunity, "the Equal Protection Clause does not prevent a State from according the two parents different legal rights."[16]

The rule of thumb that the Supreme Court seemed to be developing in these cases, namely, that an unwed biological father who had established a substantial relationship with his child had a constitutionally protected interest in maintaining that relationship, was sidelined in a subsequent decision about an unwed biological father's rights. In *Michael H. v. Gerald D.* the Court found that a California statute creating an irrebuttable presumption that a woman's husband was the father of a child she bore (that is, the husband would be the legal father no matter what facts could be presented to show that he was not the biological father, unless both the putative father and the husband's wife requested a blood test to rebut the presumption of the husband's paternity) was constitutional. A biological father, Michael H., who had lived intermittently with his biological daughter and her mother even though the mother was married to and sometimes lived with her husband as well, argued that he had a right to a hearing to establish his paternity (and, if successful, seek visitation) when the husband and wife sought to cut off his contact with the child.

Reflecting the unsettled nature of our society's current thinking about biology, nurture, and parenthood, the case produced no fewer than five opinions from a deeply fractured Court. The Justices disagreed not only over the specific question of the protection to be given to Michael and Victoria, the daughter, but also over the approach that the Court should take in order to answer this question. The plurality decision, written by Justice Scalia and joined in full only by Chief Justice Rehnquist, rejected Michael's claim. Justice Scalia contended both that the state had an interest in preserving the "unitary family," and that neither Michael nor his genetic daughter had a constitutionally protected liberty interest in maintaining their relationship. He argued that the proper method for discerning what interests are protected by the Constitution was to look at "the most specific level at which a relevant tradition protecting, or denying protection to, the asserted right can be identified."[17] Justice O'Connor and Kennedy agreed with Justice Scalia's conclusion but not his reasoning.[18] In a concurring opinion, Justice Stevens asserted, without much apparent basis, that Michael could have obtained visitation rights as an "other person having an interest in the welfare of the child," and so did not need further protection.[19] Two dissenting opinions supported Michael's right to a hearing but used quite different grounds to do so. Justice White, joined by Justice Brennan, reiterated the view he expressed in *Lehr* that biology itself creates a presumptive parental right.[20] Justice Brennan, joined by Justices Marshall and Blackmun, argued that the *combination* of biology and nurture establishes the liberty interest Michael claimed.[21] Justice Brennan suggested that once a relationship between father and child exists, the mother cannot then exclude an otherwise fit father from being heard with respect to his paternal rights. His opinion left open the question of to what extent Michael's situation was like or unlike that of an unmarried biological father of a child born to an *unmarried* woman.

These decisions do not tell us whether under the Constitution an unwed biological father has a right to veto the adoption of a newborn even if he has had no opportunity to establish the kind of relationship and provide the kind of care that the Court has declared protects parental rights. And when the Court refused to hear an appeal in the Baby Richard case it declined an opportunity to resolve the issue. The unsettled nature of constitutional doctrine concerning an unwed father's rights when the mother wishes to place the child for adoption is reflected in the great variety of state laws governing paternal consent.[22] Advocates of fathers' rights insist that unwed biological fathers do have such a constitutional right, and that when the biological mother has decided to relinquish her parental rights, a biological father, unless shown to be "unfit," is entitled to assume custody of his offspring. Advocates of mothers' rights, on the other hand, assert that, having been pregnant with the child, the mother should have the authority to make this decision without interference from anyone, including the father. For my part, I argue that this question cannot be decided without careful attention being paid to the child. The Supreme Court was correct to ground parental rights in a combination of biology and nurture, and whether any individual father should have the right to veto an adoption will depend on what *specific actions* he has taken to provide for the mother and child. Parental rights cannot be decided without considering the complex web of relationships involved in procreative activity, relationships involving mother, father, and child alike.

Fathers' Rights versus Mothers' Rights

In recent years some unwed biological fathers have claimed that, because of the mother's lack of cooperation, they have not found any way to meet the Court's demand in *Lehr* that a biological father who wants to retain his parental rights and "enjoy the blessings of the parent-child relationship" act to "grasp the opportunity" to develop a relationship with his offspring by assuming some "responsibility for the child's future."[23] Should a biological father have the opportunity to veto an adoption regardless of the wishes of the mother? Should adoption proceedings not be allowed until the unwed father has been heard? What considerations should guide us as we try to evaluate such issues? To answer these questions we need to think about both the basis of claims for custodial rights and the relative claims of biological mothers and fathers outside of marriage.

The argument that the biological father must be given custody when the biological mother chooses not to raise the child is grounded first of all in the conviction that parenthood is a significant good in the lives of men as well as women. Fathers might wish to raise their children for the same reasons mothers do—sharing intimacy and love, nurturing a child to adulthood, seeing one's genetic inheritance survive into the next generation, and passing on ethnic and religious traditions. A commitment to gender neutrality led most states to abandon an automatic maternal preference if mother and father, married or unmarried, each sought custody, and the same commitment would suggest that the law require the consent of *both* parents, if known, before the child can be adopted.

A variety of commentators support an unwed father's right to veto the adoption of his child on the grounds that fathers have an interest fully comparable to that of mothers in exercising parental rights and responsibilities. Claudia Serviss says all parents have "a constitutionally protected opportunity interest in developing a parent-child relationship."[24] John Hamilton argues that all unwed fathers have a right to be notified by the state of the existence of their offspring and be heard before any adoption can proceed, and that the state may therefore require the biological mother to identify the biological father.[25] Daniel Zinman insists that the state must not only notify the biological father of the child's existence, but also place the child with him while custody is being adjudicated, while Jeffrey Boyd argues that when the biological mother has relinquished her rights, if a father steps forward promptly to acknowledge paternity and seek custody, the state must give him preference unless he is shown to be unfit.[26]

Some courts appear receptive to these arguments for a gender-neutral standard. For example, in deciding *In the Matter of Kelsey S.*, the California Supreme Court held unconstitutional a statute that gave unwed mothers and legally recognized or "presumed" fathers a greater say in pre-adoption proceedings to terminate parental rights than it gave to unwed biological fathers. The Court declared that the statute rested on a "sex-based distinction" that bore no relationship to any legitimate state interest once the child was outside the mother's body and she had decided to relinquish custody.[27]

Deciding what actions by the unwed biological father constitute a sufficiently prompt or adequate manifestation of his intent to assume responsibility for the child is extremely difficult. For example, the various Illinois courts that heard the case of Baby Richard did not agree that the boy's biological father took adequate steps to show his concern after the baby's birth.[28] The difficulty of establishing relevant standards does not, however, mean that the effort should be abandoned.

The presumption of fitness for biological parents also avoids the dangers of subjective judgment and cultural prejudice that seem unavoidable in attempts to determine the child's best interest.[29] Use of the best interest test in cases of an infant who has lived with no adult caregiver for any appreciable period of time invites the court to make judgments about the relative merits of a whole array of "lifestyle" issues that are not subject to scrutiny when an unwed biological father does not contest a biological mother's wish to retain custody of her child. A "fitness" standard applied to unwed biological fathers would avoid the possibility that an adoption decision might rest on a judge's preference that a child be raised in a two-parent household rather than by a single male, or a judge's prediction that middle-class professionals will give a child more "advantages" than a working-class couple would. One supporter of an unwed father's right to custody argues that a best interest determination "is subject to abuse and may lead to paternalistic infringement on the parent-child relationship in the name of the child's welfare." The traditional preference for rearing a child in a two-parent home, combined with the long waiting list of prospective adoptive parents, makes a best interest test "a no-win situation for the unwed father of a newborn with whom he has not yet had the opportunity to develop an emotional tie."[30] In 1987, the Georgia Supreme Court explicitly rejected the best interest test in favor of a fitness standard and held that "If [the father] has not abandoned his opportunity interest, the standard which must be used to determine his rights to legitimate the child is his fitness as a parent to have custody of the child. If he is fit he must prevail."[31]

The question of whether an unwed biological father shall have a right to custody of his newborn infant is not simply about a biological father's "fitness," however, or even the actions he has taken to establish his parental claim. For the unmarried biological father to assume custody, the biological mother's expressed wishes concerning any other placement for the child will of necessity be overridden. Arguments that a biological father should be able to veto the adoption decision of the biological mother and assume custody run up against counterarguments that the courts should give an unwed biological mother authority to decide who shall take custody of her newborn child. These counterarguments must be considered before deciding whether an unwed biological father who is not "unfit" should have custodial rights.

Arguments for using the "fitness" standard for unwed biological fathers falsely assume that once a mother has surrendered the child for adoption she has no further relevant wishes with respect to custody. Defenders of an unwed biological father's right to veto an adoption often contrast what they portray as his laudable desire to assume custody and to care for the child with the mother's uncaring decision not to raise the child herself. The image of the "bad mother," and the assumption that the mother must be indifferent to the child she chooses not to raise, hover just beneath the surface of these depictions. But the notion that once a mother decides to relinquish her child for adoption she can have no further relevant concerns, denigrates both her experience of pregnancy and the nature of her decision. Women relinquish their newborns for adoption for many reasons: lack of money or job prospects, youth or immaturity, feelings of inadequacy or isolation. While some women may be indifferent to the placement of their children, in most cases women agonize over the adoption decision and try to make certain to do what is best for the baby.[32]

A woman's decision to place her child for adoption also does not mean that she is indifferent about the question of who raises the child. The argument that an unwed biological father should be preferred to adoptive parents because they are "strangers" to the child inappropriately ignores the biological mother's preference that the child be adopted through an agency or private placement rather than placed with a guardian or in the father's custody. If the mother has had very little contact with the father beyond the act of intercourse that led to her pregnancy, for example, the father may be as much a *social* "stranger" to her and the child as the adoptive parents, and his claim rests on genetics alone. Contrasting the biological father's rights to those of strangers obscures the fact that the fundamental or precipitating disagreement about custody is not between the adoptive parents and the biological father, but between the two biological parents. And if the mother has known the father over a considerable period of time, her unwillingness to make him the custodial parent needs to be examined to see why she feels as she does, just as it would be if the parents were married.

Are there any reasons to weigh the biological mother's wishes about who shall (or shall not) take custody of the child more heavily than those of the biological father? At the time of birth the relationship of biological father and mother to the child is neither biologically nor socially symmetrical. She has borne the child for nine months, for which there is no precise male analog; indeed, no one else can perform functions analogous to those of gestation.[33] The biological mother's "expectant" state has affected both her own physiological experience and the ways in which others view and interact with her.[34] To what extent should gestation affect the right to make custodial decisions concerning a newborn?

Some theorists argue that the fact that only the woman is engaged in the physical gestation of the human fetus should make a decisive difference in the rights given to unwed mothers and fathers in deciding on the custody of their offspring. According to sociologist Barbara Katz Rothman, parenting is a social relationship and parental rights are established by caregiving. In her view, the biological difference between mother and father is crucial and conclusive in establishing their respective claims for custody of newborns: "Infants belong to their mothers at birth because of the unique nurturant relationship that has existed between them up to that moment. That is, birth mothers have full parental rights, including rights of custody, of the babies they bore." By the same token, other persons with a genetic tie to the child do not have such rights: "We will not recognize genetic claims to parenthood, neither as traditional 'paternity' claims nor as genetic maternity in cases of ovum donation." Rothman would have the gestational mother's absolute claim last for six weeks after giving birth, and so the adoption decision would rest solely in the mother's hands during that period. After six weeks, "custody would go to the nurturing parent in case of dispute." Rothman emphasizes that her preference for the gestational mother rests on her understanding of pregnancy as "a social as well as a physical relationship," and that "*any* mother is engaged in a social interaction with her fetus as the pregnancy progresses."[35] Neither the physical interdependence nor the social relationship between the gestational mother and fetus can be fully shared by any other adult, no matter how attentive. Actual caregiving, not genetic connection, creates familial bonds and, in this case, Rothman argues, custodial rights.

Others also have argued that parental rights usually are not symmetrical, and that the social or biological bonds (or both) between mothers and children should give mothers the authority to decide who should have custody of their offspring. Nancy Erickson argues that the liberty interest that a parent has "to control the care, custody, and upbringing of the child" pertains only to the mother (not the father) of a newborn because of her role during pregnancy. At birth the mother is "not only the 'primary caretaker parent,' she is the only caretaker parent" because of her role during pregnancy.[36] Thinking about custody of older children of parents who divorce, Mary Becker argues that mothers are so frequently the primary caregivers of their children that it makes sense to adopt an automatic "maternal deference" standard rather than hold a hearing to try to determine what arrangement would be in the child's best interest: "When the parents cannot agree on a custody outcome, the judge should defer to the mother's decision on custody provided that she is fit, using the 'fitness' standard applicable when the state is arguing for temporary or permanent separation of parents and children in intact families."[37] Becker is not terribly worried that giving primacy to the mother's wishes might in some instances permit a woman to deprive a caring father of custody: "A maternal deference standard would recognize that mothers, as a group, have greater competence and standing to decide what is best for their children ... than judges, fathers, or adversarial experts. ... Mothers will sometimes make wrong decisions, but in the aggregate they are likely to make better decisions than the other possible decision makers."[38] Becker's reasoning applied to custodial decisions affecting newborns suggests that courts should defer to a biological mother, both because the woman has provided direct nurture to the fetus during pregnancy, and because, on average, biological mothers' decisions are likely to be as good as or better than those of anyone else.

Martha Fineman, similarly very critical of the best interest standard, would replace it with a "primary caregiver" standard.[39] Fineman argues that the best interest of the child standard frequently disadvantages mothers by looking to the likely future financial resources of father and mother. It would be more appropriate (both in terms of fairness to the parents and of the child's emotional well-being), Fineman asserts, to look instead at who has actually given the child physical and emotional care up to the present. In most, but not all, instances, this will be the mother. Although Fineman does not discuss custody of newborns, if courts were to apply the primary caregiver standard to the kinds of disputes I am discussing, it would suggest that the mother who has borne and given birth should make the custody decision concerning the infant.

Many arguments for giving an unwed biological father custody of an infant child whom a biological mother wishes to have adopted not only ignore the physical and social experiences of pregnancy, but invite no inquiry at all into the conditions under which the woman became pregnant. Just as looking at the biological father's actions during the mother's pregnancy would encourage men to take responsibility for their sexual acts and their offspring, so attention to the circumstances under which conception took place is reasonable to ensure that the child was not conceived as the result of abusive behavior toward the mother. In trying to determine which parent's wishes concerning adoption should prevail, it would not be unreasonable for a court to treat an unmarried biological father who had been in a long-term relationship with the mother or shared living expenses with her differently than one who engaged in casual sex or deceived the woman (perhaps saying he was single when he was in fact married), or coerced her or willfully ignored the fact that she was under the age of consent.

For all these reasons it seems clear that the existence of a genetic link alone does not give an unwed father parental rights. But the argument that a mother should have the exclusive authority to decide to relinquish her offspring for adoption runs the risk of treating some men unjustly and of locking both women and men into traditional gender roles. Barbara Katz Rothman's contention that gestational mothers always have exclusive control over custodial decisions for the child's first six weeks of life, for example, fails to acknowledge the ways in which men can either assume or disregard parental responsibility even for infants. If parental claims are properly grounded in the first instance in a combination of biological ties and nurture, then a father's genetic link by itself does not give him parental rights. Instead, the genetic relationship becomes a reason to look to see if he has attempted to assume responsibility for the child, and has done so without interfering with the mother's well-being. If, and only if, he has acted accordingly, should a court recognize his claim to custody.

A New Model

If unwed biological fathers should have some custodial claim to their children but not the extreme claim qualified only by "fitness," what standards should define the extent of their rights? The law needs to adopt stringent criteria for assessing the biological father's intention to take responsibility for and act as a parent to his child even prior to birth. Such criteria will require a shift in thinking and mode of argumentation away from an emphasis on parents as owners to parents as stewards, from abstract individualism to embodied personhood, and from parents' rights to children's needs.[40]

Many discussions of the "rights" of biological mothers and fathers reveal the inherent tension in liberal political theory and legal practice between protecting individuals and their freedoms and protecting and fostering those relationships which in fundamental ways constitute every individual.[41] The language of parental rights emphasizes the parent's status as an autonomous rights-bearer, and invoking individual rights has proved useful in minimizing the role of the state in people's procreative and childrearing decisions. For example, begetting, bearing, and raising children are for many people part of the good or fulfilling life that the liberal state is obligated to protect. Courts have recognized the importance of intergenerational ties for many people and have protected the liberty to procreate and parent a child not only in custody cases, but also in decisions prohibiting forced sterilization. And since biological parents have a variety of incentives to care for their children to the best of their ability, assigning custody to them tends to protect children's interests as well as those of adults. Giving biological parents custodial authority unless they do something to forfeit it also sets crucial limits on the exercise of state power.

Yet in other contexts, such as custody disputes at divorce, use of the language of parental rights inappropriately focuses on the individual parent rather than on the relationships that are inherent in being a "parent." Katharine Bartlett has advocated recasting many legal disputes that involve parents and children in such a way that the language used does not pit one "right" against another, but emphasizes the view that parenthood implies deep and sustained human connection and must be grounded in adult responsibility for children. "The law should force parents to state their claims . . . not from the competing, individual perspectives of either parent or even of the child, but from the perspective of each parent-child relationship."[42] Bartlett suggests that language based more explicitly on open-ended responsibility toward children would capture the nature of the parent-child relationship better than discussions framed in terms of parental rights.

When someone is considered in the role of parent, he or she cannot be viewed apart from the child that makes him or her a parent; an "autonomous" (in the sense of unfettered or atomistic) individual is precisely what a parent is *not*. A "parental right" should not be viewed as pertaining to an individual per se, but only to an individual-in-relationship with a dependent child. It is therefore entirely appropriate for the law to require that efforts be made to establish a relationship before a parental right can be recognized.

Asking a court to determine whether a man or woman has made efforts to establish a parental relationship with a newborn is, however, fraught with difficulties. Obviously, the biological father has no physical relationship to the fetus comparable to pregnancy. In addition, in assessing what kind of relationship mother and father have have established with a baby, courts need to minimize their own intrusiveness into the parents' lives and their biases about the best forms of family life. Indeed, part of the reason that both the paternal fitness test and the maternal deference standard are attractive is that each provides a fixed criterion for determining an unwed biological father's custodial claim. Unfortunately, however, the efficiency and clarity of each of these criteria are purchased at the cost of reducing the way the law talks about family relationships to an assertion of either biological fathers' or mothers' rights.

I propose that an unwed biological father have an opportunity, through his behavior, to establish his intention to parent his offspring. This approach seeks to minimize the legal effects of biological asymmetry without ignoring altogether the relevance of sexual difference. I assume that an unwed biological mother has demonstrated a parental relationship with her newborn by virtue of having carried the fetus to term, even if the pregnancy was unwanted. An unwed biological father may be required to show actual involvement with prenatal life if he wishes to have custody of the child. For example, he may have to demonstrate that he made efforts to find out whether the woman was pregnant and to provide her with both financial and emotional support during her pregnancy. The model or norm of "parent" in this case, therefore, is established not by the male who awaits the appearance of the child after birth, but by the pregnant woman.[43] Moreover, the legal norm is relationship-based rather than exclusively focused on individual rights.

Some people might object that equating pregnancy with maternal care for the fetus is an invalid assumption, especially in cases in which the mother has taken drugs or engaged in other possibly harmful behavior. As Cynthia Daniels has pointed out, the "image of the pregnant drug addict is deeply troubling, representing as it does the paradox of a woman simultaneously engaged in the destruction of life (addiction) and the perpetuation of life (pregnancy)."[44] In such cases should the mother forfeit her claim to custody or to make the decision to place the child for adoption?

It is tempting to blame, and to seek to punish, the pregnant drug user or addict when confronted by the needs of children who are physically or mentally impaired as a result of their exposure to harmful substances during gestation. It is important, however, to ascertain just what the drug-dependent mother is guilty of, and whether punishing her or taking away her right to be heard in matters concerning the custody of her child is an appropriate response to her behavior. What is the degree of a woman's culpability if, like many drug-addicted pregnant women, she sought treatment for her addiction, but was turned away? Even when it can be ascertained that fetal damage was caused by drugs or alcohol the woman took, it does not necessarily follow that she was so indifferent to the well-being of her child that she should be deprived of her right to be heard with respect to placing the child for adoption. The care the pregnant woman has given the fetus through bearing it to term and the harm her actions have caused it cannot be separated; both involve the biology and chemistry of gestation, the passage of materials across the placenta through the bloodstream. To see the pregnant drug-addict as a child abuser rather than a person who is herself in need of medical treatment is to ignore the inseparability of mother and fetus during pregnancy.[45]

The different biological roles of men and women in human reproduction make it imperative that law and public policy permit a father and mother to demonstrate commitment to their child in different ways. What is crucial is that parental rights be grounded in specific manifestations of care and demonstrable acts of parental responsibility.

What actions might a court accept as indications that an unwed biological father had made every effort to act as a parent to the child? The enormous variation in statutory provisions among the states concerning what is necessary to establish an unwed father's right to consent to adoption shows that this question is not easily answered.

Repeated attempts by the New York State legislature and courts to define the extent of a biological father's right to withhold consent to the adoption of his nonmarital child show how difficult it is to identify what actions might establish a man's intention to take responsibility for his infant offspring. In 1990, in *In re Raquel Marie X.,* the New York Court of Appeals struck down a statute that stipulated that only a father who had established a home with the mother for six months prior to her relinquishment of the child for adoption could veto the mother's adoption decision.[46] The court said that this provision imposed "an absolute condition . . . only tangentially related to the parental relationship" and allowed a woman who would not live with a man the power unilaterally to cut off his constitutionally protected interest in parenting his child.[47] It instructed the legislature to find some other way to gauge a father's commitment to his unborn child's welfare and set forth certain standards that lower courts were to follow in the meantime when judging an unwed father's parental commitment. "[T]he father must be willing to assume full custody," the court declared, "not merely attempt to prevent the adoption, and he must promptly manifest parental responsibility both before and after the child's birth."[48] In assessing the father's demonstration of responsibility, judges should look at such matters as "public acknowledgment of paternity, payment of pregnancy and birth expenses, steps taken to establish legal responsibility for the child, and other factors evincing a commitment to the child."[49]

Courts in New York have used these guidelines in resolving cases involving unwed fathers' efforts to block mothers' adoption decisions in the years since *In re Raquel Marie X.,* but New York is still without a statute governing unwed fathers' rights to consent to adoption of infants under the age of six months. Two different approaches have been evident in proposed legislation, reflecting a widely shared uncertainty over what considerations were appropriate in determining the nature and extent of an unwed biological father's custodial rights.

One approach was found in bill A 1518, introduced to the Assembly during the 1997–1998 session, and referred to the Committee on the Judiciary. The bill listed a number of actions an unwed father of an infant under six months might take to establish his right to consent to the adoption. The bill would make his consent necessary if he openly lived with the child or the child's mother prior to the placement of the child for adoption; *or* held himself out to be the father of such child during such period; *or* paid or offered to pay a fair and reasonable sum, consistent with his means, for the medical expenses of pregnancy and childbirth; *or* initiated judicial proceedings to obtain custody of the child; *or* married the child's mother.[50] Since the father needs to have taken only one of these actions, and may have initiated judicial proceedings after the child was born, this bill applies a simple "fitness" test and requires no showing of interest prior to the child's birth.

By contrast with the minimal expectations put on unwed fathers by A 1518, the Family Court Advisory and Rules Committee in its yearly Report to New York State's Chief Administrative Judge has repeatedly proposed legislation requiring a biological father to have demonstrated his commitment to his offspring in a number of ways, and to have done so both prior to and after the birth of the child.[51] In place of the "or"s in A 1518, the proposed bill of the Family Court Advisory and Rules Committee uses the conjunctive "and." This wording makes it clear that a biological father must have supported the mother or baby financially, held himself out as the father, and taken steps to initiate legal proceedings to establish paternity and assume custody of the child. This bill clearly means to grant the right to consent to an adoption only to unwed fathers who demonstrate that they have been and will be actively engaged in the care and upbringing of their offspring, and who themselves wish to assume custody; the stipulations rest on a definition of father as caretaker and nurturer, not simply as progenitor or source of sperm.

The bill proposed by the Family Court Advisory and Rules Committee is clearly more consistent with the principles set forth in this essay than is A 1518, but a fully adequate statute would go further. A court should be required to hear a mother's objections to a father's assuming custody of the child, if she has any, both because the birth of a child has resulted from a web of social interactions and relationships, and because the mother's relinquishment of the child for adoption should be viewed not as an act of abandonment but as an attempt to provide care for the child. In cases in which the mother objects to the father's assumption of custody, a court should listen to the *reasons* the mother opposes placing the child in the biological father's custody. Because parental rights must be grounded in the provision of care and the assumption of responsibility, if an unwed mother demonstrated that her pregnancy was a result of force, coercion, or deception, or that she had been under the age of consent when intercourse occurred, the father would be held to be "unfit."

Finally, a statute should provide that a pregnant woman who wishes to make plans for her child should be able to ascertain early in the pregnancy whether or not the father will step forward later to oppose the adoption. No woman should be required to notify an unwed father, but the law should provide that she may notify him in writing of the pregnancy, and the state may preclude him from a veto if he fails to act soon after receipt of such notification. Similarly, if a father is found to be entitled to veto an adoption, a mother should be able to negate her consent to the child's adoption and be put back in the same position she was in prior to her consent, that is, as one of two unwed parents each of whom seeks custody.[52]

One purpose of spelling out what actions the father needs to take to establish his claim would be to ascertain as early as possible during the pregnancy or after birth whether or not he wished custody, so that infants could be definitively freed for adoption.[53] Where the mother objected to the father assuming custody, a hearing would be necessary. A hearing would, of course, take more time than assigning custody based on a rule that any "fit" biological father prevail or that a mother be able to make the decision to place her child for adoption unimpeded by the biological father. But a hearing to ascertain whether an unwed biological father has grasped the opportunity to take responsibility for his newborn would not cause more delay than a best interest hearing. Such a hearing would be to find out facts about the unwed father's behavior and the mother's considered opinion concerning custody, not to try to project what custodial arrangement might be in the child's best interest.

These considerations leave unresolved the thorny issue of who, if anyone, has the responsibility of informing the unwed biological father of the mother's pregnancy, and of what, if any, recourse a father should have if the mother hides her pregnancy or lies to him about his paternity. In most circumstances a biological father who wishes to assume custody of his offspring should bear the responsibility of knowing of the child's existence and taking action to assume parental obligations prior to birth. Even if the mother wanted nothing to do with the father, the law might require him to enter his name on a putative fathers' registry, thereby demonstrating his commitment to a child by notifying the state, not simply the mother and his friends and family, of his intention. This would also make it clear that his purpose is to become the custodial parent of his child, not to reestablish contact with the mother.

In 1992 the New York Court of Appeals addressed the question of what effect ignorance of a woman's pregnancy should have on a biological father's right to seek custody after learning of a child's existence. Robert O. and Carol A. had been engaged and living together when Robert moved out and terminated all contact with Carol, who, unbeknownst to him, was pregnant by him. Carol did not tell Robert that she was pregnant, apparently because she believed he would think she was trying to force him to marry her. Carol contacted friends, Russell K. and his wife, and arranged for them to adopt the baby. The baby was born on October 1, 1988, turned over to Russell K. and his wife when Carol left the hospital, and formally adopted in May 1989. In January 1990, Robert and Carol reconciled and subsequently married; in March, 1990, Carol informed Robert that the baby existed and had been adopted.

Robert tried to void the adoption by arguing that his constitutional rights had been violated because neither Carol nor the state had informed him of the child's existence prior to the adoption proceedings.[54] The New York court acknowledged that "the unwed father of an infant placed for adoption immediately at birth faces a unique dilemma should he desire to establish his parental rights." His opportunity to "shoulder the responsibility of parenthood may disappear before he has a chance to grasp it." But although the father, Robert O., acted as soon as he knew of the child's existence, the adoption had been finalized ten months before. "Promptness," said the Court, "is measured in terms of the child's life, not by the onset of the father's awareness." Robert, having failed to determine in a timely fashion whether the woman with whom he had lived was pregnant, lost the right he otherwise would have had to an opportunity to show his "willingness to be a parent."[55] (By contrast, in a strikingly misogynistic assertion of the significance of genetic paternity, one defender of unwed fathers' rights proposes a jail sentence of up to two years for a woman who refuses to name the father of an infant she is surrendering for adoption.[56])

The responsibility to know of a child's existence should fall on the man who would assume responsibility for raising the child. A biological father aware of the mother's pregnancy should be required to act prior to birth and soon after he suspects his paternity; a biological father who is deliberately kept ignorant might be allowed to step forward for some specified period after birth (probably not less than eight weeks nor longer than six months). Thereafter the importance of the baby's attachment to the adoptive parents would preclude his advancing a parental claim. Given a child's need for such a relationship it should also be required that courts hear and decide disputes concerning infant adoptions expeditiously.

One way of testing the adequacy of these principles would be to see what light they shed on actual disputes concerning parental rights and adoption. The cases of Baby Jessica and Baby Richard raised such issues, although both were complicated by the fact that the biological parents became estranged before the child was born, then reconciled after the mother had relinquished the child for adoption. Even though I have been focusing on instances in which the unwed father wishes to assume custody of the child against the wishes of the mother who wants the child to be adopted, the principles I suggest can illuminate (and be illuminated by) these two cases, and also suggest important issues that go beyond adoption law itself.

Neither side in either *Baby Girl Clausen* (Baby Jessica) and *Baby Boy Janikova* (Baby Richard) grounded its position in the kinds of principles I have put forward here. The Iowa statute that Daniel Schmidt invoked to claim that Baby Jessica's adoption could not be finalized required the biological father's consent, but no showing that he demonstrate his commitment to the child before (or even after) birth.[57] The biological father's mere opposition to the adoption was a sufficient basis upon which to grant him custody. The DeBoers, for their part, based their claim that they should be allowed to adopt Jessica on the best interest standard.[58] Placing the child with the Schmidts reinforced the notion that a biological tie between man and child automatically creates a custodial claim. On the other hand, a decision favoring the DeBoers would not only have reinforced the best interest standard but might have been viewed as rewarding them for prolonging legal proceedings after Schmidt raised his claim.

The principles advanced here would probably have granted a hearing to Daniel Schmidt, but not on the basis of his biological paternity alone. While his biological tie alone did not guarantee him a hearing, the facts that Cara Clausen deceived him about his paternity during her pregnancy, that he acted immediately after learning that he was Jessica's biological father, and that he acted within four weeks of her birth, did provide such grounds. Provided that Cara Clausen did not present serious objections, he would have been granted custody. Had Clausen objected, the hearing would not have attempted to determine whether the child's "best interest" would be better served by granting custody to Schmidt or the DeBoers. Instead it would have asked whether Schmidt's actions were sufficient to establish a claim to custody, and whether Clausen's reasons for objecting were sufficient grounds for denying Schmidt custody. It seems to me that Schmidt's claim probably would have been recognized, and that the likelihood of a ruling in his favor would have been clearer to the DeBoers and their lawyer than it was under the law then in effect. That clarity might well have led them to give up their effort to adopt Jessica early on, avoiding some additional grief although not the pain of parting with Jessica and stifling their yearning to be parents.

While the principles I put forward here would, I believe, have supported Kirchner's claim to a hearing and probably his claim to custody, they are very different from those invoked by the Illinois Supreme Court. The language which Justice Heiple used in deciding in Kirchner's favor showed little regard for the complexity of the circumstances that gave rise to the litigation. Justice Heiple remarked that the adoptive parents would have to live "with the knowledge that they wrongfully deprived a father of his child past the child's third birthday." Given that the potential adoptive parents knew that Janikova had been a resident in a battered women's shelter and that she and her family took extraordinary steps to keep Kirchner from knowing the baby's whereabouts, it is neither surprising nor ill-intentioned that they initially tried to retain custody. After the trial court ruled that Kirchner had no parental claim, what else were they to do but continue to care for the child? Justice Heiple would have done better to have called for a concerted effort to clarify the law and to reform the procedures that result in protracted proceedings than to have chastised the adoptive parents for having "brought [their pain] on themselves."[59]

Justice Heiple also referred to Kirchner as the "real" father, rather than more precisely as the "biological" father, implying that "real" paternity is genetic. He criticized the lower courts for the "wrongful breakup of a natural family." The characterization of Kirchner, Janikova, and their offspring as a "natural family" again assumes that biology alone creates a family, rather than acknowledging that what we recognize as a family evolves through social practices and that legally recognized family rights and obligations are human creations. The judge's invocation of a "natural family," despite the fact that Kirchner and Janikova were not married and had stopped living together before the baby was born, seems as ill-founded as Justice Scalia's assertion that Carole, Gerald, and Victoria D. constituted a "unitary family" whose existence precluded a paternity hearing for Michael H., despite the fact that Victoria was not Gerald's biological offspring and had for a while lived with and regarded Michael H. as her father.[60] Indeed, both Justice Heiple's and Justice Scalia's decisions draw attention to the ways in which the question of what constitutes a family deserving state protection is a matter of contestation, not something self-evident from either "nature" or the "most specific level" of the "relevant tradition" of American life and law.

The principles I advocate here, grounding parental rights not only in the genetic tie but also in lived relationships of care and responsibility, suggest that certain revisions in Illinois adoption law would avoid confusion about whether an unwed biological father's efforts were adequate to establish his parental claim. Had Illinois required an unwed father to make efforts to take responsibility for his offspring from the time he learned of the pregnancy rather than within thirty days of the child's birth, it would have been clearer to the prospective adoptive parents that Kirchner had some basis to demand a hearing, since he had lived with and supported Janikova during the first seven months of her pregnancy. A stipulation requiring an unwed father to enter his name on a putative fathers' registry or otherwise publicly indicate his desire to assume responsibility for the child would be a gauge of his desire to take responsibility for the child, not simply (or primarily) to reestablish a relationship with the mother. A stipulation requiring courts to listen to any objections the mother might have to the father receiving custody of the infant might lessen an unwed mother's reluctance to reveal the identity of her child's biological father.

Adoption laws should contain incentives for biological mothers to reveal, and adoptive parents to make every effort to ascertain, the biological father's identity so that adoption can be finalized as soon as possible. Yet the law should also establish a time limit beyond which a father's claim will not be heard. As it turned out, Kirchner acted within sixty days of his baby's birth and Schmidt acted within four weeks, so under the stipulations suggested here each would have been entitled to a hearing. Because pain is inevitable in such cases, law must make clear the conditions under which a biological parent can veto an adoption so that biological fathers and mothers, prospective adoptive parents, and their attorneys can assess realistically each party's likelihood of prevailing.

When disputed adoption cases drag on, pain to the child is inevitable. To separate a child from birth parents brings with it an inevitable psychological toll. Adoption is sometimes the only and the best course for a child, but that does not eliminate the pain caused by the realization that one's earliest human relationship was disrupted and that one was given away, no matter how lovingly, carefully, and justifiably. But to remove a toddler from the only family he or she has known causes emotional trauma far beyond this sense of loss, no matter how loving the new home. To serve the well-being of the child, when an unwed father claims custody the principles embedded in the law must be just and the resolution of the conflict must take place quickly. Cases of disputed custody will also cause suffering to the adults whose claim is denied. A biological parent who loses custody will experience the loss of a child and of the intergenerational continuity that is one of the joys of parenthood. The prospective adoptive parents who are denied custody will lose not only this particular child, whom they have come to love, but also suffer the defeat (at least for the time being) of their yearning to be parents. To avoid as much trauma and pain as possible to adults and children alike, adoption laws must embody principles that are as sensitive to the complexity of such situations as we can make them.

Conclusion

The main lesson to be drawn from cases like *Baby Girl Clausen* and *Baby Boy Janikova* is that it is imperative that states formulate adoption laws that reflect the principle that parental rights are properly grounded in a combination of biology and the provision of care. Because such profound and profoundly important human relationships are at stake, courts should be required to hear and rule on disputed adoptions in a timely fashion. Another lesson may be that in certain instances it would make sense to allow some form of legal recognition that a child may have more than two "parents": genetic parents (sperm and egg donors), biological parents, stepparents, adoptive parents, social or psychological parents (that is, those who actually raise the child), and legal guardians. Some such recognition might avoid cases in which an unwed biological father who has not been reconciled with or married the biological mother seeks to block an adoption to which she has consented. Some of these cases seem motivated not so much by the man's desire to raise the child as by his fear of losing all opportunity to know a child he has sired. There may be ways of dealing with this fear short of blocking the adoption. Adoption registries that allow adopted children and birth parents to contact one another by mutual consent seem to have been helpful to biological parents, adoptive parents, and children alike. They allow for the simultaneous recognition of both biological and psychological or social parenting, and in doing so undercut the suggestion that something about adoption is shameful or is best kept hidden. Such registries also take into account the perspective of children who want to know their biological forebears, without either weakening the legal rights and responsibilities of the social (adoptive) parents or denying the primacy of the emotional bonds between adoptive parents and children.

Cases like *Matter of Robert O. v. Russell K.*, *Baby Girl Clausen*, and *Baby Boy Janikova* should also lead us to try to think about the circumstances that might lead an unwed mother to lie about or conceal the paternity of her child, such as fear of violence or harassment, or shame over an unwanted sexual relationship. Working toward justice in family relationships requires struggling to eliminate the social conditions that give rise to such fear and shame, and also requires making sure that all citizens have access to the resources that allow families to survive and flourish, so that no biological parents will be forced to relinquish custody of children they would prefer to raise themselves had they the economic resources to do so.

This analysis of disputes over paternal custody of nonmarital newborns makes it abundantly clear that the language of individual rights, so central to liberal political theory, and to the due process and equal protection guarantees of the U.S. Constitution, is not well suited to dealing with complex issues of parent-child relationships. While notions of maternal or paternal rights are not useless—for example, they allow us to think about limits to state intervention—they misdirect our attention to the adult *individual*. When no attention is paid to the distinct circumstances of male and female adult individuals who have a child outside of marriage, faulty analysis is bound to follow. In particular, the language of a father's "right" to custody of his infant child based on his genetic tie obscures the complexity of the lived relationship between parents and between parent and child. Those relationships must be at the center of the analysis of parental claims.

Because being a parent means being in a relationship with a dependent person, a parental "right" cannot properly be conceived of as something independent of the relationship. An individual can exercise a parental right, but the existence or the nature of the right cannot be explained by reference to that individual alone. Only by taking account of the dependency, reciprocity, and responsibility of family relationships; current gender inequality; and the primacy of children's needs will we be able to overturn old models of family life and move toward a world that takes seriously men's and women's equality and children's right to committed parents and to care.

CHAPTER 3

"A Child of Our Own": Against a Market in Sperm and Eggs

*D*uring the academic year 1999–2000 an ad appeared for a few weeks in the newspaper of the college where I teach: "Special Egg Donor Needed—$25,000" said the headline. The text continued, "We are a loving, infertile couple hoping to find a compassionate woman to help us have a baby. We're looking for a healthy, intelligent college student or college graduate, age 21–33, with blue eyes and blonde or light brown hair. Compensation $25,000 plus expenses. Your gift of life would bring great joy. Please contact us through our representative" (an 800 phone number followed).[1] An ad placed in some other college newspapers offered $50,000 for the eggs of an athletic, five-foot-ten woman who had scored at least 1400 on the Scholastic Aptitude Test.[2] Another ad, placed by an agency, that ran almost every week in my campus newspaper stated, "Being an Egg Donor is an Awesome Gift" and offered $5,000 plus expenses to any donor who was "healthy, age 21–30, a non-smoker, and average weight."[3] Such offers are attractive to some of my students, both those who want altruistically to help others, and those who are concerned about the financial debt they have incurred from student loans. More than personal considerations, however, should arise in thinking about whether or how to respond to such ads; "making babies" and "making families" by buying and selling eggs and sperm raises complex ethical, social, and legal issues.

The practice of buying and selling (and advertising for) eggs and sperm reflects and shapes our understanding of our relationship to our genetic material, the extent to which family bonds are created by nature and by human will, and the role the market should play in forming families. This chapter examines the practices that shape the way people form families with gametes supplied by other people and asks some of the same kinds of questions that guided my examination of adoption: Should users of donated genetic material strive to create a "match" and an "as if" family? Should they be able to select gametes on the basis of the race, religion, or other characteristics of the donor? Should the children created with donated gametes be able to learn the identity of the donor(s)? Should the sale of eggs and sperm be prohibited, regulated, or left to the open market? Discussing these questions should help us think about whether and in what ways adoption and gamete transfer are analogous or dissimilar, and what the implications are for contract pregnancy or "surrogate motherhood," which I consider in the next chapter.

As with many of the issues discussed in this book, one of the first choices to make is what to call the practice under discussion. In "gamete transfer," a person uses sperm or eggs from someone else who is not his or her spouse or life-partner and has no intention of being a legal or social parent to the child created from this genetic material. (A gamete can be *either* an egg or a sperm; a gamete is half the genetic material needed for human procreation.) This practice is usually called gamete "donation," a term that suggests that a gift is being made. Only rarely, however, do people transfer gametes without receiving money for them. (Instances of transferring gametes to another as a gift are almost always between family members.) Since one of the ethical issues I want to examine is the buying and selling of eggs and sperm, I will speak of gamete "transfer" rather than "donation." With respect to the person who is the source of the gametes, although "provider" or "vendor" would reflect the fact that he or she is paid, I will refer to this person as the "donor" to avoid possible confusion with the fertility clinic or sperm bank that is the third-party "provider" and "vendor" of genetic material (and is usually intent on maximizing profits).[4]

Compared to adoption and contract pregnancy, gamete transfer has received relatively little attention from courts and legislatures. Courts have dealt on occasion with what to do with frozen embryos when the gamete donors disagree, or when they are deceased, but transferring sperm or eggs for someone else to use to conceive a child has been largely unregulated.[5] Some state legislatures have passed laws making the husband of a woman who is inseminated with someone else's sperm by a doctor the legal father of a child so conceived. But there has been little attention to the questions that concern me here: whether someone conceived through the use of third-party gametes has a right, when an adult, to learn the donor's identity, and whether human gametes to be used for procreation should be priced by market mechanisms. I argue that states should require the release of specific identifying information about the donor to an adult who was conceived with transferred gametes if that adult requests the information, and should prohibit differential pricing of human gametes.

Thinking about adoption offers some guidance in thinking about gamete transfer. Gamete transfer can, like adoption, create a family in which the child is not genetically related to at least one parent, and ads soliciting eggs in some ways resemble those placed in newspapers by couples seeking to adopt children: "A happily married loving white couple wishes to share their warmth, laughter and hearts with a newborn. Will provide endless love and security, with close family ties. Expenses paid."[6] In important ways, however, gamete transfer is different from adoption. Only genetic material, not an actual child, is transferred between adults, and a child conceived through gamete transfer usually has a genetic relationship with one parent (this is true in both heterosexual and same-sex couples and for single mothers). That genetic relation, and the fact that one parent bears and gives birth to the child, may make the child seem more the parents' "own" than an adopted child would be.

The implications of the fact that the child is one's own, and yet was created with the genetic material of a third party, have not been adequately examined. Rather, practices surrounding gamete transfer such as anonymous donation and market pricing developed incrementally as the technology advanced and demand increased, but they bear marks of the original procedures and social context in which they developed.

Initially, only sperm could be transferred, a relatively simple procedure that doctors began recommending in the 1940s, and one that could easily be done secretly as well as anonymously. The technology created no barrier to the formation of "as if" families; for the most part, heterosexual couples used insemination to have children that resembled both parents. When egg transfer became possible after the first successful in vitro fertilization (IVF) in 1978, sperm transfer was the model, though the far more complicated procedures and scarcity of donors led to pressure to pay egg donors more than sperm donors.[7]

In the 1970s, the debates over how to think about gamete donation were complicated by social change and medical developments. The women's movement enabled single women to think about creating families without husbands.[8] And greater openness about same-sex relationships led some lesbian couples to use gamete transfer to have children. By the end of the twentieth century, therefore, gamete transfer was used to create both traditional-looking heterosexual families and less conventional-looking lesbian (and with the development of "surrogacy," gay men's) families.

But major issues raised by this widening practice remain in political, legal, and moral limbo.[9] Should we, and if so how should we, now think about and regulate secrecy, anonymity, and openness in gamete transfer? Whose interests should be considered in setting such policies? And what restrictions, if any, should be imposed on the buying and selling of human genetic material? What practical and ethical considerations need to be weighed in arriving at any policy?[10]

Some people question whether it is ever ethical for a single person or a lesbian or gay couple to use gamete transfer to procreate. While the issues involved are worthy of discussion, I leave them aside here. Whether a person should use gamete transfer to become a single parent should be discussed in the larger context of all the ways in which people become single parents, and the ethics of single-parenting in general. And whether same-sex couples should use donated gametes should be discussed in the larger context of other ways in which same-sex couples come to raise children together, including one partner gaining custody after divorce and adoption, and the ethics of same-sex relations. I would only say that I do not think that either single- or same-sex parenting is in itself immoral, and that I believe that the ethical principles that should govern gamete transfer properly apply to both heterosexual and homosexual parents.

On the general public policy issues, my conclusions are clear. I call for an end to both anonymity and open-market buying and selling. As I explain in detail below, both have developed in ways that do not take adequate account of the interests of the future child or of society. The child has an interest in identity formation and not being treated as a commodity. Society will benefit from keeping family formation as free from market forces as possible. But before taking up those arguments, it may be helpful to review the medical procedures involved in gamete transfer.

How Gamete Transfer Is Done

Prior to the 1940s, couples who wanted to raise a child but found they could not conceive might occasionally raise a relative's child, or might formally adopt a child. Gradually, some doctors began offering patients the possibility of artificial insemination when the difficulty appeared to be with the husband. Artificial insemination (more recently called "alternative" insemination since some people considered "artificial" to be misleading and disparaging) by donor (AID) was used in cases of sterility or low sperm count, or if the husband were the carrier of an inheritable disease. In alternative insemination by husband (AIH), several ejaculates from the husband were combined to offset low sperm count or motility. Alternative insemination was a simple procedure performed in a doctor's office. At the most propitious time in the woman's ovulatory cycle, the doctor collected ejaculate from the husband or donor (often waiting in a room down the hall from the examining room), placed it in a syringe, and injected the sperm in the woman's vagina as close to the cervix as possible. It enabled many patients to become pregnant.

Since a couple's use of alternative insemination was usually private, creating a family using this procedure required much less social effort and explanation than adoption. The insemination procedure could be done during a seemingly routine visit to the doctor. While the later use of transferred eggs required a more complicated medical procedure of extracting eggs, fertilizing them in a glass petrie dish ("in vitro" means "in glass"), and placing the pre-embryo into the woman's uterus, apart from the physician only those the couple chose to tell would know a couple was engaged in infertility treatment. When a heterosexual couple used AID or egg transfer, there was no need for a home study and evaluation of their fitness to be parents; there were no worries that the child might have suffered unknown physical or psychological difficulties prior to placement; and there was nearly as much physical resemblance between parents and child as in unassisted conception.[11]

Studies of the use of donated gametes to overcome infertility began appearing in medical journals in the United States in the early 1940s.[12] The doctors selected the donors, who were usually medical students, other university students, or hospital personnel. Virtually all doctors paid donors for their semen; usually $25 per ejaculate in the mid-1970s, with a low of $20 and a high of $100, rising to approximately $170 by the late 1990s. Doctors might use the same donor repeatedly; a research team at the University of Wisconsin reported that in response to a survey conducted in 1977, many doctors said that they used a donor for no more than six pregnancies, although 5.7 percent had used a donor for fifteen or more. About 50 percent of the doctors kept records on the women they inseminated, but many fewer kept medical records on sperm donors or on children born after AID.[13] Until the 1980s, little screening beyond self-reporting of medical history was done. After the transmission of AIDS (acquired immunodeficiency syndrome) became a risk, semen was tested for the HIV virus and frozen for future injection.

The fact that most early donors were medical school and university students, and that recipients were private patients of doctors affiliated with teaching hospitals, suggests that the majority of the participants were white. More recent reports of the incidence of AID indicate that race-matching is the norm, just as it was in the early years, that is, recipients use sperm from donors with the same racial identity as their partner. I have not been able to find any information on the relative number of members of various racial groups who use

AID. My guess is that recipients are disproportionately white, since there is a much larger pool of children of color available for adoption than of white children, and since in many black communities there is less emphasis on the genetic tie in constituting families.[14]

Until the 1970s, virtually all AID was used to help married heterosexual couples have a child who resembled as much as possible the biological child they would have produced. Doctors purchased the semen, and couples paid the doctor for the insemination procedure. Insemination was anonymous; the donor's identity was neither released nor obtainable. Sometimes the husband's sperm was mixed with the donated sperm so that no one would know for certain which man's genes actually produced the child. Often, not even family members and friends knew that the pregnancy had resulted from someone else's sperm. Occasionally, even the husband did not know his wife was undergoing alternative insemination.

A variety of concerns made anonymity and secrecy seem appropriate, even necessary. The association of manliness with potency, and the stigma attached to the inability to sire children, made many couples anxious to keep their use of insemination secret. Some legal and religious authorities suggested that sperm transfer might constitute an act of adultery.[15] Lawyers were unsure about whether the donor had any parental rights or responsibilities with respect to the child.[16] Parents rarely told their children that they were conceived with donated sperm; many psychologists counseled parents to protect themselves and their child from the resentment the child might feel if she learned that she was "different" from other children.[17]

The goal of AID was to create a family in which the children appeared to be the biological offspring of the husband and wife. Both the practice of "matching" the donor and the recipient's husband in physical appearance, and the practice of anonymity, supported this goal. The 1977 survey by the University of Wisconsin researchers found that the majority of doctors tried to match hair color, skin color, eye color, and height, and some tried to match religious or ethnic background, ABO blood type, and educational level.[18] Doctors took great care to make sure that the identities of neither donors nor recipients would be known, and many gynecologists who delivered babies conceived by

AID never knew that their patients had undergone alternative insemination.

The practices that grew up around AID carried with them complicated messages about what mattered in making babies and making families. On the one hand, the way AID was carried out suggested that what really made a man a father could be social, not invariably genetic, parenting. As the practice of AID grew, many state legislatures and courts declared that any child conceived within a marriage by donated sperm was to be considered the legal child of the husband and wife.[19] The fact that donors were paid a token amount, were not counseled about any possible psychological effects of their act, and were permitted or encouraged to sell sperm multiple times all suggested that the sperm were without particular significance to the man, an attitude that contrasted markedly with the later concern about an unwed father's right to veto a mother's decision to place a child for adoption, discussed in Chapter 2.[20] On the other hand, the way in which the receiving family was treated suggested that it *was* significant that they were conceiving through the use of donated genetic material. In several countries (although not in the United States) couples received extensive counseling before insemination. Doctors tried to match physical traits, took great care to keep donor and recipient from seeing one another, and kept all records confidential. When the technology to freeze sperm (called cryopreservation) developed, both anonymity and matching were easier to achieve, and there was no need for the donor to be nearby when insemination took place. Cryopreservation also meant that recipients could choose from among a far greater number of donors and match characteristics more precisely than they could when fresh semen was needed.

With the development of in vitro fertilization it became possible to acquire eggs as well as sperm from a third party, though initially IVF was used by married women who produced healthy eggs but could not conceive because their fallopian tubes were blocked. The first birth from this procedure took place in 1978. In 1984 a woman gave birth for the first time to a child to whom she bore no genetic relationship after a donor's eggs were fertilized in a petrie dish and successfully implanted in her womb. Thereafter doctors began using IVF to join the husband's sperm with donated eggs to enable couples in which the wife did not produce healthy eggs to create a child. By 1999 about five thousand egg transfers a year took place in the United States.[21]

Egg transfer is a far more complicated procedure than sperm transfer. Where AIH and AID require only a syringe for introducing the sperm, egg transfer "harvests" eggs from the donor by aspiration (suction), fertilizes the eggs in vitro, and either introduces the fertilized egg into the uterus or introduces both egg and sperm into the upper end of the fallopian tube (gamete intrafallopian transfer or GIFT). Some consider "complete surrogacy" (contract pregnancy), which I discuss in the next chapter, another form of egg transfer, in which a woman becomes pregnant through AID using her own eggs, and gives birth to a child whom she turns over to the sperm donor and his wife or partner. Here I focus on egg transfer to a woman who will carry the child during pregnancy and be the child's social and legal mother.

Both donors and recipients in egg transfer undergo medical treatment. A woman who is to donate eggs receives hormone injections to stimulate ovulation. For three weeks, a donor injects herself with Lupron, which shuts down the ovaries so that no eggs ripen or are released. Taking this drug often produces menopause-like symptoms: hot flashes, difficulty with short-term memory, and insomnia. The donor then switches medication, injecting herself for a week with the follicle-stimulating hormones Pergonal and Metrodin. These injections hyperstimulate the ovary and cause the release of an abundance of eggs, often a dozen or more. Finally, the donor receives an injection of human chorionic gonadotropin (hCG). About thirty-four to thirty-six hours after hCG administration, eggs are retrieved either by laparoscopy or ultrasound.[22]

In its early years, egg transfer was done using laparoscopy; now ultrasound is the preferred method. For laparoscopy, the woman is placed under anesthesia, and the doctor inserts a needle into her abdomen just below the navel. Carbon dioxide gas is released into the abdominal cavity, moving the abdominal wall away from the organs. Then the doctor inserts the laparoscope, a small fiberoptic instrument about a half inch in diameter, into the abdominal cavity in order to view the ovaries and fallopian tubes. When the laparoscope provides a good view of an ovary, the doctor punctures the egg follicle with a needle inserted through another small incision, applies suction, and collects the contents of the follicle in a tube or trap. The ultrasound procedure requires only local or very light anesthesia. The ultrasound reveals an image of the egg follicles by waves sent through the bladder. The doctor can then insert a needle through the vaginal wall to reach the ovarian follicles using suction to capture the eggs. Once the eggs are extracted, technicians place them in culture dishes with sperm. About twenty-four hours later, the eggs are observed for signs of fertilization, and those that appear fertilized are placed in an incubator for another twenty-four hours. By this time, successfully fertilized eggs will have divided into two, four, or even eight cells. Usually about four of these are then placed into the uterus using a small catheter.[23]

The recipient, for her part, must also undergo hormonal treatment to synchronize her menstrual cycle with that of the donor, although of course she does not experience hyperstimulation of her ovaries. The recipient often needs additional hormonal injections for a short period after egg transfer to facilitate the egg's implantation in the uterine wall.

Despite the great differences in the procedures for sperm and egg transfer, by and large the practices surrounding egg transfer followed the model of sperm transfer: recipients selected donors with characteristics they desired for their children; the identity of donors was kept secret; fertility centers and doctors served as intermediaries; and donors were paid a fee. The scarcity of egg donors, however, because of the difficulty of the procedure, led people to begin advertising to find donors which has meant that egg transfer is both far more costly and less secret than sperm transfer.

These invasive medical procedures and the high cost of egg transfer sparked renewed attention to the ethical issues gamete transfer raises. Many of the early discussions of the ethics of sperm transfer had involved the question of whether being injected with donated sperm constituted an act of adultery, and whether the genetic father had any parental rights or responsibilities with respect to the child. By the 1960s, most medical and legal writers agreed that sperm transfer was not adulterous and should carry with it no parental rights or responsibilities. Initial discussions of the ethics of egg transfer by and

large concerned only the medical advisability of placing certain restrictions (such as limiting the number of eggs that anyone could
transfer because of the unknown long-term effects of the hormone injections) and the ethics of inducing women to sell their eggs by offering large sums of money.

In the 1970s, the movement toward open adoption and the use of
AID by some single women and lesbian couples drew attention to additional ethical issues in gamete transfer. By the 1980s, some professionals, in part inspired by the movement for open adoption, were ad-
vising that children of a suitable age be told that they were conceived
through AID but not be given any information concerning the identity of the donor.[24] Moreover, the medical procedures involved made
it more difficult to keep egg transfer secret than sperm transfer. When
some single women and some lesbian couples began to use donated
sperm to have children, they were creating families different from
those produced by early AID. Whereas alternative insemination had
initially been used to create "as if" families for married heterosexual
couples, lesbian couples could now have one partner undergo alternative insemination and then raise the child together. A procedure that
many people had characterized as a minor assist to nature when used
to enable heterosexual married couples to have children was portrayed as a most unnatural practice when used to enable lesbians or
single women to have children. Some gay men also used donated eggs
and the gestational services of surrogate mothers, but they were few in
number and did not spark the same kind of outrage that lesbians' procreation without a social father generated.[25]

It is interesting to speculate whether, had egg transfer developed
before sperm transfer, different images or analogies concerning what
was involved in transferring gametes might have developed. Sperm is
easily removed from the body, ejaculation is pleasurable, and the act
can be repeated without difficulty or harm to the body. Egg transfer,
by contrast, cannot be done alone and unobserved and requires hormonal injections and surgery, both of which cause discomfort or
pain. The need to coordinate the menstrual cycles of donor and recipient suggests a cooperative relationship between donor and recipient
even when they do not know one another. Egg transfer cannot be repeated frequently because no one knows the long-term effects of hor-

monal manipulation or of the ovarian scarring that may occur during extraction. Weighty cultural values associated with "motherhood" also make egg transfer seem more portentous and troubling than sperm transfer: since time immemorial men have impregnated women to whom they are not married and have walked away without a backward glance; women, by contrast, have been expected to love and devote themselves to their children, and those who do not are deemed monstrous.[26]

At present, in the United States, the tale told by policies and practices surrounding gamete transfer is one of individuals who are free to commodify their genetic traits, consulting only their own immediate interests and values. This is not, however, the only way to conceptualize gamete transfer. A more open and less market-driven practice would reflect a less atomistic conceptualization of society. Society and public policy makers need to pay more sophisticated attention to the child's psychological experience, to the multiple relationships that create and sustain any human being, and to the variety of family forms that foster human intimacy.

An Argument against Anonymity

From the perspective of doctors and patients alike, producing a successful pregnancy through alternative insemination and a child a married couple could call their "own" was the happy ending of infertility treatment. Typically, doctors told neither donor nor recipients one another's identities.

Even after many states enacted laws stating that a child conceived by alternative insemination was the legal child of the mother and her husband, anonymity remained the norm.[27] While the donor's physiological features, intelligence, ethnic background and religious identity were important to some recipients, knowing the specific identity of the donor was unimportant, even undesirable. Most professionals associated with assisted reproduction argued that anonymity should be the norm, because it freed the donor from any legal responsibility for the child and any apprehension that the child would seek contact with him in the future. Also, the receiving couple and their child would be indistinguishable, or nearly so, from other heterosexual couples with children. With anonymity the accepted norm in adoption, it seemed all the more the case that gamete transfer, before a child existed, should be anonymous.

The practice of anonymous donation was also consonant with those aspects of liberal individualism that embraced equal opportunity and rejected linking legal or political status to accident of birth. National mythology still pictured the United States as a country populated by "self-made men" and people who had cut themselves off from their past and started life anew through immigration or migration to the western frontier. The assumption that the identity of the gamete donor was not terribly significant because the children conceived with donated gametes would become whatever they made of themselves, drew on these images of self-determination.

The individualistic understanding of the person reflected in the terms some people used to talk about gamete transfer drew upon, although it exaggerated, other developments in American family law. Increasing recognition of the individuality of each member of a family has been a trend in law and social practice since the mid-nineteenth century. Beginning in the 1850s, passage of married women's property acts in many states recognized that a wife, who previously had been subsumed in the legal personality of her husband, who acted for her in legal matters, might hold property in her own name. Later in the century, child labor laws and compulsory schooling limited parents' ability to control what their children did. Creation of legal adoption around 1850 allowed the legal bond between biological parent and child to be severed. In the twentieth century, the expansion of grounds for divorce suggested that marriage was no longer to be thought of as an indissoluble bond, that under certain circumstances individuals might reclaim their single status. In these various ways, social and political discourse presented the person "as a potentially free-standing and whole entity (an individual subject or agent) contained within an abstract impersonal matrix."[28] Bonds between family members that people had once thought of as unchangeable or "given" were now viewed as established by human intention and will. The inherent tension in American political theory and law between the individualistic and relational aspects of each person permeated the ways people talked about gamete transfer.

When doctors developed the practice of sperm transfer, the anonymity that prevailed suggested that there was no intrinsic or essential relationship between donor and sperm, nor between the person to be created and his or her genetic progenitor. "Donation linking a person to a source of genetic endowment does not necessarily link the person to another person. Indeed, twentieth-century people who talk of semen 'donation' treat it as a substance that will fertilize the maternal egg *whether or not* its identity is known."[29] Acceptance of a child who was a genetic stranger to one of the parents also reflected a belief in the social construction of the self. Couples using gamete transfer did not think that the genetic tie would make that spouse or partner more of a parent than the genetically unrelated parent. "Nurture" would be every bit as important as "nature" in the child's development, and anyone's claim to be recognized as a parent would rest upon the commitment to the marriage and to rearing the child.

At the same time, however, secrecy and anonymity suggested that the identity of the donor involved in begetting the child *was* important; if the genetic tie had no significance whatsoever, it would not need to be hidden. But what *kind* of significance might the genetic link have? One of the problems gamete donors and recipients faced was that in the past law had given biology too much significance when it gave genetic fathers claims to legal paternity or held that sperm transfer constituted an act of adultery. I believe that both donors and recipients were right to think that genetic contribution alone, without the assumption of responsibility for the child, should not give someone a claim to be regarded as a social or a legal parent.

But many people who used donated sperm or eggs to conceive a child who was genetically related to one parent attributed a different kind of significance to their genetic link to the child. Having a child genetically related to one member of the couple gave a sense of continuity both to the genetically related parent and to the spouse who would see his or her partner reflected in their child. The genetic tie linked the parents not only to their child, but also to the generations that preceded them and, through the possibility that their child would have children, to those following them. This was true for both parents who conceived with the help of AIH, for mothers who conceived through AID, and for fathers who used donated eggs. The sense of genetic continuity through the generations placed the family in a history that stretched both forward and backward in time. Parents could feel that they were passing on a legacy not only through their words and actions, but also through their bodies.

From the perspective of the child, and the person that child will become, knowledge of how and from whom one came to be is now being seen as part of the right to an identity.[30] I agree with the view that someone created with donated genetic material should have the right to learn (although not be compelled to learn) the identity of the donor, not simply medical facts or DNA profile, upon reaching the age of majority or some other specified age. The reason for this is not that genes "trump" social identity; I argued in Chapter 2 with respect to unwed fathers that the right to be treated as a legal parent follows from a genetic relationship only when the genetic parent also assumes responsibility for the child's welfare. Rather, the right to learn the identity of one's genetic forebear stems from some people's desire to be able to connect themselves to human history concretely as embodied beings, not only abstractly as rational beings or as members of large social (national, ethnic, religious) groups.[31] Children come into the world through the actions of specific persons, which now can include both "intentional" parents (those who plan their conception) and genetic donors.

It is important that society as a whole affirm the right to know one's origins. Religion, philosophy, and psychoanalysis alike contend that truth is better than either falsehood or obfuscation, and openness is better than secrecy (some form of "the truth shall make you free" is found in each of these fields of thought). Neil Leighton, a social worker, has argued that children have a right to "the development of a sense of self as a lived narrative blending action and memory [and] to participate in their own histories and their own future." He worries that "children who have no identifiable origin, no identifiable human beginning to their personal narrative may have a sense of alienation in the world in which they find themselves."[32] While not all children (or the adults they become) may experience such feelings, social policy should place the burden of proof on the person who would seal an adoption record from the adult adoptee or a medical record from the person created with donated gametes, not on the person seeking information about his or her origins.

Some who agree that people should know that they were created by gamete transfer do not agree that they should be guaranteed access to information concerning the specific identity of the gamete donor. Some assert that guaranteeing access to such information reflects a socially created need that comes from a patriarchal focus on genetic lineage, and others assert that it reflects a kind of genetic essentialism that downplays the importance of experience and social factors in the formation of a person. It should be clear by now that I reject both patriarchalism and genetic essentialism. It is good, however, when social practices reflect the fact that specific human beings are necessary for any person to come into existence, that individual actions shape the larger social whole, and that cultural development is something individuals participate in rather than something that happens to them. Law and social practice should foster the understanding that what individuals do, even on a small scale, has repercussions beyond themselves and their intimate associates.[33]

Arguing that the person created by gamete transfer has a right to learn the progenitor's identity upon reaching age eighteen or twenty-one implies that the gamete donor must be prepared to have his or her identity revealed. The donor has no responsibility to the child/adult beyond that; there is certainly no obligation to meet. Another implication may be that clinics should prohibit multiple donations (say, no more than three or five).[34] Repeated anonymous donation treats the transfer of genetic material as if it were analogous to giving blood. Yet the fact that human beings may result from gamete transfer makes it different in kind and significance from blood donation to donor and recipient alike, and repeated donation might foster an undesirable sense of detachment from the procreative potential of one's body.

Is it possible for people in this culture to accept the distinction between genetic and social parenthood, and to give each its proper due? That question (along with what constitutes each person's "proper due"), can only be answered over time. It seems to me that both discussions like this one, and people's actions, contribute to our collective deliberation. The experience of some lesbian and gay couples who chose to use known donors has suggested that it is possible to do so without generating confusion among family members about who are (or should be) the child's legal parents. In making collaborative procreation visible and validating the significance of specific family histories, these families may provide new modes of thinking and suggest new ways of acting to heterosexual families as well.[35]

An Argument against Marketing Human Gametes

The mechanism by which gametes are transferred from one person to another in the United States has largely been the market. Gamete "donation" has always been a misnomer in the United States. Human eggs and sperm have a number of characteristics that made it possible to treat them as commodities. First, they were separable from the donor and transferable to another person. Because gametes were separable from the donor they could be treated as a generalized "resource" that could be traded in the market. Control over eggs or sperm could be transferred from one owner to another—from donor to doctor or fertility clinic, and from these to the recipient.[36] The fact that once gametes are removed from the donor's body they can become part of a common store—a sperm or ova bank—from which others can obtain what they need or want, also tempts us to think of gametes as commodities. In market transactions, "an anonymously produced object becomes part of a store on which others draw."[37] Marilyn Strathern believes that "the market analogy has already done its work: we think so freely of the providing and purchasing of goods and services that transactions in gametes is already a thought-of act of commerce."[38] The practices of the market have so thoroughly shaped our culture that it is hard to imagine an alternative method by which to transfer gametes.

It is appropriate that gametes be regarded as the possession of the donor in the sense that neither the government nor a medical research facility may commandeer anyone's body, body part, or genetic material without the donor's informed consent; only the person whose gametes are to be transferred can make that decision. Further, it is appropriate that the transfer of material does not create any conceivable claim to parental rights or responsibilities on the part of the donor. I argued in Chapter 2 that only unwed fathers who assume concrete responsibility for a child or the child's mother should have any claim to be recognized as parents; gamete donors, who have no social or sexual relationship with the recipient, clearly should not be regarded as "parents."

The notion that it is acceptable for one person to agree to transfer his or her genetic material to someone else under appropriate conditions does not, however, mean that the reason this transfer can take place is that the donor *owns* that material, or that the gamete is a commodity. Unlike adoption, in which existing children have an existing social tie (albeit sometimes a very brief or nominal one) to their birth parents, in gamete transfer there can be no social relationship between donor and gamete, and the donor is not a parent. This has unfortunately led people to treat the gamete as a *possession* of the person from whom it is extracted. The marketing of sperm and eggs further suggests that the recipients can be regarded as customers or consumers, free to exercise consumer choice. "Those who seek assistance, we are told, are better thought of not as the disabled seeking alleviation or the sick seeking remedy—analogies that also come to mind—but as customers seeking services."[39] But the notion that people own their gametes mistakes the nature of their relationship to reproductive material.

The liberal ideal of "self ownership" does not mean that we can do whatever we like with all our body parts, selling off what we don't need or want. The law allows people to sell hair, and sometimes blood, but prohibits the sale of body organs. Even someone willing and able to live with only one kidney or eye may not sell the other (nor may the kidney, eye, heart, or liver from a deceased person be sold). The distinction here is not simply that between renewable and nonrenewable material, or between material necessary and unnecessary to sustain life. It also involves a judgment that some parts of the body should not be for sale either because of their nature, or because economic need might lead poor people to sell body parts.[40] What kind of "body parts" are gametes, and how should we think about the donor's relationship to his or her gametes? Donna Dickenson suggests that "the kind of ownership which we can be said to possess in relation to our gametes is conditional: we are not allowed to do anything we like with them, because they are not unequivocally ours. They are held in common with past and future generations."[41]

The practice of regarding donors as owners of their gametes has led to customer "shopping" for gametes and in some cases to the differential pricing of gametes based on their donors' characteristics. Some gamete shoppers compare the considerations that go into their choice of a donor to those that influence their choice of a spouse; is he/she tall, good-looking, smart, a baseball fan? One difference, of course, is that the gamete expresses no choice and is purchased from someone else, but recipients are free to—indeed encouraged to—exercise choice. Various social practices already reward certain traits the person was born with more than others: lighter-skinned people encounter less employment discrimination than darker-skinned individuals; men are paid more than women with comparable education. It is bad enough that these and other differences which are accidents of birth generate economic inequality in the labor market; it is far worse when these traits lead to differential compensation for the donor's gametes.

Differential pricing of gametes based on characteristics like the donor's height, skin and hair color, athletic or academic achievement, and musical ability seems to validate the assumption that persons with such attributes—both donors and as-yet-unborn (indeed, as-yet-unconceived) children—are "worth more" than others. We need to think hard about the moral and political consequences of accepting such a position. We need to think about what a child knows of the genetic material that made her or his existence possible. Knowing that the genetic material was bought for a higher (or lower) price than that of some other child is to cast further doubt on the proposition basic to United States law that all persons are of equal dignity regardless of their wealth or social status.

Using the market to transfer human gametes draws upon and perpetuates an overly individualistic understanding of human society and distorts the liberal commitment to human freedom. An open market can create undue pressure on potential donors (a student saddled with heavy student loan debt, a woman in poverty); harm children who will learn that their relative "value" depends on traits over which they have no control; and undermine the basic democratic concept of the equal intrinsic worth of all persons.

A person's relationship to his or her genetic material is better thought of as a kind of stewardship than as ownership. Thinking about what is involved in gamete transfer should turn us away from those strands of the liberal tradition that emphasize the individual and property in the body, and towards those strands that rest on a deeper understanding of the person rooted in multiple and complex relationships to family and civil society. If neither anonymity nor an open market in gametes is desirable, what then should be "the tale told by law" and public policy with respect to gamete transfer?

Transforming the Practice of Gamete Transfer

To bring gamete transfer into conformity with the ethical principles that should underlie all of United States family law, policies and practices should give as much recognition to the relational as to the individualistic aspects of human procreation and should focus attention on the potential child. Specifically, we should do away with the market in human gametes, and we should do away with the sealed (or nonexistent) records that make it impossible for an individual created by gamete transfer to identify his or her specific genetic forebear(s).

The experiences of other countries suggest that donors can be persuaded to donate without a guarantee of anonymity and without high payment. Swedish legislation allows the offspring of a donor access to the donor's name once the child is sufficiently mature. Canadian and German reports have recommended that children be given a legal right to know their origins. In the United Kingdom, law requires all donor insemination centers to keep identifying information on donors whose gametes are used for conception, and permits their offspring, after reaching age eighteen, to request information about their genetic origins. Although the intent of the law is to provide nonidentifying information in cases of medical necessity, it does not prohibit the release of identifying information about the donor. New Zealand and Australia also moved toward greater openness and the right of children to information about their origin. In New Zealand, arguments for every child's right to know the identity of his or her genetic forebears have been joined by arguments that indigenous peoples, in particular, have a right to their specific heritage.[42] Some of these countries explicitly protect the donor from unwanted contact with the child/adult, which seems appropriate.

In the early years of AID, the donor's anonymity was regarded as central, and only a few voices suggested that the child might have significant psychological needs or other interest in knowing his or her origin.[43] While secrecy and anonymity still predominate, some psychologists, counselors, social workers, and others have begun to urge greater openness, and public policy in some countries has responded.[44]

The understanding people have of what it is they are doing in gamete transfer—whether it's a charitable or profitable act, for instance—naturally affects their behavior as well as others' understanding of the meaning of the practice. If someone regards gamete transfer as a market activity akin to selling a product or one's labor, then selling it for the highest possible price makes sense. But if someone thinks about gamete transfer as a way to collaborate in others' efforts to conceive a child, then other models suggest themselves. Monica Konrad reports that egg donors she interviewed spoke of what they did as "donating means or a way of helping others," and chracterizes their accounts as "narratives of assistance" and of "social efficacy . . . on behalf of others."[45] The act of transferring gametes makes donor and recipient part of a web of social and biological relationships that form part of the person-to-be's identity. Both have obligations generated by that person's claims to human dignity.

Defenders of the open market in gametes argue that payment to sperm donors, and high remuneration to egg donors, are necessary to get men and women to donate sperm and eggs.[46] Again, data from other countries does not bear this out. In France, sperm donors were initially paid, but when it became possible to freeze sperm (and so the donors could come to a fertility center at their convenience) they ceased being paid. The majority of the centers "maintained a policy that the semen donation be simply that, a gift for which no payment is received as is the case for organ donation." In 1979 doctors reported that "donations have kept pace with semen demands," although a constant recruitment effort was necessary as demand continually increased.[47] Requests for donors appealed to those who understood the longing for a child, and potential recipients were urged to talk about donor insemination to increase public acceptance and encourage donations. More recently, England prohibited remuneration of more than 15 pounds sterling (about 24 dollars) for egg donors. Some commentors regard this amount as inadequate to recruit a sufficient number of egg donors and suggest setting a uniform payment (usually somewhere between 300 and 400 pounds sterling, or about 700 dollars) as remuneration for the inconvenience and discomfort of donating eggs (as distinguished from the eggs themselves), while others advocate holding fast to unpaid donation.[48] England and Canada have had some success in encouraging "egg sharing," whereby a woman undergoing IVF using her own eggs donates to someone else any eggs that were harvested but that she did not use.

The United States is the only western country in which there are no national restrictions on the marketing of human ova, although the selling of human organs is prohibited by statute. The question is whether it would be proper, and possible, to change this. Reimagining gamete transfer as something other than a market activity will be an uphill struggle, but not one that is doomed to fail. While the difficulties and risks that are part of egg transfer may make it impossible to abolish payment altogether, it would be possible to remunerate people for undergoing the medical procedure at a single set fee, while prohibiting differential pricing of gametes.

In a thought-provoking paper, Hawley Fogg-Davis suggests that a possible basis for establishing gamete transfer on an ethical foundation would be to regard transfer as a form of work or labor, for which donors could be paid, and then to bring their labor under the jurisdiction of Title VII of the Civil Rights Act of 1964. Because Title VII prohibits discrimination on the basis of race, sex, religion, or national origin, Fogg-Davis believes it could be used to prohibit mention of the donor's race in any catalogue or other materials relating to the gamete. It is both impracticable and immoral, she argues, to ascribe "race" to gametes, since racial categories are not biological facts but social constructions, and the law should prohibit sperm and egg banks from listing the race of donors.[49]

Although, like Fogg-Davis, I take a constructivist view of race, do not regard the gamete as a person, and find racism abhorrent, I am not convinced that recipients should not be allowed to choose donors based on physical appearance, including racial features. People's motives in reproductive decision-making are tremendously complex;

while some white infertile couples may turn to gamete transfer solely because they do not want to adopt a child of color and create a mixed-race family, others may turn to gamete transfer because they want to experience pregnancy and raise a child from birth, and have a child with a genetic connection with one parent, and a connection to a particular historical heritage.[50] These desires are not illegitimate or base.[51]

While there is a danger that some recipients of gamete transfer will use it to perpetuate white racial privilege, there are also dangers in treating the act of donating gametes as a form of work falling under Title VII's prohibitions on employment discrimination and in treating the egg or sperm as "raceless." Bringing gamete transfer under Title VII could result in treating egg donation like any other labor market activity, and treating genetic material as a "product," a product that becomes part of a "pool" of gametes without a specifiable relationship to their origin.

Fogg-Davis's fears that gamete transfer may be used to perpetuate social and economic privilege might be mitigated if the open market in gametes and anonymity were abolished. While it would be ideal to make gamete transfer a real "gift" by forbidding all payment, the main harms of a market system would be avoided if a uniform fee for donating and for receiving gametes was put into effect; affluent recipients could not bid up the price of gametes from donors with certain characteristics. Children created by gamete transfer would not bear the burden of wondering (or knowing) what they "cost" compared to other children. Abolishing anonymity would remind us that the child—although unambiguously and irrevocably the child of the recipients, the social parents—has come into being not only because of the parents' desire and choice, but also because of the actions of another person. Allowing recipients some choice in the physical and social characteristics of the donor, along with the provision that the donor's name will be disclosed at the request of the grown child, counteracts the risk that children created with donated genetic material will be imagined as the genetic offspring of "nobody" or of "anybody," rather than of specific individuals.[52]

The families formed by gamete transfer greatly increase the variety of families in the United States. Collaborative procreation is used by both heterosexual and homosexual couples, and by some single persons. Some families choose to approximate the appearance of a family in which genetic parents and social parents are one and the same, others do not. Some families choose to keep the parents' use of gamete transfer private, others do not. Some families make the donors known to the children when the children are young, others do not. (Chapter 5 discusses some issues that have arisen when lesbian couples have encouraged a social relationship between their donor and child.)

Pluralism in family forms is not only unavoidable but desirable. Respect for families does not mean that all must adhere to the same form or way of being in the world. Instead, respect for families—and in particular respect for children and the persons that they will become—requires that family formation not be absorbed by the market and that gametes not become differentially priced and anonymous commodities. Creating uniform payments and costs for egg transfer and for sperm transfer, and guaranteeing every person's right to a specific account of origin, are policies that reflect commitment to these ethical principles.

The practices, regulations, and laws that shape the way in which gamete transfer is carried out in the United States affect not only how we regulate our conduct, but also the categories and terms we use to characterize what it means to be a "parent" or a "child." At stake in these debates are the images and ways of thinking that inform our own and others' understanding of what it is to be a member of a family.

Gamete transfer forces us to rethink the ways in which people have tended to regard families either as inevitable and "natural" or as voluntaristic and contractual associations. New reproductive technologies, along with birth control and abortion, encourage voluntaristic models of thinking about family relationships because having children by buying genetic material or gestational services introduces choice and contingency into what was long thought to be inevitable. As anthropologist Marilyn Strathern notes, "However one looks at it, procreation can now be *thought about* as subject to personal preference and choice in a way that has never before been conceivable." Where formerly the child was "regarded as a social being" whose birth "reproduced . . . a set of social relations" (the relationship between the parents themselves and the relationships among the parents and other kin), "now the child is literally—and in many cases, of course, joyfully—the embodiment of the act of choice." The child embodies "the desire of its parents to have a child."[53]

This tension between our social and legal understandings of the family as a biological creation involving only one woman and one man who are married to each other and as a conventional or voluntaristic entity seems to me unavoidable, but also overly dichotomous. Neither model alone is persuasive. The traditional model assumes that there is only one form of family given in nature: it is heterosexual, with rigidly defined gender roles, and is headed by a male. The voluntaristic model, for its part, suggests that the rights and obligations of those engaged in gamete transfer are to be decided strictly by the will of the parties involved, often through market negotiations.

Any theory of the family worth its salt must view people alternately—even simultaneously—both as individuals and as persons whose identity is formed through relationship to other people.[54] Respect for the moral autonomy of the person is very different from atomistic individualism.[55] Liberal society and law regard every individual as having property in the person, that is, as being capable of self-government and of assuming responsibility for his or her acts, a notion quite different from having property in the body itself.

Respect for the child (and the person the child will become) sets limits to the ways in which people can exchange or transfer gametes in efforts to procreate. Discussions of the ethics of gamete transfer have overwhelmingly centered around the interests of recipients, donors, and physicians, with only rare mention of the person-to-be. But that person must be central to moral reasoning about procreative practices. Gamete transfer has not existed long enough for many children and adults created with third-party genetic material to share their perspectives, although these will be very important to future moral reasoning. In the present absence of such first-person testimony I would suggest that respect for the equal worth of human beings precludes setting different monetary values on genetic material to be used in procreation. And respect for each individual's right to establish his or her own sense of identity requires that society not withhold from anyone information about his or her origins.[56] The deep conceptual transformations necessitated by the creation of families from gamete transfer are not encompassed by a false dichotomy suggesting that family bonds are grounded either in "nature" or in "convention." Rather, these transformations require us to frame an ethic of interpersonal and intergenerational responsibility under conditions of unprecedented choice. It is possible to change both our thinking about and the policies governing the transfer of human gametes to be used in procreation, and we should do so for the sake of all those involved.

CHAPTER 4

"Surrogate" Motherhood: The Limits of Contractual Freedom

*T*he "Baby M." case, which riveted the attention of much of the country in the late 1980s, remains the best-known legal contest involving "surrogate motherhood" in the United States. For nearly an entire year, people fiercely debated the question, "What makes someone a parent?" and, more particularly, "Who should be declared the legal parent of 'Baby M.'?" in newspaper columns and law journals, on television talk shows, and at gatherings of co-workers and friends.

The facts of the case are heartwrenching.[1] Mary Beth Whitehead agreed to be inseminated with the sperm of William Stern and to give up any resulting child to him and his wife for a fee of $10,000. Ms. Whitehead gave birth to a baby (whom she called Sara and the Sterns called Melissa) on March 27, 1986. Three days later she took the baby home from the hospital and turned her over to the Sterns. Shortly thereafter, Ms. Whitehead appeared at the Sterns' house, apparently distraught, and begged the Sterns to let her take the baby temporarily, promising to return with her later. Fearful that in her state of distress Ms. Whitehead might harm herself, the Sterns entrusted her with the baby. The next week, Ms. Whitehead called the Sterns and told them that she had changed her mind and could not relinquish the baby. The Sterns went to Ms. Whitehead's home accompanied by police, and while they were talking with relatives in the living room, Ms. Whitehead passed the baby through a bedroom window to her husband who was waiting outside. The next day the Whiteheads took the baby with them to Florida, where Ms. Whitehead's parents lived. Over the next three months Ms. Whitehead kept moving from one motel to another with the baby, periodically speaking with Mr. Stern by phone to tell him that the baby was all right and trying to work out an agreement.

At the end of July, Florida police invaded the home of Ms. Whitehead's mother while Ms. Whitehead was in the hospital with a kidney infection, took possession of the baby, and turned her over to New Jersey authorities, who delivered her to the Sterns. Ms. Whitehead began a custody proceeding in New Jersey courts. On March 31, 1987, Judge Harvey R. Sorkow ruled that the contract by which Ms. Whitehead had agreed to bear the child for the Sterns was valid, and that Mr. Stern was the legal parent. Immediately after rendering his decision, he called the Sterns into his chambers and issued an order of adoption making Elizabeth Stern the baby's legal mother.

Ms. Whitehead appealed. On February 3, 1988, the New Jersey Supreme Court reversed Judge Sorkow's decision. Chief Justice Wilentz held that a surrogacy contract that provides payment for a woman to be impregnated, bear a child, and turn the child over at birth to the commissioning parties is invalid and unenforceable. Judge Wilentz ruled that since Ms. Whitehead was the child's legal mother, Elizabeth Stern's adoption of the baby was invalid. The court granted custody to Mr. Stern but ordered that Ms. Whitehead be allowed visitation with the child, leaving it to the trial court to work out what kind of visitation would be in the child's best interest.

Surrogate motherhood contracts like that entered into by Mary Beth Whitehead and William Stern raise issues that are similar to and different from those raised both by adoption and by agreements to buy sperm or eggs.[2] In "complete surrogacy" (like that of Ms. Whitehead) a woman becomes pregnant through alternative insemination and so has a genetic relationship to the fetus. In "gestational surrogacy," doctors transfer an embryo created in vitro into the uterus of a woman who is not the egg donor but who will carry this genetic "stranger" to term. The major focus of my attention will be on an issue that affects *both* forms of surrogacy: a woman's selling her gestational services. I argue that while pregnancy agreements should not (and in reality cannot) be prohibited, women's biologically based experiences of pregnancy dictate that such contracts should not be enforceable. I argue in addition that the only way to avoid replicating current hierarchies of race and class in the United States is to prohibit payment for gestational services. I realize that this will substantially reduce the number of women willing to act as surrogates, but I do not regard this as a social loss or as an improper restriction on the freedom of either potential surrogates or potential commissioning parents.

The different viewpoints about whether it is liberatory or oppressive to women to be free to make contracts and to be paid for this use of their bodies are reflected in arguments over what to call a commissioned pregnancy. Proponents tend to use the term surrogate motherhood, while those with reservations resist calling a woman who bears a child a "surrogate" mother (although some regard her as functioning as a "surrogate wife" to a man who commissions the pregnancy). I review these disputes in some detail. I first set out the considerations that lead some people to argue that prohibiting surrogacy would violate women's autonomy, self-determination, and freedom to do with their bodies as they choose and that it would also infringe on the commissioning parties' "right to procreate."[3] I then take up the considerations that make some people, including me, argue that while surrogacy agreements should not be prohibited, they should not be regarded by society or treated by law as binding and enforceable contracts.[4]

While contract pregnancy clearly can be viewed from the perspective of those who commission a pregnancy, I put the woman who bears the fetus, and the child who will be born, at the center of my analysis. I do so not only because, as with adoption, I think it is crucial to listen to the woman who tends to be economically vulnerable and socially stigmatized, but also because I seek to focus discussion on three clusters of considerations that extend beyond contract pregnancy. The first is the importance we give to human embodiment—and hence to sexual difference—in our understandings of the "self" and its freedom; this requires that we pay attention to the pregnant body and the child "of woman born." The second is the tension between the exercise of individual choice through contract on the one hand, and the recognition and preservation of noncontractual human relationships on the other. The third is the importance of taking social context and social facts into account when deciding what is ethical and legally permissible.

Many of the issues I have already considered in this book cast light on the ethical issues involved in surrogacy. The principle that providing care to and assuming responsibility for a child must be an important component in the establishment of parental rights, is central to my views about surrogacy. Any appeal to individual freedom (or individual rights) in family formation must pay attention not just to individuals per se but also to the role of relationships, including sexual, biological, and reproductive relationships, in developing every individual's sense of self. And the specific social circumstances in which a woman experiences her pregnancy are relevant to the ethics of regulating surrogacy.[5]

"Woman's Body, Woman's Right":
Considerations in Favor of Pregnancy Contracts

It is no wonder that many feminists have welcomed contract pregnancy as a way to demonstrate that childbearing and child rearing are two quite distinct human functions and that child rearing need not and should not be assigned exclusively to the woman who bears a child. A woman's agreement to bear and then to relinquish custody of a child offers concrete resistance to the overly close connection that law and social practice have often made between women's childbearing capacity and other aspects of their personalities. Motherhood has often been taken as women's preeminent, even defining, characteristic, and possession of a womb has often been deemed reason enough to disqualify women for most activities of public life.[6] Separating the responsibilities of parenthood from gestational activity allows us to see childbearing as one thing a woman may choose to do, but by no means as the definition of her social role or legal rights. In a somewhat parallel fashion, a man who commissions a pregnancy undertakes "fatherhood" quite consciously and might be more involved in caring for the child than men traditionally have been. Marjorie Shultz believes that contract pregnancy is thus a way to make the assumption of parental responsibilities more gender-neutral: it can "soften and offset gender imbalances that presently permeate the arena of procreation and parenting."[7]

Just as "surrogacy" emphasizes that not all women who bear children (or who have the capacity to bear children) need to be thought of as mothers, it allows women who cannot bear children to assume the responsibilities of parenthood. This can also be done through foster care and adoption, of course, but a contract pregnancy allows a couple to take responsibility for a child even before conception; in a heterosexual couple it enables at least the man and sometimes the woman to have a genetic relationship to the child. The "heightened intentionality" of contract pregnancy makes it possible for any number of persons of either sex to commission a pregnancy. While most contracts to date have involved married couples, there is no technological reason why anyone, male or female, married or not, could not provide or purchase sperm and, using artificial insemination, impregnate a "surrogate" to obtain a child by contractual agreement.[8]

Carmel Shalev regards the gestational mother's obligation to relinquish the child she bore for the commissioning party as an expression of her freedom to undertake whatever work she chooses. She argues that "the refusal to acknowledge the legal validity of surrogacy agreements implies that women are not competent, by virtue of their biological sex, to act as rational, moral agents regarding their reproductive activity." Like other defenders of contract pregnancy, Shalev places great emphasis on the consent which is at the heart of any valid contract. "If the purpose is to increase the voluntariness of the decision, attention should focus on the parties' negotiations before conception. If conception is intentional and the surrogate mother is an autonomous agent, . . . why should she not be held responsible for the consequences of her autonomous reproductive decision?"[9] The same liberty that in her view should protect a woman from any governmental effort to prohibit birth control or abortion or to force sterilization also protects her freedom to agree to carry a child for someone else. The slogan "Woman's body, woman's right," succinctly captures the notion that a woman herself—not a husband, not a doctor, not the state—must make those procreative decisions that affect her.

Those who see contract pregnancy as an exercise of freedom particularly emphasize that consent is given prior to conception: "The surrogate consciously enters into the agreement and voluntarily consents to give up the child even before she becomes pregnant. Rather than being unwanted, the pregnancy is actively sought."[10] Or again, "If autonomy is understood as the deliberate exercise of choice with respect to the individual's reproductive capacity, the point at which the parties' intentions should be established is before conception."[11] Defenders of contract pregnancy seek to distinguish it from baby-selling, arguing that it is not the child or fetus for whom the woman receives payment, but her gestational services.

But how can one be sure a woman's agreement is really voluntary, her consent truly informed? Advocates of contract pregnancy propose a variety of safeguards to help ensure that pregnancy contracts will be fair and noncoercive. For example, so that women fully understand what kind of physical and emotional experiences to expect from pregnancy, the law could allow only women who have previously given birth to contract to bear a child for someone else. All parties to a contract pregnancy could be required to undergo counseling before the conception, during the pregnancy, and after the birth. To avoid financial exploitation of poor or economically vulnerable women, only those with a certain level of financial resources could be allowed to enter a pregnancy contract.[12] The emphasis in all these proposals is on the combination of reason and will that are involved in consent. "In contract law, intent manifested by a promise and subsequent reliance provides the basis for enforceable agreements. Typically, the mental element is the pivotal element in determining legal outcomes."[13] If the choice is a free one, argues Marjorie Shultz, then "the principle of private intention [should] be given substantial deference and legal force."[14] Attention should focus on whether conditions under which the mind can be held to have freely acceded to the bargain pertained when the contract was made.

Feminist proponents of contract pregnancy argue that those who would allow a "surrogate" to change her mind about relinquishing custody fall into the age-old trap of assuming that women are not as rational as men or that their reason can be overridden by instinct or sentiment. "The paternalistic refusal to force the surrogate mother to

keep her word denies the notion of female reproductive agency and
reinforces the traditional perception of women as imprisoned in the
subjectivity of their wombs."¹⁵ One surrogate mother quoted approv-
ingly by Lori Andrews insisted that "a contract is a contract. . . . It's
dangerous to say that we are ruled by our hormones, rather than our
brains. You don't have a right to damage other people's lives [i.e., those
of the expectant couple deprived of a child when a surrogate reneges]
because of your hormones." Robin Bergstrom, a legislative aide in the
New York State Senate, remarked in the same vein, "I truly can't understand the feminists who are now arguing against women's rights
[i.e., to prohibit payment to surrogates and to make pregnancy contracts revocable]. . . . Women's rights have been cut back in the past
based on male perceptions that women are incompetent to make decisions, but this time women will be putting it on themselves."¹⁶

It is important to notice that these arguments about a woman's
free consent to bear a child assume, implicitly or explicitly, that the
"work" of pregnancy is analogous to other kinds of human labor.
What distinguishes legal rules that allow a surrogate to change her
mind from the kind of state interference in women's contractual capacity implicated in much protective labor legislation? In the early
twentieth century many feminists supported legislation to protect
women from oppressive working conditions, although the U.S. Supreme Court had struck down protective labor legislation for men as
a violation of freedom of contract.¹⁷ But by the 1990s most advocates
of women's rights had come to argue that women should not receive
protections unavailable to men. When some states and then the federal government extended rights to maternity leave to women—by
definition unavailable to men—many feminists advocated gender-
neutral parental leave policies instead.¹⁸ Many argued that even when
work involved substances that might cause fetal damage, pregnant
women should not be barred from such jobs. If, after appropriate
medical and psychological counseling, a woman freely consents to a
pregnancy contract, then allowing her later to renege on her agreement and keep custody of the child she bears—or to share custody
with its biological father—smacks of the legal paternalism that many
feminists have long opposed. Is it not antithetical to all that feminists
have worked for, ask proponents, to argue that women's reproductive

experience should be the grounds for allowing the law to treat their contracts concerning pregnancy as less binding than other contracts; does it not suggest that women are less bound than others by their freely given words?

Defenders of contract pregnancy assume not only that gestation of a fetus is work that is analogous to other forms of wage labor, but also that selling one's labor for a wage is a manifestation of individual freedom. From this perspective, prohibiting a woman from receiving payment for her services bearing a child denies her the full and effective proprietorship of her body. One ethicist argues that surrogacy is a service that is "simply an extension ... of baby-sitting and other child-care arrangements which are very widely practiced" and that it is "irrational" to allow payment for the latter services and not for pregnancy.[19] Shalev similarly believes that "the transaction under consideration is ... for the sale of reproductive services. ... A childless couple is regarded as purchasing the reproductive labor of a birth mother." Banning the sale of procreative services will "reactivate and reinforce the state's power to define what constitutes legitimate and illegitimate reproduction," while allowing payment will "recognize a woman's legal authority to make decisions regarding the exercise of her reproductive capacity."[20]

The consequence of prohibiting pregnancy contracts or banning payment for gestational services is suggested by the question of the surrogate who asked, " 'Why am I exploited if I am paid, but not if I am not paid?' "[21] When the state forbids payment for contract pregnancy, it treats reproductive activity as it has traditionally treated women's domestic labor—as unpaid, noneconomic acts of love and nurturing, rather than as work and a real economic contribution to family life. Even Margaret Radin, who opposes pregnancy contracts, acknowledges that prohibiting paid pregnancy creates a "double bind." Contract pregnancy could "enable a needy group—poor women—to improve their relatively powerless, oppressed condition, an improvement that would be beneficial to personhood."[22] To forbid people to labor or be paid for using their bodies as they choose when no harm is done to others seems extraordinarily hard for a liberal polity to justify, a point which proponents of the decriminalization of prostitution emphasize.[23] Proponents of contract pregnancy emphasize the value of allowing individuals to determine their activities and life courses as they choose. When the contract between the gestational mother and the commissioning parents reflects the procreative intentions of both parties, enforcement of the contract is the only way both to give force to the desire and commitment of those who seek to raise a child and to recognize the autonomy of the gestational mother.

Although I deeply value self-determination, I believe that pregnancy contracts should not be enforceable. I would not, however, prohibit "gift surrogacy" in which only payment of medical and living expenses would be allowed. Such surrogacy agreements could be treated like pre-adoption agreements that leave the birth mother free to decide not to relinquish custody at birth. I am ambivalent about whether any further payment should ever be permitted.[24] On the one hand, it seems odd to forbid compensation in recognition of the discomforts of pregnancy and the pain of giving birth in a freely entered agreement. On the other hand, the possibilities that allowing payment will lead some women to enter pregnancy contracts solely out of economic necessity, and will reinscribe racial and class privilege, are so great that banning payment is justified in the contemporary United States.

"Our Bodies, Our Selves": Considerations against Irrevocable Contracts

The most perplexing problem in treating pregnancy contracts like other employment contracts is that the "product" is another human being who did not exist at the time the agreement was struck. As we have seen, most advocates of contract pregnancy insist that the payment the gestational mother receives is not for the child, but for gestational services.[25] This distinction, however, seems hard to sustain when the fetus develops from the gestational mother's ovum. In such cases, the woman is contributing more than the labor of her womb; she is also selling her genetic material, and it becomes difficult to see how the exchange escapes the charge of baby-selling. In addition, as Margaret Radin has pointed out, selling an ovum along with gestational services entails pricing all of a woman's personal attributes—race, height, hair color, intelligence, artistic ability—as well as reproductive capacity, and in a society in which women's bodies are already highly commodified by advertisers, pornographers, and promoters of prostitution, it seems especially damaging to commodify a woman's physical attributes.[26]

In "gestational surrogacy," when the childbearing woman has no genetic relationship with the fetus, the assertion that the commissioning couple is purchasing only gestational services is stronger than it is in "complete surrogacy," in which the intentional father's sperm is introduced into the surrogate's womb to fertilize her egg. The incidence of gestational surrogacy has risen markedly in the past decade. By 1990 there had been some eighty known cases in the United States in which an embryo had been introduced into another woman's womb after having been fertilized in vitro.[27] The practice of gestational surrogacy increased from about 5 percent of contract pregnancies in 1988 to over 50 percent in 1998.[28] It appears that some couples turned to gestational surrogates because, though the wife produced eggs, she could not carry a pregnancy to term, or because the couple perceived (correctly) that a gestational surrogate would have a harder time winning a dispute about custody or visitation than would a complete surrogate.

The attitude that the genetic tie, more than the experience of relationship, creates a parental right was reflected in the decision of Judge Richard N. Parslow in the California case in which Anna Johnson bore a child conceived by in vitro fertilization from the ovum and sperm of Crispina and Mark Calvert. While pregnant, Ms. Johnson sued to have her contract declared invalid and to retain custody of the child after birth. Judge Parslow awarded custody to the genetic parents and commented that the contract was binding: "I see no problem with someone getting paid for her pain and suffering.... They [gestational mothers] are not selling a baby; they are selling pain and suffering."[29] To Judge Parslow the contract appeared to be an agreement about work, and his remarks raise the question of how the "pain and suffering" of pregnancy are analogous to the physical and psychological demands of other kinds of labor.

Arguments for contract pregnancy depend, it seems to me, on a strong analogy between the "work" of pregnancy and other forms of wage labor. The analogy seems to rest on two main considerations: pregnancy involves the body, culminating in the extraordinary physical exertion of "labor" and giving birth; and pregnancy ends with the appearance of something new in the world, a tangible "product" of gestational work.

What seems to distinguish human gestation from other kinds of productive work, however, are the ways in which it involves both a woman's physical and psychological being, and the distinction between the human being that results from a pregnancy and other kinds of products. The basic issue is the separability of the mother's body and the fetus. The more we can see the two as separate the easier it is to regard the child, once born, as a "product" of a woman's body.[30] But the experience of pregnancy as described by women seeking to understand their connection to the being growing within them suggests that mother and fetus are not yet, or are not in every way, distinct entities. Neither are they the same being. In her 1945 poem about abortion, "The Mother," Gwendolyn Brooks cries out against the inability of language to express the relationship between mother and fetus: "you are dead. / Or rather, or instead, / You were never made. / But that too, I am afraid, / Is faulty: oh, what shall I say, how is the truth to be said?"[31] In her analysis of "The Mother," Barbara Johnson notes that "the poem continues to struggle to clarify the relation between 'I' [the woman] and 'you' [the fetus], but in the end [the language of the] poem can no more distinguish between 'I' and 'you' than it can come up with a proper definition of life."[32] Like Brooks, Adrienne Rich testifies to her experience of the fluidity of the boundary between self and other during pregnancy. "In early pregnancy, the stirring of the foetus felt like ghostly tremors of my own body, later like the movements of a being imprisoned within me; but both sensations were *my* sensations, contributing to my own sense of physical and psychic space."[33] Iris Young points out that while for observers pregnancy may appear to be "a time of waiting and watching, when nothing happens," for the pregnant subject "pregnancy has a temporality of movement, growth and change. . . . The pregnant woman experiences herself as a source and participant in a creative process. Though she does not plan and direct it, neither does it merely wash over her; rather, she *is* this process, this change."[34] Mother and fetus are at one and the same time distinct and interrelated entities, and this fundamental fact of human embodiment means that to speak of the "freedom" of the mother as residing in her intention as an "autonomous" agent misunderstands both the relationship between woman and child and of the woman to her ongoing self.

The interrelatedness of mother and fetus makes it difficult to specify exactly what gestational labor entails. Unlike other work, gestational labor is not consciously controlled; the bodily labor of pregnancy goes on continuously, even while the pregnant woman is asleep. Whether the "work" is done badly or well is only marginally within the mother's control; she can refrain from smoking, drinking, and using drugs, eat properly, and get an appropriate amount of exercise, but whether the fetus grows to term, has a safe birth, and is free of genetic abnormalities are otherwise largely beyond her control.

In her critique of contract pregnancy, Carole Pateman argues that while all wage labor involves selling some aspect of oneself to some degree, the alienation involved in selling gestational services is so extreme as to make it illegitimate. The problem, she says, is that the "logic of contract as exhibited in 'surrogate' motherhood" sweeps away "any intrinsic relation between the female owner, her body and reproductive capacities. It ignores the fact that the work of pregnancy involves women's emotional, physical and sexual experiences and understandings of themselves as women. It objectifies women's bodies and their reproductive labor in a manner and to a degree that are wholly unacceptable."[35]

Elizabeth Anderson echoes this point when she argues that any form of paid pregnancy involves "an invasion of the market into a new sphere of conduct, that of specifically women's labor—that is, the labor of carrying children to term in pregnancy." In her view, "[t]reating women's labor as just another kind of commercial production process violates the precious emotional ties which the mother may rightly and properly establish with her 'product,' the child." When a woman is required "to repress whatever parental love she feels for the child, these [economic] norms convert women's labor into a form of alienated labor." The forfeiture of self involved in contract pregnancy is an extreme instance of the alienation involved in many labor contracts. Market norms may be legitimate and useful in their proper sphere, but when "applied to the ways we treat and understand women's reproductive labor, women are reduced ... to objects of use."[36]

The distinction between complete surrogacy and gestational surrogacy pushes this argument about what is entailed in the "labor" of gestation, and whether the existence of a genetic tie between fetus and woman should make any difference to whether the law enforces pregnancy contracts. In some people's eyes the existence of a genetic tie significantly alters the relationship between pregnant woman and fetus. Heléna Ragoné reports that some women who agree to be gestational surrogates say that they would refuse to be complete surrogates. These women say that they would feel as if they were giving up their own child if the child were conceived with their egg, but that they do not feel related to a child to whom they have no genetic relationship.[37] Judge Parslow distinguished the case before him in *Johnson v. Calvert* from the *Baby M.* case by pointing out that Anna Johnson, unlike Mary Beth Whitehead, had no genetic relationship to the child she carried.

Countering the implications of the testimony of gestational surrogates who have refused to be complete surrogates, however, are studies that show that many women consider the gestational tie to be as central as the genetic tie to their sense of themselves as a "parent." Mary Mahowald reports on two studies in which both women and men said that gestation was significant when asked whether they would choose to have the mother (either themselves or their partner) of their child be the gestational or the genetic mother, although women gave more importance to gestation than did men.[38] Each man in one of the studies was asked whether he would prefer both himself and his partner to be genetically related to their child, without the woman being pregnant or giving birth, or would prefer that only he be genetically related to a child conceived through IVF to whom his partner gave birth. Interestingly, almost 75 percent of the men chose having a child with a genetic relationship to both partners but gestated and birthed by another woman, while just under 50 percent of the women chose this. Clearly women saw gestational and genetic ties as equally valuable to parenthood, while men emphasized the genetic tie.

If gestation is at least as important in establishing parenthood as the genetic tie, in *Johnson v. Calvert* the claim of the gestational mother, Anna Johnson, should have been regarded as equal to that of either one of the Calverts. Judge Parslow's characterization of Anna Johnson as doing nothing more than "selling pain and suffering" paid too little attention to the claims generated by the activity of gestation. The California Supreme Court, for its part, regarded both gestation and genetics as grounds for legal motherhood. It held that "two women have each presented acceptable proof of maternity," one by gestation and the other by genetics. The Court held that when the woman with the genetic tie is not the woman giving birth, "she who intended to bring about the birth of a child that she intended to raise as her own" has a claim to custody as the "natural" mother.[39] I would give greater weight to gestation and require a hearing.[40]

When trying to determine what public policy with respect to surrogacy should be, it is important to take into account that payment for gestational service does not occur in some gender- and race-neutral environment. Rather, in our society many of our institutions and interactions are shaped by relationships of unbalanced power between women and men, and between black women and white men and women. To talk about the freedom of the self-possessing individual to do what she will with her own body while ignoring these imbalances flies in the face of lived experience. I think it is possible (barely) to imagine conditions in which it would be legitimate for a woman to receive payment for bearing a child to whom she had no genetic relationship, provided always that she retained the power to assert custodial rights before or at birth. At a minimum, such conditions would include an economy free from wage labor undertaken in order to survive; rough economic equality between men and women and between people of color and whites; a culture in which the "ideology of motherhood," which asserts that childbearing is women's natural and preeminent calling, did not contribute to some women deriving their sense of self-worth from being pregnant; a society free from the objectification and commodification of women's sexuality; and a politics uninfluenced by gender and racial hierarchies. Descriptions of contract pregnancy that depict the practice as nothing more than womb rental in a supposedly neutral market fail to take account of the profoundly gendered nature of the transaction. Contract pregnancy can as appropriately be described as enabling economically secure men and women to purchase economically vulnerable women's procreative labor and custodial rights as allowing women the freedom to sell procreative labor. And in this context contracts should be unenforceable and payment beyond expenses should be prohibited.

This argument that a person should be released from an agreement that she could fulfill rests on a judgment that the person's self or sense of self may change in such a significant way that enforcing the contract would do violence to that self. The fact that many people think that the freedom to choose at one point in time does not capture what is most important about human freedoms in a liberal society is reflected in prevalent attitudes towards divorce. Prior to the midnineteenth century, divorce on any ground other than a wife's adultery was impossible in most states. Yet many states now permit "no fault" divorce, which entails releasing people upon their request from the promise to be husband or wife "until death do us part." States will not enforce a promise to live intimately with another person for life, nor prohibit the formation of a new relationship through remarriage. Divorce law reflects in part society's determination that the law cannot permit people to be bound to a promise when they and their relationship have fundamentally changed. Not to allow a woman to revoke her consent during pregnancy or at birth seems to ignore the possibility of a somewhat analogous change that simultaneously affects the self as an individual and as a person-in-relationship.

These considerations lead me to think that pregnancy contracts should be unenforceable. To assume that only irrationality or mindless flightiness would induce a woman to change her mind about relinquishing a baby she has borne through months of pregnancy ignores the months she has spent *in relationship with* a developing human being. It is this relationship that may change her, and it is this relationship that is severed if a pregnancy contract is enforceable. Defenders of pregnancy contracts argue eloquently, and with much truth, that intentional parents have also been in relationship with their child-to-be, imagining the role the child will play in their lives, planning for its care, and loving it as it develops *in utero*. Marjorie Shultz argues that it is the relationship between intentional parents and fetus that must be protected by enforcing reproductive contracts. "To ignore the significance of deliberation, purpose and expectation—the capacity to envision and shape the future through intentional choice—is to disregard one of the most distinctive traits that makes us human. It is to disregard crucial differences in moral meaning and responsibility. To disregard such intention with reference to so intimate and significant an activity as procreation and child-rearing is deeply shocking." When a surrogate reneges on her promise to relinquish custody, it is wrong "to say to a disappointed parent, 'go get another child.'" Such a judgment "offends our belief in the uniqueness of each individual. It inappropriately treats the miracle and complexity of particular individual lives as fungible. By contrast, surrogacy and other reproductive arrangements transfer the life and parental responsibility for a particular unique child." Hence, argues Shultz, "Although it may seem counter-intuitive, the extraordinary remedy, specific performance of agreements about parenthood, in some sense confirms core values about the uniqueness of life."[41]

The claims on behalf of both the intentional parents and those of the gestational mother rest, then, on assertions about the relationship between parent and fetus. Defenders of contract pregnancy are deeply disturbed by the prospect that allowing a gestational mother to void her contractual agreement "expresses the idea that the biological experience of motherhood 'trumps' all other considerations. . . . [I]t exalts a woman's experience of pregnancy and childbirth over her formation of emotional, intellectual and interpersonal decisions and expectations, as well as over others' reliance on the commitments she has earlier made."[42] Yet even Shultz's eloquent plea and my own commitment to gender-neutral law do not persuade me that promises to relinquish custody should be enforced against the wishes of the gestational mother. Her later judgment based on her experience of the pregnancy *does* "trump," and what it trumps is her own earlier promise, upon which the intentional parents' claim to sole custody depends. It trumps because enforcement of a pregnancy contract against the gestational mother's wishes, whether or not she also has a genetic tie to the child, would constitute a legal refusal to recognize the reality of the woman and fetus as beings-in-relationship, which the law should protect as it does many other personal relationships. Yet the biological father or the commissioning couple also have parental claims. The claims of those denied custody might be recognized by granting and enforcing visitation rights, although if this proved disruptive courts might cut off visitation.[43]

I find my thoughts on the importance of the actual embodied relationships of gestational mother and fetus to be akin (with certain significant exceptions) to those of Robert Goldstein, who argues in *Mother-love and Abortion* that most discussions of abortion, whether put forward by regulationists or pro-choice advocates, err in regarding pregnant woman and fetus as distinct individuals with competing rights.[44] As he points out, "rights talk" in this context emphasizes what Ferdinand Schoeman refers to as "the appropriateness of seeing other persons as separate and autonomous agents," whereas "the relationship between parent and infant [or fetus] involves an awareness of a kind of union between people. . . . We *share our selves* with those with whom we are intimate."[45] A correct approach, says Goldstein, would not "define personhood as if it were a solitary achievement of the fetus and its DNA that precedes rather than presupposes participation in the primary community of woman and fetus." With regard to abortion, respect for this "primary community" requires that the law recognize the pregnant woman as the person who must make decisions about the dyad she and the fetus constitute; she must be accorded "a privileged position as dyadic representative that is superior to that of other would-be dyadic participants," such as the biological father, the state, or potential adoptive parents. In Goldstein's analysis, the privacy and autonomy that the *Roe v. Wade* decision protects, then, "belongs not only to the woman as an individual but also to the dyadic, indeed symbiotic, unit of woman and fetus. This dyad constitutes the relevant community for understanding the abortion decision."[46] In the case of surrogacy, the embodied relationship of the gestational mother (who may or may not be the genetic mother) is stronger than that between the commissioning parent(s) and fetus, or her own "intentional self" and the fetus prior to conception. In Kenneth Karst's expressive phrase, a critically important aspect of the right of "privacy" is not to isolate people from one another, but to protect and foster what he calls "the freedom of intimate association."[47] A legal rule enforcing a pregnancy contract would reinforce notions of human separateness and insularity rather than recognizing that the development of individuality and autonomy takes place through sustained and intimate human relationship.

Putting It in Context:
Gender, Race, and Class and the Ethics of Surrogacy

The issues that arise in contract pregnancy overlap with those that arise in adoption and gamete donation. As in adoption, the child is transferred from the gestational mother to people who will be the child's legal and social parents, but, unlike adoption, the child has a genetic tie to the prospective father and perhaps the prospective mother. As in other forms of gamete donation, the prospective parents purchase an egg from the surrogate in complete surrogacy, and the child has a genetic relationship with the other parent. Unlike gamete donation, the prospective parents also purchase gestational services.[48] These characteristics of surrogacy mean that this practice can be regulated neither exactly like adoption, nor exactly like gamete transfer, but that all these practices need to be shaped in accordance with the same ethical concerns.

Like those who purchase eggs, prospective parents who turn to complete surrogacy to obtain both an egg and gestational services engage in "matching" the characteristics of the donor and themselves. Intentional parents usually look for a surrogate with the same racial features, physical build, and hair color as the intentional mother. As with other kinds of gamete donation, people sometimes choose surrogacy because having a child genetically related to one of the social parents is important to them for a variety of reasons. Sometimes, again like some instances of gamete donation, white parents turn to surrogacy to avoid adopting (or being asked to adopt) a child of a different race. As I argued in Chapter 3, some of the reasons people turn to gamete donation or surrogacy are far better than others: parents, doctors, and counselors alike need to think hard about what they are doing and about the implications of their actions not only for a particular couple, gestational mother, and child, but for the shaping of widely held social values. There is a strong case to be made for encouraging people to adopt existing children, and while that goal should not preclude surrogacy, it should make policy-makers reflect very hard on the values that are both reflected in and shaped by how we approach surrogacy.

I suggested above that balancing the values of liberty, relationship, equality, and care could be met if pregnancy contracts were allowed, but unenforceable. Both the intentional parents and the woman willing to gestate a fetus would have the liberty to make an agreement, but legislatures and courts would not regard freedom of contract as the only value at stake in surrogacy agreements. Equally important would be the recognition of the many relationships between multiple adults and the child-to-be: the initiative of the intentional parents, the contribution of gamete(s), and the activity of gestation. Both the intentional parents, if they contribute to the pregnant woman's welfare during pregnancy, and the pregnant woman herself, provide care to the child. Acknowledgment of the importance of both genetic donors and gestational mothers to the future child requires the recognition of sexual difference in achieving equality.

All the adults involved in contract pregnancy have a responsibility to make available to the person being created by their actions full information about the identity of the egg donor and the gestational mother (who will be the same person in complete surrogacy). The reasons for this duty are the same as those discussed with respect to gamete donation. It is important that persons upon reaching adulthood be able to learn the name of as well as other social facts about the woman who gave them birth, whether or not she is also the egg donor. Regulations affecting surrogacy must reflect the judgment that gestation is one of the activities that gives rise to parental rights, as are genetic ties, intention, and caregiving. The significance of gestation is clear if one considers the perspective of the future child, who owes his or her existence not only to genetic donors but also to the woman who carried the fetus as it developed.

Public policy could hold that when a surrogate changes her mind about relinquishing custody of the child during pregnancy or very soon after birth, there would be a hearing to decide on custody. Were this public policy, intentional parents would have very strong incentives to make certain that the gestational mother had been thoroughly counseled about her action and was acting voluntarily and with a great deal of self-knowledge. Miscalculation or self-deception on the part of the intentional parents would subject them to stressful and costly legal proceedings, might in addition cost them the money they had spent supporting the gestational mother, and might subject them to the tremendous emotional pain of losing sole custody of the child.[49]

The policy of nonenforceable contracts would not, however, be adequate to guard against exploitation and adverse consequences in all cases. Thinking about gestational surrogacy shows how deeply threatening the possible commodification of women's bodies is to the freedom of all women, but, in this society, particularly to women of color. In a society where employment opportunity is as stratified by race as it is in the United States, it is not irrational to think that black and hispanic women would often agree to be gestational surrogates for a lower fee than would white women. Because our society tends to regard both genetics and race as natural and essential components of personal identity, in cases in which the gestational mother and the child share no genes and are of different races, the temptation to regard the child as a "product" wholly separate and distinct from the pregnant woman will be very strong. In such cases the temptation to view the agreement to bear a child as a binding employment contract will be particularly great. The separability of the gametes from the donors' bodies makes them appear like commodities, and the resulting child like a product produced with those raw materials. If the gestational surrogate and the intentional parents have different racial features, in a society in which race is such a strong social marker, the tendency to view the (white) child as utterly distinct from the (black) mother will be great, as indeed it will be if a black child is born to a white woman.[50]

The danger that racial difference will compound the difficulty of getting legislatures and judges to recognize the importance of the relationship between pregnant woman and fetus to any custody dispute was evident in Judge Parslow's decision in *Calvert v. Johnson*, when he distinguished the Calvert case from the Baby M. case by pointing out that Anna Johnson, unlike Mary Beth Whitehead, had no genetic relationship to her child. Judge Parslow did not mention race in his decision, but because the media described Anna Johnson as black, Crispina Calvert as Filipina, and Mark Calvert as Caucasian, the case raised the fear that Anna Johnson would be the first of many black women who would bear white or mixed-race children with whom courts would assume they had no relationship worthy of legal recognition.[51] Commenting on the *Calvert* case, Jeremy Rifkin and Andrew Kimbrell worried that

> Minority women increasingly will be sought to serve as "mother machines" for embryos of middle and upper-class clients. It's a new, virulent form of racial and class discrimination. Within a decade, thousands of poor and minority women will likely be used as a "breeder class" for those who can afford $30,000 to $40,000 to avoid the inconvenience and danger of pregnancy.[52]

These concerns resonate with those Twila Perry and others raised with respect to both domestic and intercountry transracial adoption. I argued in chapter 1 that the risk of treating poor women of color as resources for children for more affluent women might be reduced in adoption by doing away with closed records, so that all the adults involved would have a direct reminder of their responsibility to the child and to the adult that child will become. What I have said about the error of (and the social harm stemming from) turning gamete donation and gestational services into market transactions supports my conclusion that when the gestational mother changes her mind about relinquishing the child to the intentional parents, the care she has provided to the fetus and her relationship to the newborn child entitle her to a custody hearing.

Prohibiting anonymous donation and refusing to enforce pregnancy contracts without first holding a custody hearing could be sufficient to prevent exploitation in cases of complete surrogacy. In a society like the United States in which race plays a significant role in shaping personal identity and distributing social power, however, nonenforceability might be insufficient in cases of gestational surrogacy. A poor woman who has borne a child for a couple of a different race would be more likely to be regarded as providing nothing more than gestational labor than would a woman who also shared a genetic connection with the fetus. She would also be less likely to seek custody herself because she would face all the stigma and difficulty attending a multiracial family. To guard against exploitation in gestational surrogacy it would be necessary to get rid of the monetary inducement to bear the child, making surrogacy a "gift" relationship.

I want to argue against regarding gestation as just another employment opportunity for women, just as I did against regarding human sperm and eggs as commodities. The incursion of the language, images, and practices of the market into both of these aspects of procreative activity poses a tremendous threat to respect for both adults and for the children who come into being as a result of these activities. Acceptance of the market as the way to regulate procreative activity misunderstands or ignores the multiple ways in which the relationships that form an intrinsic part of human life impose limits on what people can legitimately choose to do with their bodies and their genetic material.

None of these considerations means that it is wrong for a woman to agree to bear a child for someone else or to decide to relinquish a child for adoption. Law should not force a woman to retain physical custody of her child once it is born. In adoption, a birth mother may decide that placing the child in someone else's care may be best for her, for the child, and for the new custodial parent(s). But the ethics of adoption and "gift" pregnancy must be distinguished from those of contract pregnancy regarded as just another form of female employment. Even though birth mothers in adoption may mourn for children they entrust to others to care for and raise, they have made their decision to separate from an existing human being, not from a potential one. Their actions, which may bring relief as well as (or as much as) sorrow, are not the consequence of an agreement that ignores or dismisses the relevance of the experience of pregnancy and of the human and embodied relationship between woman and fetus to our understanding of human freedom and choice. The implications of what it means for human beings to be embodied creatures are as relevant to both complete and gestational surrogacy as they are to adoption. Human embodiment affects what both woman and child are due in a society that recognizes the reality of human relationship and interdependence even as it cherishes and promotes human freedom and choice.

CHAPTER 5

Lesbian Co-Mothers, Sperm Donors, and Fathers: How Many Parents Can a Child Have?

O ne dramatic change in the ways in which people choose to live and to define themselves as a family has been lesbian and gay partners' use of third-party gametes (and, in the case of gay men, a surrogate mother) to have children together. These families challenge both the notion of family as beginning with a heterosexual couple, and the notion that every child has two (and only two) parents to both of whom the child is biologically related.

Some lesbian couples are raising children born to one of the partners during a previous marriage, while others use alternative insemination and have children who have two female parents and a male sperm donor. To date, obtaining legal recognition of the parental status of the nonbiological mother in lesbian families has only occasionally been successful. To some extent, the nonbiological mother in a lesbian family formed after a previous marriage is in the same position as other stepparents, except that she is legally barred from marrying her partner. In families in which the lesbian couple uses alternative insemination, the lack of legal recognition of same-sex marriage makes securing parental rights for the nonbiological parent much more difficult than it is for heterosexual married couples. But even among those who support legal recognition for lesbian families, and protection for the relationship between lesbian co-mothers and their children, there is no consensus about the proper grounding of parental rights for the nonbiological parent. Nor is there agreement about whether known sperm donors of the children of lesbian partners should have any kind of parental or quasi-parental rights.

In this chapter I look at different ways to ground the parental rights of nonbiological parents in lesbian couples that have used alternative insemination, and ask whether or not a sperm donor who is known to and involved in the life of his genetic offspring should have any right to visitation or other legal status. (This analysis can apply to gay men, with added attention to the ethical concerns involved in using a surrogate mother, discussed in Chapter 4.) Both questions involve aspects of the question, "What gives someone the right to be recognized as a legal parent?"

Two prominent cases in which courts considered the parental status of lesbian co-mothers, *Alison D. v. Virginia M.*[1] and *Thomas S. v. Robin Y.,*[2] provide concrete examples of the kinds of issues that arise under current law, and of the very different views of both judges and scholars about the proper grounding of legal parenthood. A reading of these cases is valuable in two ways. These cases push hard against traditional definitions of the family, show the difficulties of modeling legal rules to govern homosexual family relationships on those that govern heterosexual families, and suggest ways of framing appropriate rules and practices. And in raising the question of whom the law should recognize as a legal parent, the controversies in *Alison D.* and *Thomas S.* are relevant not only to lesbian families but to a wide variety of families in contemporary America.

Because the implications of these cases are far-reaching and contested, I review the decisions themselves, examine scholarly comment on the proposed rationales for assigning legal parenthood in these cases, and then offer my own reflections on the grounding of legal parenthood. Current law has not yet found an adequate way to ground the parental rights of adults in various situations who are raising children to whom they are not genetically related. A child-centered approach to family policy requires that the law protect relationships that are fundamental to a child's sense of self and well-being, including the

parental status of a lesbian nonbiological mother. It is the recognition
of a child's right to a permanent, nurturing relationship, more than of
an adult's right to parent a child, that is the proper grounding of the
parental status of biological and nonbiological parents alike.

Case Histories:
Alison D. v. Virginia M. and *Thomas S. v. Robin Y.*

The issue in *Alison D. v. Virginia M.* was whether a lesbian co-
mother had standing to seek visitation rights with a child after she and
the child's biological mother separated. Alison D. and Virginia M. began living together in 1978, and in March 1980 decided to have a child.
They agreed that Virginia would use alternative insemination to become pregnant and that they would share all the responsibilities of
child rearing. In July 1981 Virginia gave birth to a baby boy, A.D.M., to
whom they gave Alison's last name as his middle name and Virginia's
last name as his last name. Alison shared in all birthing expenses and
after birth continued to support him financially. During the first two
years of A.D.M.'s life she and Virginia shared child rearing equally. In
November 1983, when A.D.M. was a bit over two years old, Alison and
Virginia ended their relationship and Alison moved out of their
jointly owned home. They agreed that Alison would continue to pay
half of the mortgage and major household expenses and that she
would visit with A.D.M. several times a week. This arrangement continued for three years, at which time Virginia bought out Alison's interest in the mortgage and then began to restrict Alison's visits with
A.D.M. Alison moved to Ireland to pursue career opportunities, but
she continued to try to keep in touch with A.D.M. Virginia, however,
terminated all contact between Alison and A.D.M. and began returning all the gifts and letters Alison sent to him. Alison then sued
for visitation; Virginia was found to be a fit parent, and the issue before the court was whether Alison had standing to seek visitation.

The trial court, the Appellate Division, and the Court of Appeals
of New York State (the state's highest court) all agreed that Alison did
not have standing to seek visitation under Domestic Relations Law
§70. The relevant statute declared that "either parent may apply to the
Supreme Court . . . and [the court] may award the natural guardian-
ship, charge and custody of such child to either parent . . . as the case

may require." The judges of the Court of Appeals found in a divided decision that Alison was "not a 'parent' within the meaning of section 70," because "although [she] apparently nurtured a close and loving relationship with the child," she was neither A.D.M.'s biological mother, nor his legal mother by adoption.[3] The court noted that New York had not adopted language similar to that of Oregon, whose law declared that "any person including but not limited to a foster parent, parent, stepparent, grandparent . . . who has established emotional ties creating a parent-child relationship with a child" may seek "visitation or other right of custody."[4] Because New York had not created such an expansive category, the courts construed "parent" to refer only to biological or adoptive parents.

The only dissenter to this opinion was Judge Judith Kaye, who argued that the court had the authority to define "parent" as it saw fit, since the term was not defined in the statute. The proper course for the Court of Appeals, said Judge Kaye, was to send the case back to the trial court to determine whether Alison "stands in loco parentis to A.D.M. and, if so, whether it is in the child's best interest to allow her the visitation rights she claims."[5]

For those who want to secure legal recognition of gay and lesbian family relationships and protection for children of gay and lesbian families, *Alison D.* was a severe disappointment. Here was a couple who planned together to have a child, lived together with the child for two years, and shared responsibility for and care of the child until the child was over five years old. A.D.M. had a strong attachment to Alison and called her Mom and her parents Grammy and Granddad.[6] Even among Alison D.'s supporters, however, views differed about what exactly should have grounded or justified a decision to give Alison standing to seek visitation. I will return to those differences shortly.

Where *Alison D.* concerned a dispute between mothers, *Thomas S. v. Robin Y.* concerned lesbian parents who were united in their opposition to a sperm donor's efforts to establish parental rights over a child conceived with his sperm, and their determination to maintain what they saw as the integrity of their family against disruption by a man they portrayed in court papers as an "outsider."

The mothers, Robin Y. and Sandra R., met in 1979 and established a monogamous lesbian relationship. Early in their relationship, they decided to have children and chose Jack K. to be the sperm donor. Robin, Sandra, and Jack agreed that Jack would not have parental rights or obligations and that Jack would allow himself to be known to the child if she ever asked about her biological origin. Sandra underwent alternative insemination with Jack's sperm, and Cade R.-Y. was born in May 1980. Sandra and Robin then decided that Robin should bear a child. They enlisted Thomas S., like Jack a gay man, to be the sperm donor. Again, all three adults agreed that any resulting child would be raised by Robin and Sandra as co-parents; that Thomas would have no parental rights or obligations; and that he would make himself known as the biological father if the child asked about his or her biological origins. Robin was successfully inseminated, and Ry was born in November 1981. Like Cade, she was given Sandra's and Robin's last names.

In early 1985 Cade, who was almost five, began to ask about her biological origins. Sandra and Robin contacted Jack and Thomas and asked whether they would meet the children. Both agreed, and Sandra, Robin, Cade, and Ry traveled from New York to San Francisco to meet both men. The meeting was by all accounts successful and pleasant for everyone. Subsequently, Jack developed a drinking problem and no longer gave much attention to Cade. Sandra and Robin asked Thomas to treat both Cade and Ry equally, and he agreed. Between 1985 and 1991, Thomas visited with Robin, Sandra, and the girls several times a year.

Initially, all contacts between Thomas and the girls were at the discretion of their mothers, and this seemed to cause no difficulty. In late 1990 or early 1991, however, Thomas asked that Ry visit him and his biological relatives in California by themselves, without Robin and Sandra. Robin and Sandra felt that Thomas's request to have the girl visit him and meet his biological family undermined the understanding that the two women were equally mothers to both girls, and that the girls were fully sisters, regardless of their biological relationship. The mothers also worried that were Robin to die, Thomas or his biological family might seek custody of Ry. They refused Thomas's request to have the girls visit him without them. Thomas commenced a proceeding for an order of filiation (that is, a legal determination that he was Ry's father) and visitation rights.

Judge Kaufmann of the Family Court in New York County denied Thomas's petition for an order of filiation, and said that were it granted, he would deny Thomas's application for visitation. In making his ruling, Judge Kaufmann invoked the doctrine of equitable estoppel, which says that a person may not ask for enforcement of a legal right where his or her action or inaction has led someone else to act in a way that could be held against them if the right were now to be enforced. Thomas's actions, Judge Kaufmann held, had consistently indicated that he had no intention of seeking recognition as Ry's father, and so the mothers had allowed a relationship to develop between him and Ry.[7] Having acted as he did, leading the mothers to encourage his relationship with Ry, trusting that he would not seek recognition of legal paternity, he could not now request an order of filiation based in part on the existence of that relationship. The Appellate Court reversed in a 3-to-2 decision. The majority ruled that Robin could not seek "to deny [Thomas's] right to legal recognition of [his parental] relationship." The Court granted filiation, and sent the case back to Family Court for a hearing on visitation. The dissenting justices, however, agreed with Judge Kaufmann's decision denying Thomas's petition on the grounds that equitable estoppel of Thomas's action would serve "the best interests of this child."[8]

Robin announced her intention to appeal, and the New York Court of Appeals said no order of filiation should be granted until the appeal process was completed. Thomas, stating that his health was deteriorating (he had AIDS), declined to oppose the appeal.[9] This ended the litigation without his being granted an order of filiation. Nonetheless, the Appellate Division ruling stands as the declared law of New York. Litigation concerning Ry's legal parents ceased, but the issues raised by the case were scarcely resolved.

Proposed Rationales for Assigning Legal Parenthood in *Alison D.* and *Thomas S.*

I find four major positions arising from statutes, court decisions, and legal commentators concerning the question of what should give someone a claim to be recognized as a legal parent. For some people, the actual genetic link between adult and offspring is fundamental; this position would make it reasonable to give parental rights to a biological lesbian mother, while denying them to her partner, and to allow gamete donors to seek legal recognition of their parenthood. Others believe that people should be able to use contract or indications of intent to control what is done with their genetic material; this position would make it possible for a caregiver who was genetically unrelated to a child to assume parental status by agreement or contract. Others think that adults who perform the social and psychological functions of parents should be given parental rights; this position would recognize the parental claims of nonbiological caregivers like lesbian co-mothers. A fourth group would focus not on adults but on the child, trying to determine the child's best interest, what meets a child's needs, or to what kind of care a child has a right; such a viewpoint tries to adopt the perspective articulated by or attributable to the child. Each of these perspectives appeared in the various judicial decisions and scholarly discussions about *Alison D.* and *Thomas S.* In my view, the child-centered rationale is the most persuasive of the four. Placing the child at the center of analysis would lead us to better thinking about *all* parent-child relationships.

Genetic Grounding of Parental Status

In both *Alison D.* and *Thomas S.* the courts laid heavy emphasis on the presence or absence of a genetic tie between adults and child. As we have seen, at the present time granting parental status to persons other than the genetic parents requires explanation and justification; the burden of proof rests on anyone who would ground parental rights in something other than the genetic tie.

One of the best-known proponents of this position is law professor John Robertson, who has taken the position that being the source of genetic material used in procreation should give people parental rights unless they explicitly give them up. In his eyes, the right to control what happens to one's genetic material is part of what it means to be a self-possessing individual: "Although the bundle of property rights attached to one's ownership of an embryo may be more circumscribed than for other things, it is an ownership or property interest nonetheless. . . . [T]he persons who provide the egg and sperm have the strongest claim to ownership of the embryo."[10]

Several of the judicial opinions in both *Alison D.* and *Thomas S.* reflected the view that the law should regard the egg and sperm donors as the legal parents of a child. The majority of the Court of Appeals relied on a biologically based understanding of the parent-child relationship when it said that Alison did not have standing as a parent and so was not entitled to a hearing concerning visitation with A.D.M. The court did not pay attention to Alison's and Virginia's joint decision to procure sperm and inseminate Virginia, nor to Alison's part in child rearing or her years acting as a parent to A.D.M. The only relevant fact, the court contended, was that Virginia was A.D.M.'s genetic and gestational mother and therefore a parent, while Alison, a genetic and "biological stranger" to him, was not.

The dispute in *Alison D.* was between lesbian ex-partners, while *Thomas S. v. Robin Y.* pitted a biological mother in an intact lesbian relationship against a sperm donor seeking an order of filiation. Thomas's brief relied on genetic arguments and spoke of Robin's position as analogous to that of an unwed mother. His brief stated that nothing stood in the way of declaring him to be Ry's father because "a known donor of a child conceived by an unmarried woman as the result of artificial insemination is the legal father of the child."[11] An order of estoppel such as Robin was seeking, he argued, can defeat a claim of paternity only when the mother is married and the paternity order would make the child "illegitimate." The Appellate Court followed Thomas's lead. It rejected the trial court's assertion that the case involved a threat to an "established family unit." Instead the court treated the case as analogous to disputes concerning visitation between an unwed father and an unwed mother.[12] Like the Court of Appeals decision in *Alison D.*, it held that while a genetic parent has a prima facie claim to be declared the legal parent, a person who assumes a parental role in the absence of a genetic tie does not.

Intentional or Contractual Grounding of Parental Status

Reflecting a different perspective, one that emphasizes intention rather than genetics, Marjorie Shultz has proposed that when more than two persons plan for the conception of a child, the law "should recognize the importance and legitimacy of individual efforts to project intentions and decisions into the future." Spurred primarily by her dissatisfaction with the uncertainty surrounding the legal status of "surrogate motherhood" contracts, Shultz argues that when procreative agreements are "deliberate, explicit and bargained for, where they are the catalyst for reliance and expectations, as they are in technologically assisted reproductive arrangements, they should be honored."[13] Enforcing such contracts would "enhance individual freedom, fulfillment and responsibility." For one thing, respect for individual autonomy and sense of self would enable people planning collaborative procreation to decide themselves what to do with their sperm or ova. For another, individuals planning collaborative procreation are already assuming some responsibility for the child even prior to conception. Nonbiological lesbian co-mothers can assume financial responsibility for procuring sperm, the insemination procedure, and prenatal care. Furthermore, because contractual provisions can reflect whatever division of labor and household responsibilities the parties choose, such contracts might encourage greater flexibility of gender roles than statutory provisions have traditionally done.

Although often used to support parental status for nongenetic parents like Alison D. or Sandra R., as well as to bolster the parental claims of commissioning parents in surrogacy arrangements, intention-based theories of parental rights are related to genetic-based theories because they both assume that individuals should be able to control the use of their genetic material. Someone with a right of ownership or control can alienate or transfer that right to another; positive agreement among persons who collaborate in procreative activity should determine whom the law recognizes as a legal parent. John Robertson argued that "preconception rearing intentions should count as much as or more than biologic connection" in establishing legal parenthood; he saw "compelling reasons for recognizing the preconception intentions of the parties as the presumptive arbiter of rearing rights and duties, as long as the welfare of the offspring will not be severely damaged by honoring these intentions."[14]

Certainly many supporters of Alison D. and of the custodial rights of nonbiological co-mothers in general argue that they should be recognized as parents because they planned their partner's pregnancy, supported her through the pregnancy, and cared for the child after birth. Robertson found that the human relationships recounted in *Alison D.* "directly challenge the importance of bloodline in determining parenting relations." And Robertson thought that Alison's interest in maintaining her relationship with A.D.M. might be worth protecting, even though she is not a biological parent, as it would be in the case of adoptive parents.[15]

Enforceable contracts could settle disputes between known sperm donors and lesbian co-mothers as well as disputes between co-mothers. Contracts could stipulate in advance the extent of involvement of a known sperm donor. A donor could renounce any parental rights and agree to assume a limited role in the child's life. A contract could preclude both his seeking more extensive rights *and* the mothers' excluding him altogether from the child's life. If the parties later disagreed, the pre-conception contract would settle their dispute. As Robertson put it, "if the parties who have contracted to rear are adequate child rearers, their preconception agreement should trump the claims of donors or surrogates who later insist on a different rearing role than they had agreed upon."[16]

Interestingly, despite the sizable scholarly literature arguing that intent or contract should provide the basis upon which to settle disputes over parental status, none of the court decisions in either *Alison D.* or *Thomas S.* looked to the pre-conception understandings of the parties to resolve their conflicting claims. Instead, those who argued against equating genetic and legal parenthood either looked to see who had acted as functional parents, or they invoked the best interest of the child.

Functional Grounding of Parental Status

A number of legal theorists insist that persons' *actions,* not simply their stated intentions, should establish the right to be recognized as the legal parents of a child. This position supports arguments that if the gestational mother in a surrogacy arrangement changes her mind about relinquishing the child, she should not be bound by her pre-conception contract. The surrogate's action in carrying the fetus to term creates a right to be heard in a custody dispute with the people who commissioned the pregnancy. It also supports parental status for lesbian co-mothers who plan for and take care of a child, and for gay men who jointly raise a child. A functional theory of parental rights based on the existence of a social and psychological relationship lies

behind the proposal that in divorce proceedings custody should be
determined by the amount of time each parent spent physically caring
for or being with the child, and awarded to this "primary caretaker,"
rather than being equally divided, or decided by the parents, or judi-
cially determined according to the child's future "best interest."[17]

In her dissent in *Alison D.*, Judge Kaye's view that the trial court
should find Alison to be a "parent" rested on her understanding of
theories of functional parenting. Judge Kaye cited Katharine Bartlett's
argument that the law should grant certain rights to people who can
demonstrate that they have actually assumed a parental role and dis-
charged parental responsibilities over a significant period of time.[18] To
claim such rights, people who are neither biological nor adoptive parents would have to demonstrate that they have had physical custody of
the child for at least six months; that their motive for seeking parental
status is "genuine care and concern for the child," and if the child is
old enough to express herself that this is also the perception of the
child; and that the relationship with the child began with the consent
of the child's legal parent or under court order.[19] In a similar vein,
Nancy Polikoff has proposed "expanding the definition of parenthood to include anyone who maintains a functional parental relationship with a child when a legally recognized parent created that relationship with the intent that the relationship be parental in nature."[20]
The gestational mother is to be considered a parent unless shown to be
unfit, and another person can be recognized as a parent if he or she has
assumed care for the child with the consent of the gestational mother.
Nancy Polikoff contended that Alison and Virginia were "like divorc-
ing parents." Alison should have had standing to be heard in court and
probably should have been granted visitation because she performed
the functions of a parent with the consent of the legally recognized
parent. Courts should preserve the bonds of parenthood when a family dissolves because they "consider it critical to a child's well-being to
protect the child from the traumatic and painful loss of a parent."[21]

These criteria for recognizing someone as a "functional parent"
would give parental status to Sandra, Robin's partner, since Sandra
planned for Ry's conception and took care of her since her birth, all
with Robin's consent. Even some commentators who felt that Thom-

as's genetic relationship to Ry, combined with the social ties he had established with her, entitled him to seek visitation, found Thomas's effort to portray himself and Robin as Ry's (only) two "parents" troubling. Thomas's effort to make his situation analogous to that of an unwed father seeking visitation was an "offhand, even cynical, dismissal of gay/lesbian concerns" and of Sandra's role in both Robin's and Ry's lives.[22] The notion of "functional parent" would make it clear that Sandra could not be excluded from membership in Ry's legal family, nor could Robin be denied recognition as Cade's co-mother.

There was considerable disagreement, however, over the question of whether Thomas himself had *any* claim to be considered as some kind of "functional parent." The Appellate Court, while relying mainly on Thomas's genetic relationship with Ry in granting him standing to seek an order of filiation, mentioned that Thomas also had established some social relationship with Ry. "[T]he nature, duration and constancy" of Thomas's relationship with Ry during the six years prior to his petition demonstrate his "interest and concern for his child."[23] Several commentators argued that Robin and Sandra had themselves initiated and encouraged Thomas's relationship with Ry, and subsequently with Cade, and were wrong to seek to cut him off and sever an existing bond.[24] Even those who were sympathetic to Thomas were not certain, however, that he should be designated Ry's legal "parent" with all its attendant rights and responsibilities. Some proposed a new category called "limited parenthood" to deal with situations such as Thomas's, a proposal I discuss later, in the last section.

Child-Centered Groundings of Parental Status

The "best interest of the child" standard is a well-established and frequently invoked element of family law. Judges frequently justify placing the child in the custody of one or another parent or with someone else by saying that it is in the "best interest of the child." The strength of the best interest standard is that it places the child at the center of the analysis and allows (indeed invites) a particularized ruling in the light of the specific facts of a given child's situation. It distinguishes the grievances adults have with one another from their respective abilities to provide for and nurture a child. The best interest standard directs attention not to adults' self-ownership, intent, or action, but to how best to provide a particular child with physical sustenance and psychological nurture.

Given the long history of courts invoking the best interest standard for settling disputes over child custody, placement, and visitation, it is not surprising that in her dissenting opinion in *Alison D.*, Judge Kaye used the best interest of the child standard to argue that Alison D. should be given standing to argue her case for visitation. Judge Kaye cited precedent that held that "the best interest of the child has always been regarded as superior to the right of parental custody," reflecting the principle that "a child is a person, and not a subperson over whom the parent has an absolute possessory interest."[25] She asserted that the majority's refusal to exercise the power to define "parent" in applying the New York Social Service statute "close[d] the door on all consideration of the child's best interest in visitation proceedings" unless the person seeking visitation is a biological parent. She argued that the case should be returned to the trial court with instructions that the court begin to develop some more inclusive definition of "parent" in order to prevent situations in which a consideration of the child's best interest would be ruled out altogether.[26]

Whereas Judge Kaye thought that recognizing Alison D. as a parent was in the child's best interest, the dissenters from the Appeals Court ruling that Thomas, as a genetic father, had a right to a hearing, said that Ry's best interest would be served by rejecting Thomas's claim. They focused their analysis on the *consequences* that would stem from "a dramatic abrogation" of Ry's understanding of her family: "While the child has always known that petitioner is her biological progenitor, it had consistently been demonstrated by petitioner himself that this factor did not confer upon him any authority or power over her life, that it did not mean that Sandra R. was less her mother than Robin Y., and that it did not mean that her sister was not her full sister." The order of filiation, the dissent believed, would lead to further litigation concerning visitation and possibly custody, if not by Thomas then by his parents or other relatives. Even if no other legal action transpired, "the constant, frightening potential for it is a burden that the child . . . should not have to bear."[27]

Like Judge Kaye, the dissenters on the Appeals Court hearing

Thomas S. said that "[i]f the child's best interests are to be the touch-stone of the analysis, the attempts by both parties to argue the equities of their own respective personal positions are not germane."[28] Rather, the relevant consideration was what configuration of parental rights and responsibilities would be best for Ry. They concluded that the emotional repercussions of giving Thomas legal status as Ry's father would not be in her best interest.

While sympathetic to looking at a child's best interest when adjudicating family disputes, Barbara Woodhouse has observed that the ideal can fall short of its promise. It does so either because judges' own beliefs and prejudices influence their assessment of a child's needs and wants, or because children are voiceless and powerless in defining their needs. Woodhouse would replace or supplement the best interest standard with what she calls "a generist perspective." That perspective "affirm[s] the centrality of children to family and society" and "define[s] parenting as the meeting of children's needs." The term is meant to evoke words "like 'generation' and 'regeneration,' 'genius' (guardian spirit), 'genus' (ours is *homo* as in *homo sapiens*), and 'generous' (willing to share, unselfish)." Generism would view parenthood "as stewardship, not ownership" and would value "highly concrete service" to meeting children's needs.[29] Woodhouse's generist theory rejected not only genetic and intentional models of parental rights, but also functionalist approaches that assume that adults can "earn" the right to custody of children. Woodhouse's generist approach did not confer parental status on the basis of genetic tie, intention, or the performance of certain actions, but started with a consideration of children's needs, and bestowed parental status on those who could—and should—fulfill those needs.

In the dispute between Alison and Virginia, Woodhouse saw little ambiguity in assessing whether A.D.M. had regarded Alison as his parent. Unlike the trial court, Woodhouse believed that the biological connection between Virginia and A.D.M. gave Virginia no superior custodial claim if Alison provided emotional, physical, and financial prenatal care to Virginia (which was in effect to provide support to A.D.M. as well). From A.D.M.'s perspective, the two mothers who held and cuddled him after birth gave similar care (even if Virginia breast-fed A.D.M., this did not make her so much more involved with his care as to justify excluding Alison). Woodhouse sharply criticized the legal approach that suggested that Virginia might bar Alison from future contact with A.D.M. She insisted that "Our focus on individual rights and dyadic relationships masks the fact that children need us to care not only for them but for one another. A truly child-centered family law recognizes and sustains the child's network of care."[30] While Woodhouse would not expect Virginia and Alison to reunite, she would regard them as having a mutual responsibility to protect the network of A.D.M.'s relationships, including his relationship with each of his mothers.

The same emphasis on sustaining "the child's network of care" that led Woodhouse to support Alison D.'s claim led her to reject Thomas's: "To Ry, Thomas S. is an outsider attacking her family, refusing to give it respect, and seeking to force her to spend time with him and his biological relatives, who are all complete strangers to her." Woodhouse remarked that Judge Kaufmann's decision was unusual, and correct, in taking Ry's perceptions as the proper starting point for assessing the adults' claims. "[T]he child's network of care . . . and not traditional parents' rights, is the reason for protecting a functioning unitary family from destructive intrusion and for seeking ways to minimize conflict and stress when families do separate."[31] Similarly, Woodhouse applauded the dissenters on the Appeals Court who looked at Ry's understanding of her family in rejecting Thomas's request for an order of filiation.

Reflections on the Groundings of Legal Parenthood

One of the disturbing aspects of the controlling decisions in both *Alison D.* and *Thomas S.* was, as Kate Harrison said, that they "read down the role of the non-biological mother, to a point where she is not even the functional equivalent of one member of the heterosexual couple." Rather than stand in a privileged position as a member of a parenting couple, she stood as an outsider, "[akin to] child care workers, baby-sitters, and housekeepers," a dismissal both of her status and of the integrity of the family unit of which she was a part.[32]

There is, of course, a sense in which the genetic tie *should* be relevant to the establishment of legal parenthood: the custody of a child is not up for grabs at birth. Notions of self-ownership and of each person's right to control the disposition of something so central to one's sense of self as genetic material should prohibit the government or anyone else from appropriating a person's ova, sperm, or offspring without carefully constructed and rigorously enforced procedures, including the consent of the genetic donor. Where heterosexual couples living together are concerned, absent a strong showing of cause or voluntary relinquishment, it is proper to presume that the biological parents are the custodial parents. But society is not well-served by regarding an individual's relationship to his or her genetic material as a proprietary one, or by elevating the genetic tie alone over the actual assumption of responsibility for a child's welfare and daily care as the foundation for establishing legal parenthood.

I find the claims of the nonbiological mother to be grounded in the child's need for and right to her care, an approach that moves the legal focus away from the entitlement of adults to own or claim custody of a child. In asking what a child needs and who fulfills those needs, this approach pays less attention to adults' claims than it does to a child's present and future well-being.

This approach is similar to but not the same thing as the traditional "best interest of the child" standard. That standard ran the danger of opening the door to judgments based on cultural preferences or prejudices, favoring the party with greater financial resources (usually men), and inviting repeated visits to court. And such lack of finality often had detrimental effects on a child. Thus, while the best interest standard focused on the child as the most relevant person in any custody dispute, the term itself exaggerated the degree to which a court can know what is going to be most conducive to a child's future well-being.

Adopting the perspective of the child and protecting a child's relationships, however, is a child-centered approach that avoids the pitfalls of the traditional best interest standard. For example, Barbara Woodhouse's call for recognizing the importance of the "network of care" and maintaining the involvement of various significant parent figures in a child's life places "children, not adults, firmly at the center and take[s] as its central values not adult individualism, possession and autonomy, as embodied in parental rights, nor even the dyadic intimacy of parent/child relationships," but a child's multiple relationships.[33] Made an integral component of or substituted for the best interest test, respecting networks of care would both validate relationship rights based on care and leave room for different degrees of connectedness between a child and the adults in her life. Had both Alison and Virginia wanted custody of A.D.M., their dispute should have been decided by a court as if they were married parents, and the noncustodial parent would have been awarded visitation. As it happened, Alison agreed that Virginia should have physical custody, but she appropriately expected to remain an important part of A.D.M.'s life.

A more difficult problem to resolve is the proper relationship of a third party—the sperm donor—to a lesbian family with children. Or rather it is difficult to resolve the proper place of a *known* sperm donor, since a donor whose identity is unknown until the child reaches adulthood is not in a position to make familial claims. The problem arises when the known donor seeks greater involvement with a child than one or both of the co-mothers wish. How people think about the role the known donor may take in the life of a child depends in part on how our discourse and the language we use characterize gamete transfer: is the sperm donor the seller of a product, the forever-unknown source of genetic material, a friend of the family, a father, or something else? And on what basis and for what reasons should society make that decision?

One answer is clear from previous chapters: in these cases the genetic tie alone is not the basis on which to establish legal parenthood. That theory not only overvalues the genetic connection but negates the possibility of legal parenthood for the nonbiological co-mother who may be deeply involved in the child's life, and may indeed be the primary caregiver. The genetic tie deserves some recognition, however, particularly from the perspective of the person who may someday wish to know the identity of the gamete provider.

Grounding parental rights in the intent of all three collaborating adults in cases of third-party transfer of genetic material has more promise than genetic entitlement. In "collaborative procreation," when the genetic progenitors and the adults raising the child are not (all) the same people, scholars like John Robertson and Marjorie Shultz have argued that we should look not to genetic link but to the *intentions* of those involved to decide disputes over custody. Lesbians and sperm donors have described the kinds of considerations that entered into their decisions to engage in (or not to engage in) collaborative procreation.[34] An intention-based theory of parental rights can lead to a recognition of the parental status of both co-mothers and may involve additional caring adults in a child's life. It also can satisfy the desire of many people to know their biological and genetic origins.

But grounding parental rights in intention alone has drawbacks. When parties to an intentional arrangement come into conflict and dispute the terms of access to a child, the provisions of the original agreement may not suit the present circumstances of the child. And the ensuing dispute will inevitably be harmful to a child old enough to be aware of it. This was clear in the litigation over Thomas's claim of filiation. For the first three years of her life, Ry did not think of herself as having a known father. Thereafter, she began a social relationship with Thomas whom she regarded as an adult who cared for her, her mothers, and her sister. Prior to the litigation she understood the complexity and unconventionality of her family; she had two mothers and a sister, who were "family" despite the asymmetry of their genetic ties to one another, and she knew that she had a biological father whom she had been encouraged to regard as someone more than a "stranger." But once litigation commenced, she came to regard Thomas as a threat, and the inability of the three adults to reach an agreement on terms of visitation ruptured the bonds of affection.

Adding functional theory that would grant full parental rights to the co-mothers (who are the social and psychological parents) would reinforce the adults' agreement by giving weight to those who are fulfilling the child's need for care. In order for an agreement to establish some kind of ongoing involvement by the gamete donor or surrogate mother, a functional approach would require that person to engage in some practical caregiving under agreement with the co-mothers. Combining intention-based and functional theories reduces some of the concerns about grounding donors' rights in agreement alone. The danger of functional theory alone, as discussed earlier, is the possibility of widening legal entitlements of access to a child to anyone who has been in some caring relationship with her.[35]

Grounding legal recognition of parent-child relations can focus either on adults (the source of the genetic material, the gestational mother, the people expressing their intent, the caregivers) or the child (the person who may wish someday to have access to the identity of the gamete or gestation provider, the person in need of care). I think the focus should be on the child. But adopting the child's perspective does not in itself answer the question of whether some new legal status should be devised for a known and involved sperm donor (or an egg donor or a gestational mother). Some commentators argue that a rigid distinction between legal parents on the one hand and nonparents on the other perpetuates overly rigid and dichotomous categories. In their view, the law should be changed to accommodate those who have a relationship to a child somewhere *between* that of "parent" and "stranger." Some have made the case for the creation of a legal category of "limited father" for sperm donors who are known to and involved in the lives of their offspring.[36] Advocates of some legal recognition for "limited fathers" identified a conjunction of factors, all or some of which might be necessary for someone to claim such status, including genetic tie, repeated contact between the adult and child and mutual acknowledgment of the nature of their relationship, and a pre-conception agreement among co-mothers and limited father that he will assume that role. In other words, most defenders of the legal recognition of limited fatherhood drew on a mixture of genetic, intentional, and functional understandings of parenthood.

Advocating this approach, Kate Harrison insists that all-or-nothing grants of parental rights "fail to grasp the mid-point reality of a limited father's position." She points out that if such a category had been available to Thomas, his painful dispute might have been avoided by having "both the validity and the limitations of his claim" recognized.[37] She argues further that denying Thomas and other involved sperm donors any standing to seek visitation would undermine "the most radical aspect of many lesbian and gay families: that children do have ongoing relationships with multiple 'parents,' some biologically related and some not, who live both inside and beyond their household, with differing levels of responsibility for them and different types of relationships with them." Instead of reinscribing the model of the two-parent nuclear family against efforts to reconfigure and expand responsibility for child-rearing, "[m]any lesbian families have been successfully constructed around men who have agreed to, and are acting as, limited fathers."[38]

Harrison contended that Judge Kaufmann's reliance on Ry's understanding of who was a parent "drew a line around the adults who were directly involved in her day-to-day care, [excluding] anyone in a noncustodial parental position, including someone who was acting as a 'limited father.'" In fact, the decision "sets a high performance threshold for someone trying to establish they are a functional parent, almost assuring that only daily caregivers, living with the child, will qualify."[39] Instead of following this approach, says Harrison, if both the co-mothers and the sperm donor agree that he should play a role in the child's life, the law should guarantee him continuing access to the child [through the creation of a new status] by creating a "limited parent" status.[40]

The value of a new legal category of limited parenthood is that it would expand the number of adults who could claim some right of access to and be assigned some responsibility toward a child (and might be granted to some surrogate mothers and egg donors as well as some sperm donors). And acceptance of limited parent status could legitimate diverse family forms and undermine the hegemony of the dyadic, heterosexual couple and their children as the normative (because "natural") model of family. It might also lead more women to use known rather than anonymous sperm donors. Women often choose anonymous donors out of fear that genetic fathers will seek legal recognition of their parental rights. If such disruption were precluded by law, it would be desirable from the child's perspective that the identity of the genetic father be knowable, whether such knowledge led to a social relationship or not. As I have said, the value of this knowledge is its importance to constructing one's sense of self and one's place in a family's and community's history.

Despite these desirable effects, basing a sperm donor's connection to a child on a contractual or quasi-contractual basis gives me pause.

On the one hand, introducing the practice and language of contract into procreative relationships may suggest that children, or the genetic materials that make their existence possible, are objects of trade. On the other hand, formalizing the agreement between the mothers and the sperm donor can clarify the relationship among them all and prevent later misunderstanding and litigation. It is hard to see what could ground collaborative procreation other than explicit agreement among all adults involved, and a pre-conception agreement may be the *mechanism* by which to establish someone's willingness to be a known sperm donor and a "limited" father.

Imagining all the various configurations to which adults collaborating to procreate might agree alerts us to the fact that pre-conception parenting contracts may rest on "a concept of the child fulfilling the needs and desires of parents rather than on the parents fulfilling the needs and desires of the child."[41] A theory of parental rights must begin not with adults but with children, and not with volition but with need. While we may use mechanisms of consent or agreement, or look at what the adults have in fact done (or not done) to care for the child as evidence that they have assumed or relinquished parental rights and responsibilities, law and language must make it clear that the needs of the child, not adults' acts of will, create those rights and responsibilities. Even some function-based theories of parental rights, while a huge step forward from the proprietary models of genetic-based and some intention-based theories, continue to focus on adult volition and activity both on the part of the adults who relinquish or decide to share authority and on the part of those who assume parental responsibilities. This being said, however, an adult who functions as a child's parent establishes to some degree what that child needs; thenceforth the child needs that relationship. An adult's willingness to meet a child's need for social and psychological parenting, a willingness manifested in word and deed, is the proper justification for accepting pre-conception agreements.

There is a further tension between protecting the child's relationships with adults other than primary caregivers and achieving stability by protecting the authority of the primary caregivers and the autonomy of the family unit they have created. Thinking about limited parenthood raises the question of how exclusive the exercise of paren-

tal rights and responsibilities should be. On the one hand, it is not always in a child's interest to maintain active ties with adults outside the
household. A child needs stability, and this need justifies parental authority and autonomy (and could block the interference by a "limited
parent" just as it can block a noncustodial parent after divorce). On
the other hand, adults have an obligation to adjust or enable their
children to maintain ties with people who have acted as parentlike
figures.[42] As Woodhouse noted, the bestowal of legal parenthood
means "not only the right to give children our love but the power to
give and withhold children's love from others. Parental autonomy becomes the freedom to deploy and redeploy children . . . as enhance-
ments to shifting adult relationships."[43] Adults who cut others off
from access to a child not for the child's well-being but for their own
perceived interest, shift consideration from the child's need to the
adult's volition. Had Thomas *not* threatened the stability of Ry's family as he did, I believe that Woodhouse's principle would have placed
an obligation on Robin and Sandra to allow him to continue to have
contact with Ry even if doing so had become inconvenient or financially burdensome.

One lesbian mother, Martha Gaines, whose children have strong
social ties to the men from whose sperm they were conceived objected
to the term "limited father" to refer to these men because she felt it did
not convey the signficance of their relationship to her children.

I find it difficult to embrace the term "limited father." In what way are [my
children's] fathers "limited"? True, they don't have daily contact—but that
doesn't seem necessary to the definition of fatherhood. Is a father who has divorced the mother of their children a limited father if the mother moves out
of town with the kids so that the family can make ends meet financially? I
don't think we would allow him to be called that. Is a father who from necessity works in another city from his wife and children but is with them on
weekends a limited father? Neither he nor his wife would accept that.

I guess what doesn't sit well with me is the (for me) negative connotation
of the word "limited," which, in a sense, reinforces the dyadic notion of parenthood. The father must be "limited" because there are already two parents.
But I don't think of our Dads as "limited"—I think of them as extraordinary
men who serve as powerful role models for our kids of generosity of spirit and
financial generosity. They are available as a resource on everything from
homework, to visits to the Museum of Natural History, to video arcades.

They teach them about art and culture, they take them on trips, they come to soccer games and swim meets, they accompany the kids to father/daughter and father/son events. They are especially empowered in a sense, because they know these kids but don't spend so much time with them that they stop noticing things like I think one sometimes does as a parent when the important stuff becomes camouflaged by the quotidian morass. Does this make sense?[44]

Clearly the complex relationships in her family make sense to Gaines. The mothers and sperm donors have created a "network of care" (which includes the adults' siblings and parents) that the co-mothers feel sustains their children, but which gives these men no legal status. Gaines also recognizes that under current law the pre-conception contract that the three adults signed "is not worth the paper it is written on." Nor, she notes, would she want it to be, since it declared that the fathers would have "no rights and responsibilities" toward the children. Gaines's objection to the term "limited parent" is not that it would give men like the genetic fathers of her children too much recognition but too little (although she would not have them be custodial parents). The dispute over what to call the known and involved sperm donor reflects the deeper issues of the extent to which such a man should be involved in the life of the children, and of whether he or the child should be guaranteed some right to visitation. The dispute grows out of the effort to bring socially unprecedented and hence unnamed relationships into legal discourse. It shows how much sharing of experiences, discussing, thinking, and theorizing remains to be done by those concerned with making family law respond to current practices and meet children's needs.

Providing children with stability and care is among the most pressing needs of contemporary American society. The primary source (although not the only one) of such stability and care is a child's family. It is clear, however, that law today is inadequate to the task of identifying who should be regarded as a child's "parents" in various nontraditional family situations. Law is also grappling with the question of whether adults besides the legal parents should be given some rights of access to or visitation with a child in some postdivorce blended families, families formed by open adoption, and families formed by gamete donation or gestational services. The issues posed by disputes over who is a legal parent in some cases involving lesbian mothers have implications for a wide range of heterosexual as well as homosexual families, single as well as multiparent families; addressing them may lead to greater justice for all parents and children. In prodding us to recognize the centrality of caregiving to both family and social life, thinking about these issues may also enrich not only family law but liberal political theory as well.

EPILOGUE

A New Liberal Ethics
for Family Law and Policy

*A*s the preceding chapters have discussed, debates about "family values" in the United States today tend to reflect one or another of two major approaches. Some people argue that the only legitimate family is that which is rooted in "nature" or the "longstanding traditions" of society, and that individuals behave ethically only when they conform to that model. Others argue that there is no single normative model of family, and that law should recognize many kinds of relationships as worthy of the protections and responsibilities offered to legally recognized families. The former of these two competing visions is "grounded in longing for the stability traditionally associated with a two-parent heterosexual family," while the latter is "based on a recognition of the many changes in family form and structure."[1] This book is an effort to find an ethical grounding for a pluralistic vision of family that suffers from neither the male-centered and heterosexual norms of the traditional model nor the overly individualistic and voluntaristic norms of some proponents of diversity.

In my effort to develop principles that could guide thinking about new family forms, I have looked at a variety of controversies in contemporary debates about family law and policy, including adoption, gamete donation, and contract pregnancy. My work on ethics and family policy is motivated by my belief that the assertion that there is a single normative form of family given in nature or tradition is contradicted by voluminous anthropological and historical evidence and is socially harmful. This puts me at odds with those who insist that "family values" properly understood means that only a married heterosexual couple and their biological or adopted children should be supported by public policy and recognized by law as "family." I am also at odds, however, with many of those who would ground new ways of establishing family relationships in people's right to make whatever agreements about family and procreative life that they choose. I have therefore looked for other principles, language, and images to guide policy in an age in which not all committed couples are heterosexual, not all marriages will be for life, not all families will have two (or only two) parents, and increasing numbers of children will not be the genetic offspring of the parents who raise them. Modes of reasoning and public discourse shape the collective understanding of what constitutes a family and family relationships, influence people's expectations and behavior, and shape the legal rules and public policies that affect family formation and family life.

I have suggested that instead of invoking as absolute values either nature or tradition on the one hand, or choice or contract on the other, policy-makers and citizens should consider a *cluster of values* in regulating family formation and family life: liberty, equality, relationship, and care.

Two of these values, liberty and equality, have been fundamental to the traditional liberal political theory that has permeated our political culture from the Declaration of Independence and the Constitution to the present day, theory that has focused on the moral autonomy and political agency of every individual. "Liberal" in this sense does not mean the opposite of conservative, but rather the opposite of aristocratic or hierarchical.

Two other values, relationship and care, reflect the increasing concern of political and social theorists for connections among human beings, both between adults in marriage and among family members (particularly parents and children). These theorists understand that no individual exists apart from relationships with others, and that human beings are invariably both the recipients and givers of care.[2] While attention to relationships is sometimes contrasted with liberal individualism, I have argued that a respect for relationship is integral to liberal theory properly understood, and integral to a new liberal ethics for family law.

Respect for liberty means that society must allow individuals as much freedom as possible in making choices about how to live. The great range of human diversity means that some adults will choose to live alone, others to marry, others to live together but not to marry; some will choose to have or raise children, some will not; some will raise children with a partner; some will do so alone, some will do so with another adult such as a child's grandparent or aunt. A pluralistic liberal state must allow individuals the freedom to form a wide variety of families.

Despite my respect for freedom and diversity, however, I also insist that the choices people may exercise are not unlimited. In particular, I reject contractual language and imagery that is frequently used to defend people's right to form diverse kinds of families. For example, the model underlying proposals for a market in human eggs and sperm or for pregnancy contracts—the model of a self-possessing individual linked to others only by private agreement—fails to do justice to the complex interdependencies involved in family relations and child rearing. Reliance on private ordering in these matters wrongly interprets freedom as the ability to determine and pursue one's individual goals without interference from government or other individuals, and wrongly interprets obligation as arising only from specific acts of the will.[3] In reality, family formation always involves obligations created by spousal or parental relationship. In particular, the obligations of parents to support and nurture their children are not subject to negotiation or choice, although society as a whole may debate how some rights of children will be met—for example, rights to education and health care.

I believe that equality, particularly sexual equality, is a value of fundamental importance to any ethics of family formation and family life. Despite the advances prompted by the feminist movement of the last quarter of the twentieth century, much thinking about family life remains permeated by assumptions about proper gender roles that all too often leave women—and the children for whom they may be responsible—economically vulnerable, and limit the freedom of men and women alike. John Stuart Mill pointed out over a century ago that the decision to marry for many, many women could scarcely be called "free." Given women's low wages, scarcity of jobs, and lack of opportunity for higher or even secondary education, the choice to marry was for women of his day a "Hobson's choice," that or nothing.[4] Women today have more choices, but many cannot raise children without the help of a second wage-earner. The fact that many women may deeply love their husbands does not eliminate the fact that marriage may be an economic necessity for some of them.

The concern for equality is not, then, simply a concern that women be able to support themselves and their children if their partner leaves them or dies. It cannot be met by insuring equal civic rights, equal access to jobs outside the home, and equal pay for equal work, although it entails all of these. It also means that in multiparent families the parents share the responsibility for domestic tasks and the physical and psychological nurture of children. This does not imply some uniform or mathematically precise division of time spent on various tasks; people's particular talents, preferences, and strengths should be reflected in their activities. But the current gender-based structure of economic opportunity in the world of waged labor, and the gender-based division of labor in families, are so pervasive that real sexual equality in family life is elusive.

Adequate attention to the practical measures necessary to achieve equality is too often missing even from proposals to strengthen families in desirable ways. For example, a recent booklet, *A Call to Civil Society*, authored by a group of well-known academics, public officials, journalists, and other public intellectuals of various political affiliations and published by the Institute for American Values, strongly advanced an ambitious agenda of pro-family policies. The authors advocated greater economic and civic involvement for women, greater "hands on" involvement with their children for men, and stronger public supports for families and children than we have at present.[5] How will this be achieved? The authors of *A Call to Civil Society* propose that the federal government ameliorate the pressures put on families by workplace demands by giving tax credits to parents who stay home to take care of young children. They also call upon businesses to expand opportunities for flexible working hours, job sharing, tele-working and career breaks. These measures would "permit parents to spend more time with their children," an admirable and necessary goal in my view. Workplace demands keep far too many adults from spending enough time with their children, and it is appropriate that government policy and business practices alike support family-friendly policies.

But in this context "parents" is misleading in its gender neutrality. Given the employment and wage structure in the United States, far more *mothers* than fathers will leave the workplace to take care of children. While tax credits that can be applied to education and job-training will decrease the economic disadvantage experienced by parents who leave the paid labor force, the authors fail to address the persistence of occupational segregation and differential wages for "male" and "female" occupations. Occupational segregation and differential wages often dictate that it is the woman in a heterosexual couple who leaves her job to care for a child or an infirm parent, regardless of what she or the couple might prefer or otherwise choose. At no point do the authors call upon the employers in large companies to provide on-site childcare so that mothers who wish to continue in the paid labor force can do so.[6] At no point do they suggest that fathers have an obligation—not only to their wives but also to their children—to take concrete action to work toward greater sexual equality in their own families and in the larger society. At no point do the authors suggest that occupational segregation, low wages, and lack of medical and pension benefits create vulnerability for women in both family and public life. The concern to acknowledge the important claims of interdependency and community must not drive out concern to create greater gender equality.

Those who worry that the unity of the home and family are at risk must not remain blind to the fact that a certain kind of family unity is purchased at the cost not only of women's economic vulnerability, but is also premised on a gendered division of labor that can lead to the diminution of the human capacities of both women and men. The ancient Greeks certainly thought that the greatest human activities (and those activities that were specifically "human") took place in the public realm, an attitude that they bequeathed to liberal theorists.[7] Insistence that the tasks of the private realm—of caregiving, nurture, socialization of the young, support of the elderly—are important to the full development of human capacities is a new departure in the tradition of Western political thought. But a full human life for both women and men must include activities both of intimacy and care, and of citizenship.

Empathy and nurture are important human capacities that enrich individual lives, and the division of the capacities for public and private action between men and women stunts the relationships possible among human beings. The best, richest, fullest relationships among adults are those grounded in equality. The sex-based division of labor confines or limits the sharing and intimacy possible between adult partners as well as stunting the caring capacities of men and the civic capacities of women.

The gendered division of labor also affects children. It is not simply that at divorce many mothers will be economically vulnerable while many fathers will lack extensive caregiving experience; it is also that even in intact families children will not be able to relate as fully to either parent when parents' roles and capacities are limited by gender rather than defined by their individual capacities and inclination. Nor will children have before them models of adults able to assume the responsibilities and enjoy the rewards of both public and private, civic and domestic life.

Family law and policy must go beyond an extension of traditional liberal values of liberty and equality to include the values of relationship and care, since relationship is the basis of family life. The relationships in families are not transient or superficial, but play a major role in making family members who they are. This is certainly true of children, who are shaped by their interactions with their parents, but it is also true of spouses and partners. Family relationships are not something one can enter into or exit from unaffected, because as family members we are each "embedded in a network of relationships with others that is the very basis for our sense of our individuality and our capacity for meaningful choice."[8] Moreover, because our identities are shaped by the attachments we form, "obligation may arise not simply through consent, but from shared experience in relationship with another."[9] The course of these relationships, and the obligations they generate, are not completely subject to individual control.

The importance of intimate relationships both to every individual's sense of self, and the obligations and responsibilities that arise from these relationships even without explicit agreement, make the maintenance and protection of relationship a proper concern of family policy and law. The right to familial privacy, for example, is not grounded simply in an individual's right to be left alone, but in the need of family members for a zone of intimacy in which they can establish those deep bonds that are formative of the self. To protect this zone of intimacy in children's relationships with their psychological and social parents while at the same time protecting the right of adults not raised by their biological parents to know their full history if they choose, requires measures to clarify the rights of birth parents and of known and involved genetic donors. My desire to encourage respect for the importance of various relationships to an individual's sense of self leads me to advocate the right of people, upon reaching adulthood, to discover the identity of their birth parents and genetic progenitors, without this entailing any right to have a social relationship with them.

Care is at the core of what family members owe one another, and generally of what they wish to provide one another. The parental obligation to provide care to their children is the most stringent of these obligations, because children cannot take care of themselves. But there is also an obligation and desire to care for spouses and domestic partners, the sick or disabled, and elderly parents and other family members.[10]

The desire to give care and obligations of care are generated by family relationships. Even if family situations change, the obligations to care may endure. For example, in custody disputes courts must attempt to find ways to recognize and preserve a number of relationships each of which may have importance to adult and child alike. In divorce proceedings, courts may issue visitation orders that limit the parents' freedom to move out of the state, even to take a better job.

The obligation to provide care to children falls both on custodial parents and on society at large. This means that government has a responsibility to create the conditions and provide the services that allow children and families to thrive. Children have a right not only to food, shelter, and education; but also to the services that would allow the parents to continue caring for them. Even people who care deeply about families sometimes place less responsibility than I would on society as a whole to make certain that families are supported, not ruptured because of remediable need. For example, the authors of *A Call to Civil Society* urge local governments, social work professionals, and faith communities "to strengthen and expand the institution of adoption, including transracial adoption" in order "to ensure that more children will grow up with two married parents." In supporting adoption, and transracial adoption, this recommendation echoes my call to recognize diverse ways of creating families and to care for existing children. But supporting adoption on the grounds that married two-parent families are better than single-mother families is not fully consonant with the values I advance here. For one thing, some proposals to induce people to form two-parent families are not sufficiently attentive to gender equality. Social scientists like William Julius Wilson have demonstrated the link between men's economic opportunity and their willingness to marry. These scholars have urged that jobs be created in impoverished neighborhoods to decrease the incidence of single-parenthood. I support the creation of such jobs, but not the rationale that the goal of employment is simply to create *male* breadwinners.[11] Efforts to make sure that every family has a wage-earning male ignore the fact that this solution by itself does not challenge the occupational segregation and lower wage scales for women that give men disproportionate power in both the family and the public spheres.

In addition, supporting the adoption of children of single mothers by two-parent families gives too little recognition to the ethical principle that family relationships are to be sustained when possible. That principle places an obligation on all members of society to make certain that it will not be necessary to remove a child from the custody of a parent solely because of poverty, or because two-parent households have more resources that enable them to raise children.

Government policies that treat two-parent families preferentially by withholding benefits from single parents or their children would create unjustifiable inequalities among children and, in effect, punish them for the actions of their parents, failing to acknowledge the extent of public responsibility for children's well-being. For example, proposals to deny access to subsidized housing for single parents or to bar their children from programs like Head Start would deprive children of care they need. It is a collective, societal, and therefore governmental responsibility to make sure that members of the community, particularly children, do not lack access to basic housing, food, and health care.[12]

The ethical principles I have put forward in this book—respect for a diversity of family forms; commitment to sexual equality; recognition of the personal and social responsibility to sustain viable families; and acknowledgment of the responsibilities generated by family relationships, particularly the protection and nurture of children— are principles that should underlie public policy and law regarding *all* families, however formed. These values apply equally, for example, to legal conflicts involving postdivorce blended families, single-parent families, and "skipped-generation" families. Moreover, these values should guide the formation of public policies intended to strengthen families in crucial ways beyond the confines of family law.

Discussion of the ways in which these values should be reflected in family law and public policy must involve all members of society, not only lawyers, academics, and public officials. For all members of society to decide what principles should inform family policy requires a broad democratization of political and legal decision-making. The quest for a just family policy needs the voices of people from every perspective on gender, race, religion, national origin, class, and sexual orientation. Only by listening to a broad spectrum of voices in this diverse society will policy makers be able to formulate laws and policies that encourage liberty while sustaining relationship, and that advance equality while promoting care.

People's expectations and behavior are both reflected in, and shaped by, legal rules and public policies. Given the vast changes in ideology, changes in family structures, and developments in reproductive technologies in recent years, no single model of family life seems likely to replace the common-law paradigm of the unitary, dyadic, heterosexual, patriarchal family. There can be no more important task, however, than reformulating the concepts and terms in which the various "tales told by law" influence our experience of family life. Vibrant and enduring family relationships are indispensable to our well-being as individuals, and as members of civil society.

Notes

Introduction

1. Part of the reluctance to recognize a wider variety of family forms may stem from concerns about the stability of the American state, which many people have viewed as rooted in a particular kind of family. Concerns about changes in understandings of the nature and functions of families may reflect deep-seated fears about the continued viability of American culture itself. See Alice Hearst, "Constructing the Natural Family: American Identity and Family Law," unpublished manuscript, Smith College, Northampton, Mass., 2000.

2. Rose M. Rubin and Bobye J. Riney, *Working Wives in Dual-Earner Families* (Westport: Praeger, 1994), 17. See also Kingsley Davis, "Wives and Work: A Theory of the Sex-Role Revolution and Its Consequences," in *Feminism, Children, and the New Families,* ed. Sanford M. Dornbusch and Myra H. Strober (New York: Guilford Press, 1988), 67–86.

3. Judith Stacey, "Backward toward the Postmodern Family: Reflections on Gender, Kinship, and Class in the Silicon Valley, in *Rethinking the Family: Some Feminist Questions,* rev. ed., ed. Barrie Thorne and Marilyn Yalom (Boston: Northeastern University Press, 1992), 91–118, 93.

4. Kingsley Davis, "Wives and Work: A Theory of the Sex-Role Revolution and Its Consequences," in *Feminism, Children, and the New Families,* ed. Sanford M. Dornbusch and Myra H. Strober (New York: Guilford Press, 1988), 78–79.

5. Myra H. Strober and Sanford M. Dornbusch, "Public Policy Alternatives," in *Feminism, Children, and the New Families,* ed. Sanford M. Dornbusch and Myra H. Strober (New York: Guilford Press, 1988), 336.

6. Nancy Dowd, *Redefining Fatherhood* (New York: New York University Press, 2000); Suzanne Braun Levine, *Father Courage: What Happens When Men Put Family First* (New York: Harcourt, 2000).

1. Transracial and Open Adoption

1. Readers familiar with debates in political theory will recognize that this examination of adoption engages aspects of the dispute between liberals and communitarians, particularly the contrast Michael Sandel draws between the "unencumbered individual" and the "embedded self." See Sandel, *Liberalism and the Limits of Liberal Justice* (Cambridge: Cambridge University Press, 1982), and *Democracy's Discontent* (Cambridge, Mass.: Harvard University Press, 1996).

2. Elizabeth Bartholet, "Where Do Black Children Belong? The Politics of Race Matching in Adoption," *University of Pennsylvania Law Review* 139 (1991); Randall Kennedy, "Orphans of Separatism: The Painful Politics of Transracial Adoption," *The American Prospect* 17 (Spring 1994): 38–45; Richard Banks, "The Color of Desire: Fulfilling Adoptive Parents' Racial Preferences Through Discriminatory State Action," *Yale Law Journal* 107 (1998); Hawley Fogg-Davis, "Choosing Children: A Proposal for Race-Neutral Adoption Policy," unpublished paper, University of Wisconsin, Madison (1999).

3. Twila L. Perry, "The Transracial Adoption Controversy: An Analysis of Discourse and Subordination," *New York University Review of Law & Social Change* 21 (1993–94): 33–108; Ruth-Arlene W. Howe, "A Review of *Family Bonds,*" *Golden Gate University Law Review* 24 (1994): 299–305, and "Transracial Adoption (TRA): Old Prejudices and Discrimination Float under a New Halo," *Boston University Public Interest Law Journal* 6, no. 2 (Winter 1997): 409–472; James S. Bowen, "Cultural Convergences and Divergences: The Nexus between Putative Afro-American Family Values and the Best Interest of the Child," *Journal of Family Law* 26, no. 3 (1987–88): 487–544.

4. A. D. Kraft et al., "Some Theoretical Considerations on Confidential Adoptions. Part III: The Adopted Child," *Child and Adolescent Social Work Journal* 2 (Fall 1985): 139–153. Jerome Smith reviews some of the literature in which reservations about open adoption are expressed in *The Realities of Adoption* (Lanham, Maryland: Madison Books, 1997), 40–44.

5. A. Baran and R. Pannor, "Open Adoption," in *The Psychology of Adoption,* ed. D. M. Brodzinsky and M. Schechter (New York: Oxford University Press, 1990); Jeanne Lindsey, *Open Adoption: A Caring Option*

(Buena Vista, Calif.: Morning Glory Press, 1987); Katharine Bartlett, "Rethinking Parenthood as an Exclusive Status: The Need for Legal Alternatives when the Premise of the Nuclear Family Has Failed," *Virginia Law Review* 70, no. 5: 879–963; Barbara Yngvesson, "Negotiating Motherhood: Identity and Difference in 'Open' Adoptions," *Law & Society Review* 31, no. 1 (1997): 31–80.

6. Janet Farrell Smith, "Analyzing Ethical Conflict in the Transracial Adoption Debate: Three Conflicts Involving Community," *Hypatia* 11, no. 2 (Spring 1996): 1–33.

7. Smith, "Analyzing Ethical Conflict in the Transracial Adoption Debate," 2.

8. Barbara Woodhouse has developed a child-centered analysis in many of her writings on family law; see "Hatching the Egg: A Child-Centered Perspective on Parents' Rights," *Cardozo Law Review* 14 (1993): 1747, and "'Out of Children's Needs, Children's Rights': The Child's Voice in Defining the Family," *Brigham Young University Journal of Public Law* 8 (1994): 321. Hillary Rodham, "Children Under the Law," *Harvard Educational Review* 43, no. 4 (November 1973): 487–514, took a child-centered approach to constitutional issues involving children, schools, and families.

9. Michael Grossberg, *Governing the Hearth: Law and the Family in Nineteenth-Century America* (Chapel Hill: University of North Carolina Press, 1985), 268–284. On the history of adoption law in the United States, see Jamil S. Zainaldin, "The Emergence of a Modern American Family Law: Child Custody, Adoption, and the Courts, 1796–1851," *Northwestern University Law Review* 73 (1979): 1038–89; and Stephen B. Presser, "The Historic Background of the American Law of Adoption," *Journal of Family Law* 11 (1971): 443–516.

10. David M. Schneider, *American Kinship: A Cultural Account* (Chicago: University of Chicago Press, 1968), 24.

11. Barbara Yngvesson and Maureen Mahoney, "'As One Should, Ought and Wants to Be': Belonging and Authenticity in Identity Narratives," *Theory, Culture and Society* 17, no. 6 (December 2000), 85. On the ways in which U.S. culture emphasizes blood ties see Dorothy E. Roberts, "The Genetic Tie," *University of Chicago Law Review* 62 (1995): 207–273, and Schneider, *American Kinship.*

12. Rickie Solinger, *Wake Up Little Susie: Single Pregnancy and Race before Roe v. Wade* (New York: Routledge, 1992).

13. Andrew Billingsley, *Climbing Jacob's Ladder: The Enduring Legacy of African-American Families* (New York: Simon and Schuster, 1992); Patricia Hill Collins, *Black Feminist Thought* (Boston: Unwin Hyman, 1990); Jaqueline Jones, *Labor of Love, Labor of Sorrow* (New York: Vintage

Books, 1986); Herbert Guttman, *The Black Family in Slavery and Freedom 1750–1925* (New York: Pantheon, 1976); Carol Stack, *All Our Kin* (New York: Harper and Row, 1974).

14. Joyce Ladner observed that most blacks considered a child born out of wedlock to have a right to live in the community without stigmatization. Joyce Ladner, *Tomorrow's Tomorrow: The Black Woman* (Garden City, N.Y.: Doubleday, 1972) cited in Twila Perry, "Transracial and International Adoption: Mothers, Hierarchy, Race, and Feminist Legal Theory," *Yale Journal of Law and Feminism* 10 (1998): 112.

15. On the causes of the change in attitudes toward unwed (white) mothers see E. Wayne Carp, *Family Matters: Secrecy and Disclosure in the History of Adoption* (Cambridge, Mass.: Harvard University Press, 1998), and Solinger, *Wake Up Little Susie.*

16. Solinger, *Wake Up Little Susie,* 24.

17. See Joan Heifetz Hollinger, "Aftermath of Adoption: Legal and Social Consequences," chap. 3 in *Adoption Law and Practice,* vol. 2, ed. Joan Heifetz Hollinger (New York: Matthew Bender, 1998), suppl. 2000.

18. Carp, *Family Matters,* 102, 109–112, and see generally chapter 4, 102–137. Carp viewed the unwed mothers' demand for privacy as the prime reason for the trend toward secrecy, but it seems more likely that it was pressure from adoptive parents—the ones paying the agencies—that led to greater secrecy.

19. S. Katz, quoted in Ruth-Arlene Howe, "Adoption Practice, Issues, and Laws, 1958–1983," *Family Law Quarterly* 17 (1983): 178.

20. Grossberg, *Governing the Hearth,* 275.

21. Barbara Yngvesson, "Un Niño de Cualquier Color: Race and Nation in Intercountry Adoption," in Jane Jenson and Boaventura de Sousa Santos, eds., *Globalizing Institutions: Case Studies in Regulation and Innovation* (Aldershot: Ashgate Press, 2000). On the notion of a "clean break" in intercountry adoption see William Duncan, "Regulating Intercountry Adoption—an International Perspective," in Andrew Bainham and David S. Pearl, eds., *Frontiers of Family Law* (London: John Wiley, 1993).

    The Hague Convention on Protection of Children and Co-operation in Respect of Intercountry Adoption speaks both of a child's right to the preservation of its identity (Article 30) and favors adoptions that sever the tie between adoptee and birth parents (Articles 26 and 27).

22. Yngvesson, "Un Niño de Cualquier Color," 171.

23. Schneider, *American Kinship,* 38.

24. *Palmore v. Sidoti,* 466 U.S. 429 (1984).

25. Carol Sanger, "Separating from Children," *Columbia Law Review* 96, no. 2 (March 1996): 375–517.

26. Quoted in Yngvesson and Mahoney, " 'As One Should, Ought, and Wants

to Be,'" 91. The bill passed by the Vermont legislature in May 1996 provided for unsealing adoption records on a case-by-case basis, a more limited measure than Sears and others had sought.

27. States have taken various approaches to the question of making identifying and non-identifying information available to adult adoptees. Most permit the release of non-identifying background information about birth parents if the adoptee requests it. Several have a "mutual consent registry" whereby both birth parent(s) and adoptee must consent to the release of identifying information. Some have "search and consent" procedures, whereby if an adult adoptee requests her birth record, the state must search for the birth parents and request their consent to release the record. If the birth parents cannot be found, or withhold their consent, the adoptee can petition the court to release the record on a showing of good cause. See Peter Swisher, Anthony Miller, and Jana Singer, *Family Law: Cases, Materials, and Problems* (Matthew Bender, 1995), 750–752. My thanks to Milton C. Regan, Jr., for this reference.

   Naomi Cahn and Jana Singer, "Adoption, Identity, and the Constitution: The Case for Opening Closed Records," *University of Pennsylvania Journal of Constitutional Law* 1 (December 1999): 150–194, make a strong case for not opening all adoption records retroactively but requiring the state to conduct a confidential search for the birth parents and to request their consent to the release of identifying information.

28. A Tennessee statute reflects the kind of approach I am advocating. It states that an adult adoptee over the age of 21 may obtain identifying information about her birth parent(s) upon request. Birth parents, however, may register to prevent contact by the adoptee, and an adoptee who despite this contacts the birth parent(s) may be subject to legal liability. The statute was upheld against a constitutional challenge in *Doe v. Sundquist,* 106 F.3d 702 (6th Cir.), cert. denied, 118 S. Ct. 51 (1997). My thanks to Milton C. Regan, Jr., for this information and reference.

29. Yngvesson, "Negotiating Motherhood," 71.

30. Smith, "Analyzing Ethical Conflict in the Transracial Adoption Debate," 5.

31. National Association of Black Social Workers, position paper, April 1972, quoted in Elizabeth Bartholet, *Family Bonds: Adoption and the Politics of Parenting* (Boston: Houghton Mifflin Company, 1993).

   James Bowen described survival skills as "abilities to ignore racial insults, to decipher the appropriateness of fighting back or submission, to emphasize black strength, beauty and worth as a countermeasure to the denigration of Blacks in America." Bowen, "Cultural Convergences and

Divergences," 510. Eloquent testimony to the difficulties white parents face in transmitting survival skills to black children came from white as well as black parents. For example, J. Douglas Bates writes of the errors and oversights he and his wife committed in raising their two black daughters in *Gift Children: A Story of Race, Family, and Adoption in a Divided America* (New York: Ticknor & Fields, 1993).

32. Testimony before the Senate Committee on Labor and Human Resources, 99th Cong. 1st Sess., June 25, 1985, quoted in Perry, "The Transracial Adoption Controversy," 47.

33. Witness after witness at congressional hearings on the ICWA testified that Native American children placed away from Native American families were frequently placed in a series of foster homes or institutions and did not find permanent homes. Moreover, those children raised without any knowledge of or exposure to Native American culture seemed to fare less well psychologically than those who were raised with an appreciation of Native American culture. Hearings at 46–47, quoted in Alice Hearst, "The Indian Child Welfare Act," unpublished paper, Smith College, Northampton, Mass. (1996), 17–18.

34. 25 U.S.C.A. sec. 1902. For testimony before Congress see *Indian Child Welfare Act: Hearings on S. 1214 Before the Senate Select Comm. on Indian Affairs*, 95th Cong., 1st Sess. (1977); *Indian Child Welfare Program: Hearings Before the Subcomm. on Indian Affairs of the Senate Comm. on Interior and Insular Affairs*, 93rd Cong., 2d Sess. (1974).

35. James S. Bowen, "Cultural Convergences and Divergences: The Nexus between Putative Afro-American Family Values and the Best Interests of the Child," *Journal of Family Law* 26 (1987–88): 487–544, esp. 522–32.

36. Bowen, "Cultural Convergences and Divergences," 523, 531.

37. 42 U.S.C.A. §5115a (West 1995).

38. 42 U.S.C.A. §1996b (1) sec. 1808.

39. Martha Minow explains the difference as stemming from Congress's perception that the "extraordinarily frequent wrenching of Indian children from Indian parents, and the cultural insensitivity of child welfare agencies removing those children," made Indian children a special case. The differences also stem from the residence of many Indians on reservations, the distinct constitutional status of Indian tribes, and the existence of tribal courts that may make decisions regarding the custody of Indian children. Martha Minow, *Not Only for Myself: Identity, Politics, and the Law* (New York: The New Press, 1997), 75.

40. Bartholet, "Where Do Black Children Belong?," 1163.

41. Bartholet, "Where Do Black Children Belong?," 1164–65.

42. Bartholet, "Where Do Black Children Belong?," 1166.

43. Judith K. McKenzie, "Adoption of Children with Special Needs," 3 *Future of Children* 62 (1993), 68–69.

44. Bartholet, "Where Do Black Children Belong?," 1248.

45. Randall Kennedy, "Orphans of Separatism: The Painful Politics of Transracial Adoption," *The American Prospect* 17 (Spring 1994): 38–45; see also Kennedy, "How Are We Doing with *Loving*?: Race, Law, and Intermarriage," *Boston University Law Review* 77 (October 1997): 815–822.

46. Hawley Fogg-Davis, "Choosing Children: A Proposal for Race-Neutral Adoption Policy," unpublished paper, University of Wisconsin, Madison, 1999, 4–5.

47. R. Richard Banks, "The Color of Desire: Fulfilling Adoptive Parents' Racial Preferences Through Discriminatory State Action," *Yale Law Journal* 107 (1998): 880.

48. Hawley Fogg-Davis, *The Ethics of Transracial Adoption* (Ithaca: Cornell University Press, forthcoming).

49. The contrast between this view of racial navigation and racial self-definition and the view of racial identity and group membership underlying the ICWA is striking. Under the ICWA, if one of a child's parents is a tribal member, and the child fits the criteria for membership in that tribe, the tribe has jurisdiction in all custody matters concerning the child, or any state court must try to place the child with a tribal member or another Indian family. In the case of Indian children, racial identity is relevant to adoptive placement, and that racial identity is transmitted by blood or tribal membership.

50. Banks, "The Color of Desire," 909.

51. Kennedy, "Orphans of Separatism," 45.

52. Perry, "The Transracial Adoption Controversy," 65–67, 77–78.

53. Kennedy, "Orphans of Separatism," 42.

54. Fogg-Davis, "Choosing Children," unpublished paper, 1999, 4.

55. Rita J. Simon and Rhonda M. Roorda, *In Their Own Voices: Transracial Adoptees Tell Their Stories* (New York: Columbia University Press, 2000).

56. Yngvesson, "Un Niño de Cualquier Color," 173

57. Sanger, "Separating from Children," 445.

58. Sanger, "Separating from Children," 490.

59. Yngvesson, "Negotiating Motherhood"; Yngvesson and Mahoney, "As One Should, Ought, and Wants to Be." Adam Pertman, *Adoption Nation: How the Adoption Revolution Is Transforming America* (New York: Basic Books, 2000), advocates open adoption, drawing on social science data; interviews with birth parents, adoptive parents, and adoptees; and his own experience as an adoptive parent.

60. Maureen A. Sweeney, "Between Sorrow and Happy Endings: A New Par-

adigm of Adoption," *Yale Journal of Law and Feminism* 2, no. 2 (Spring 1990): 329–369, 335.

61. Sweeney, "Between Sorrow and Happy Endings," 335.

62. Donna Goldsmith, "Individual vs. Collective Rights: The Indian Child Welfare Act," *Harvard Women's Law Journal* 13 (1990), 8.

63. *To Amend the Indian Child Welfare Act: Hearings on S. 1976 Before the Senate Select Comm. On Indian Affairs,* 100th Cong., 2d Sess. 48, 1988, 97–98 (Statement of Evelyn Blanchard).

64. "If the Afro-American child's extended family shall establish a different order of preference [than that drawn up by the court] by resolution, the agency or court effecting the placement shall follow such order. . . . Where appropriate, the preference of the Afro-American child or parent shall be considered." Bowen, "Cultural Convergences and Divergences," 539.

65. Perry "The Transracial Adoption Controversy," 81.

66. Perry, "The Transracial Adoption Controversy," 106.

67. Twila Perry, "Transracial and International Adoption: Mothers, Hierarchy, Race, and Feminist Legal Theory," *Yale Journal of Law and Feminism* 10 (1998), 121.

68. Dorothy Roberts, *Killing the Black Body: Race, Reproduction, and the Meaning of Liberty* (New York: Pantheon, 1997), 276.

69. I do not think that obliterating the voice of the mother is necessary to defend tribes from unjustifiable incursions by state courts. It is important to liberal society that people be able to change affiliations, such as religious affiliation. Although he may not share these particular views, my thinking about respecting both liberal principles and cultural pluralism is indebted to Will Kymlicka, *Liberalism, Community and Culture,* esp. 162–182.

70. Banks, "The Color of Desire," 943–944.

71. For some accounts of these efforts see Roberts, *Killing the Black Body;* Angela Y. Davis, *Women, Race and Class* (New York: Vintage, 1983); Peggy Cooper Davis, *Neglected Stories: The Constitution and Family Values* (New York: Hill and Wang, 1997); Harriet Jacobs, *Incidents in the Life of a Slave Girl, Written by Herself,* ed. Jean Fagan Yellin (Cambridge: Harvard University Press, 1987); Elizabeth V. Spelman, *Fruits of Sorrow: Framing Our Attention to Suffering,* chap. 3 (Boston: Beacon Press, 1997).

72. Yngvesson and Mahoney, " 'As One Should, Ought and Wants to Be,' " 86.

73. Yngvesson, "Negotiating Motherhood"; "Un Niño de Cualquier Color"; Yngvesson and Mahoney, " 'As One Should, Ought and Wants to Be.' "

74. Mona Harrington, *Care and Equality* (New York: Knopf, 1999); Eva Feder Kittay, *Love's Labor* (New York: Routledge, 1999).

75. Drucilla Cornell, "Reimagining Adoption and Family Law," in *Mother Troubles: Rethinking Contemporary Maternal Dilemmas,* ed. Julia E. Hanigsberg and Sara Ruddick (Boston: Beacon Press, 1999).

2. Fathers' Rights, Mothers' Wrongs, and Children's Needs

1. *In the Interest of B. G. C.,* Supreme Court of Iowa, No. 207/91–476, 92–49, September 23, 1992, and *In the Matter of Baby Girl Clausen,* Michigan Court of Appeals, No. 161102, March 29, 1993.

2. *In re Doe* (Baby Boy Janikova), 627 N. E.2d 648 (Ill. App. Ct. 1993) and *In re Doe* (Baby Boy Janikova), 638 N. E.2d 181 (Ill.), cert. denied, 63 U.S.L. W. 3313 (U.S. Nov. 7, 1994) (No. 94–615), and cert. denied, 63 U.S.L. W. 3109 (U.S. Nov. 7, 1994) (No. 94–236).

3. See *In re Doe* (Baby Boy Janikova), 627 N. E.2d 648, 654 (Ill. App. Ct. 1993).

4. See *Baby Boy Janikova,* 638 N. E.2d at 182.

5. An excellent review of current laws and of the proposed Uniform Adoption Act is found in Joan Heifetz Hollinger, "Adoption and Aspiration: The Uniform Adoption Act, the DeBoer-Schmidt Case, and the American Quest for the Ideal Family," *Duke Journal of Gender Law and Policy* 2, (1995): 15–40. A summary of the different statutory provisions in all fifty states regarding who must give consent to an adoption and under what conditions is found in *Adoption Laws: Answers to the Most-Asked Questions* (Rockville, MD: National Adoption Information Clearinghouse, n.d.).

6. For example, see Jeffrey S. Boyd, "The Unwed Father's Custody Claim in California: When Does the Parental Preference Doctrine Apply?" *Pepperdine Law Review* 17 (1990): 969–1010; John R. Hamilton, "The Unwed Father and the Right to Know of His Child's Existence," *Kentucky Law Journal* 76 (1987–88): 949–1009; Jennifer J. Raab, "*Lehr v. Robertson:* Unwed Fathers and Adoption—How Much Process Is Due?" *Harvard Women's Law Journal* 7 (1984): 265–287; Claudia Serviss, "*Lehr v. Robertson's* 'Grasp the Opportunity': For California's Natural Fathers, Custody May Be Beyond Their Grasp," *Western State University Law Review* 18 (1991): 771–790; Daniel C. Zinman, "Father Knows Best: The Unwed Father's Right to Raise his Infant Surrendered for Adoption," *Fordham Law Review* 60 (April 1992): 971–1001. Wolfgang Hirczy argues that the law should insist that the paternity of every child be established at birth, a necessary prerequisite for an unwed father's assertion of paternal rights; see "The Politics of Illegitimacy: A Cross-National Comparison," paper presented at the Annual Meeting of the American Political Science Association, Chicago, Illinois, September 3–6, 1992.

7. Mary Becker, "The Rights of Unwed Parents: Feminist Approaches," *Social Service Review* 63 (December 1989): 496–518; Nancy S. Erickson, "The

Feminist Dilemma over Unwed Parents' Custody Rights: The Mother's Rights Must Take Priority," *Journal of Law and Inequality* 2 (1984): 447–472; Nancy S. Erickson, "Neither Abortion nor Adoption: Women without Options," paper presented at the American Association of Law Schools (AALS), San Francisco, January 6, 1990, p. 39 n. 22; Barbara Katz Rothman, *Recreating Motherhood: Ideology and Technology in a Patriarchal Society* (New York: Norton, 1989).

8. Becker, "The Rights of Unwed Parents: Feminist Approaches," 498.
9. William Blackstone, *Commentaries on the Laws of England*, 9th ed. (1783), ed. Berkowitz and Throne (1978), vol. 1, 453. On coverture in general see Mary Lyndon Shanley, *Feminism, Marriage and the Law in Victorian England* (Princeton: Princeton University Press, 1989). Hendrik Hartog, *Man and Wife in America: A History* (Cambridge: Harvard University Press, 2000). On custody laws in the early United States, see Michael Grossberg, *Governing the Hearth: Law and the Family in Nineteenth-Century America* (Chapel Hill: University of North Carolina, 1985).
10. Also important was the rise in both social and judicial attention to childhood and its particular needs. See Jamil S. Zainaldin, "The Emergence of a Modern American Family Law: Child Custody, Adoption, and the Courts, 1796–1851," *Northwestern University Law Review* 73 (1979): 1038–1089, and Grossberg, *Governing the Hearth*.
11. *Weber v. Aetna Casualty & Surety Co.*, 406 U.S. 164 (1972); *Gomez v. Perez*, 409 U.S. 535 (1973); and *Trimble v. Gordon*, 430 U.S. 762 (1977).
12. *Stanley v. Illinois*, 405 U.S. 645 (1972); *Quilloin v. Walcott*, 434 U.S. 246 (1978); *Caban v. Mohammed*, 441 U.S. 380 (1979); *Lehr v. Robertson*, 463 U.S. 248 (1983); *Michael H. v. Gerald D.*, 491 U.S. 110 (1989).
13. *Stanley v. Illinois*, 405 U.S. 645 (1972), at 651.
14. *Caban v. Mohammed*, 441 U.S 380 (1979), at 385.
15. 441 U.S. 380 at 392, n. 11.
16. *Lehr v. Robertson*, 463 U.S. 248 (1983), at 268.
17. *Michael H. v. Gerald D.*, 491 U.S. 110 (1989).
18. Id., at 132 (O'Connor, J., concurring in part), at 127–28 n. 6.
19. Id., at 133 (Stevens, J., concurring in the judgment).
20. Id., at 159–63 (White, J., dissenting).
21. Id., at 142–43 (Brennan, J., dissenting).
22. See National Adoption Information Clearinghouse, *Adoption Laws: Answers to the Most-Asked Questions;* Joan H. Hollinger, "Consent to Adoption," in *Adoption Law and Practice*, ed. Joan H. Hollinger, (New York: Matthew Bender, 1990, Suppl. 2000), vol. 1, app. I-A.
23. *Lehr v. Robertson*, 463 U.S. 248, at 262.
24. Serviss, *"Lehr v. Robertson's* 'Grasp the Opportunity,' " 788.
25. See Hamilton, "The Unwed Father," 998–1001, 1008–09.

26. See Zinman, "Father Knows Best," 996–1001, and Boyd, "Unwed Father's Claim in California," 1007–10.

27. 823 P.2d 1216, 1236 (Cal. 1992).

28. See *In re Doe* (Baby Boy Janikova), 638 N. E.2d 181, 182–83 (Ill.), cert denied, 63 U.S. L. W. 3313 (U.S. Nov. 7, 1994) (No. 94–615), and cert. denied, 63 U.S.L. W. 3109 (U.S. Nov. 7, 1994) (No. 94–236); *In re Doe* (Baby Boy Janikova), 627 N. E. 2d 648, 649–51 (Ill. Ct. App. 1993).

29. Katharine T. Bartlett, "Re-Expressing Parenthood," *Yale Law Journal* 98 (1988): 293–340, 303.

30. "Recent Developments: Family Law—Unwed Fathers' Rights—New York Court of Appeals Mandates Veto Power over Newborn's Adoption for Unwed Father Who Demonstrates Parental Responsibility," *Harvard Law Review* 104 (1991): 800, 807.

31. *In re Baby Girl Eason,* 257 Ga. 292 at 297, 358 S. E. 2d 459, at 463 (1987), quoted in Zinman, 993–994.

32. Maureen A. Sweeney, "Between Sorrow and Happy Endings: A New Paradigm of Adoption," *Yale Journal of Law and Feminism* (Spring 1990): 329–370; Erickson, "The Feminist Dilemma over Unwed Parents' Custody Rights," 459 n. 65, and 1990, 39 n. 22; Susan Wadia-Ells, ed., *The Adoption Reader: Birth Mothers, Adoptive Mothers, and Adopted Daughters Tell Their Stories* (Seattle: Seal Press, 1995).

33. The Supreme Court has recognized the significance of this asymmetry between mother and father during pregnancy by holding that a wife is not required to obtain her husband's consent or to notify him before getting an abortion. *Planned Parenthood of Central Missouri v. Danforth,* 428 U.S. 52 (1976) and *Planned Parenthood of Southeastern Pennsylvania v. Casey,* 510 U.S. 833 (1992).

34. On the social construction of the experience of pregnancy and childbirth see Emily Martin, *The Woman in the Body: A Cultural Analysis of Reproduction* (Boston: Beacon Press, 1987), and Barbara Katz Rothman, *In Labor* (New York: Norton, 1982).

35. Rothman, *Recreating Motherhood,* 245, 255, and 97.

36. Erickson, "The Feminist Dilemma over Unwed Parents' Custody Rights," 461–462.

37. Becker, "Maternal Feelings: Myth, Taboo, and Child Custody," 972.

38. Ibid.

39. Martha Albertson Fineman, *The Illusion of Equality: The Rhetoric and Reality of Divorce Reform* (Chicago: University of Chicago Press, 1991).

40. In "Adoption and Aspiration," Hollinger thoroughly and sensitively discusses the sections of the Uniform Adoption Act that reflect standards similar to those I suggest here.

41. Virginia Held, *Feminist Morality: Transforming Culture, Society, and Poli-*

tics (Chicago: University of Chicago Press, 1993); Jennifer Nedelsky, "Reconceiving Autonomy," *Yale Journal of Law and Feminism* 1 (1989), and "Law, Boundaries, and the Bounded Self," *Representations* 30 (1990): 162–189; Sara Ruddick, *Maternal Thinking* (Boston: Beacon Press, 1989); and Joan C. Tronto, *Moral Boundaries* (New York: Routledge, 1993).

Issues involving children raise in a particularly acute manner the tension between protecting people as individuals and protecting family associations or family ties; see Kenneth L. Karst, "The Freedom of Intimate Association," *Yale Law Journal* 89 (1980): 624–692.

42. Bartlett, "Re-Expressing Parenthood," 295.

43. See Eisenstein, *The Female Body and the Law* (Berkeley: University of California Press, 1988), 79–116.

44. Cynthia R. Daniels, *At Women's Expense: State Power and the Politics of Fetal Rights* (Cambridge: Harvard University Press, 1993), 98. See also Patricia Boling, ed., *Expecting Trouble: Surrogacy, Fetal Abuse and New Reproductive Technologies* (Boulder: Westview, 1995), and *Privacy and the Politics of Intimate Life* (Ithaca: Cornell University Press, 1996).

45. Note, "Rethinking Motherhood: Feminist Theory and State Regulation of Pregnancy," *Harvard Law Review* 103 (1990), 1325, 1333–1334; Iris M. Young, "Punishment, Treatment, Empowerment: Three Approaches to Policy for Pregnant Addicts," *Feminist Studies* 20 (1994): 39–43; Shelley Burtt, "Reproductive Responsibilities: Rethinking the Fetal Rights Debate," *Policy Studies* 27 (1994): 170–191.

46. *In Matter of Raquel Marie X.,* 76 NY 2d 387 (1990).

47. *In Matter of Raquel Marie X.,* 76 NY 2d 387 (1990), at 426.

48. "Recent Developments: Family Law—Unwed Fathers' Rights," *Harvard Law Review* 104 (1991): 803.

49. *In Matter of Raquel Marie X.,* 76 NY 2d 387 (1990), at 428.

50. New York State Legislature, Assembly, A 1518, January 15, 1997, introduced by Member of the Assembly Lopez and referred to the Committee on the Judiciary. Mr. Lopez had supported such legislation since at least 1993.

51. *2001 Report of the Family Court Advisory and Rules Committee to the Chief Administrative Judge of the Courts of the State of New York* (December 2000), 168–172.

52. Nancy Erickson, "Proposal for a Model Law on Unwed Fathers' Adoption Rights," unpublished paper, Brooklyn, N.Y., n.d. [1991].

53. Timely placement of all children is one of the goals of the federal Adoption and Safe Families Act of 1997; Pub. L. No. 105–89, 111 Stat. 2115 (1997). States need to develop legislation to implement this legislation and expedite permanency planning for children in foster care. This underscores

"the importance of clarifying the rights of biological parents at the earliest possible point in children's lives. . . . Whether a child has truly been abandoned or whether there is, in fact, a biological parent with an interest in the child must, therefore, be clarified as early as possible." *2001 Report of the Family Court Advisory and Rules Committee*, 168.

54. *Robert O. v. Russell K.*, 604 N. E. 2d 99 (N.Y. 1992).

55. *Robert O. v. Russell K.*, 604 N. E. 2d 99 (N.Y. 1992), at 102–105.

56. Hamilton, "Note: The Unwed Father and the Right to Know of His Child's Existence," 1002 n. 407.

57. See Iowa Code Ann. §600A.9 (West 1981).

58. See *B.G.C.*, 496 N. W. 2d, at 245.

59. *Baby Boy Janikova*, 638 N. E. 2d, at 190 (supplemental opinion on denial of rehearing).

60. See *Michael H. v. Gerald D.*, 491 U.S. 110, 123 (1989).

3. "A Child of Our Own"

1. *The Miscellany News* (newspaper of Vassar College), vol. 133, no. 11 (December 3, 1999), p. 22. The same ad appeared in *The Michigan Daily* on October 12, 1998, p. 5A, and undoubtedly in other college newspapers.

2. *New York Times*, Metropolitan ed., March 3, 1999, p. A10.

3. *The Miscellany News* (newspaper of Vassar College), vol. 133, no. 18 (March 24, 2000), p. 5.

4. "In most cases of sperm 'donation' and some cases of egg 'donation,' the term 'vendor' more accurately describes the gamete provider." Mary B. Mahowald, "Genes, Clones, and Gender Equality," *DePaul Journal of Health Care Law* 3 (Spring/Summer 2000): 495–526, n. 172.

5. A good discussion of gamete donation, frozen embryos, and relevant court cases is found in Christine Overall, *Ethics and Human Reproduction* (Boston: Allen & Unwin, 1987) and *Human Reproduction: Principles, Practices, Policies* (Toronto: Oxford University Press, 1993), chap. 5, "Frozen Embryos and 'Fathers' Rights': Parenthood and Decision-making in the Cryopreservation of Embryos," 81–104.

6. *Poughkeepsie Journal*, September 23, 2000, p. 8D.

7. See Gina Kolata, "Price Soars for Eggs, Setting Off a Debate on a Clinic's Ethics," *New York Times*, February 25, 1998, p. A1. The article reports that in contrast to the ready availability of sperm, eggs are in short supply and recipients must sometimes wait up to a year for donor eggs. To increase the number of donations, one infertility clinic now pays $5,000 for one month's "harvest" of eggs, twenty times the amount paid ten years before when the practice began.

8. See Melissa Ludtke, *On Our Own: Unmarried Motherhood in America* (Berkeley and Los Angeles: University of California Press, 1997), for a dis-

cussion of unmarried motherhood since 1945, whether resulting from divorce, unintentional out-of-wedlock birth, or intentional (either through sexual intercourse or sperm donation) single motherhood.

9. A thorough review of the legal issues involved in gamete transfer is found in Joan Heifetz Hollinger, "From Coitus to Commerce: Legal and Social Consequences of Noncoital Reproduction," *University of Michigan Journal of Law Reform* 18 (Summer 1985): 865–932.

10. When biomedical technology made it possible to fertilize an egg outside of the human body, "a potentially new legal and social entity had come into the world in the form of the human embryo in the very early stages of development, alive but outside the parental body. How to think it [the nature of the embryo outside the body], that is, imagine it and make it real, became a matter for debate." Marilyn Strathern, *Reproducing the Future: Essays on Anthropology, Kinship and the New Reproductive Technologies* (New York: Routledge, 1992), 4.

11. When same-sex couples use AID, if the nonbiological parent wants to secure parental rights through second-parent adoption, a home study must be done.

12. Frances I. Seymour and Alfred Koerner, "Artificial Insemination: Present Status in the United States as Shown by a Recent Survey," *Journal of the American Medical Association* (June 21, 1941): 2747–2749, reported that at least 9,500 pregnancies had been achieved by alternative insemination, two-thirds of them using the husband's sperm. This figure was sharply criticized as unsubstantiated and probably far too high by Clair E. Folsome, "The Status of Artificial Insemination," *American Journal of Obstetrics and Gynecology* 45, no. 6 (June 1943): 915–927. Martin Curie-Cohen, Lesleigh Luttrell, and Sander Shapiro, "Current Practice of Artificial Insemination by Donor in the United States," *New England Journal of Medicine* 300, no. 11 (March 15, 1979): 585–590, review early literature and describe the practices surrounding use of donor sperm.

13. Curie-Cohen, Luttrell, and Shapiro, "Current Practice of Artificial Insemination" (1979), 586–587.

14. See Dorothy E. Roberts, "The Genetic Tie," *University of Chicago Law Review* 62 (1995): 209–273.

15. In 1948, the Report of a Commission Appointed by His Grace the Archbishop of Canterbury recommended that donor insemination be considered a criminal offense; courts in the United States were uncertain about whether AID constituted adultery. See Ken Daniels and Karyn Taylor, "Secrecy and Ownership in Donor Insemination," *Politics and the Life Sciences* 12, no. 2 (August 1993): 155–170, 156.

16. See the articles and cases cited in *In Re Adoption of Anonymous*, 74 Misc. 2d 99, 345 N.Y.S.2d 430 (Surrogates Court of New York, Kings County,

1973), in *Family Law: Cases and Materials,* 2d ed., ed. Judith Areen (Mineola, N.Y.: The Foundation Press, 1985), 878–884.

17. See both Douglas J. Cusine, "Legal Aspects of AID," and Christine Manuel, Marie Chevret, and Jean-Claude Czyba, "Handling of Secrecy by AID Couples," in *Human Artificial Insemination and Semen Preservation,* ed. Georges David and Wendel S. Price (New York: Plenum Press, 1980), 485–489, 419–429.

18. Curie-Cohen, Luttrell, and Shapiro, "Current Practice of Artificial Insemination" (1979), 587.

19. *In re Adoption of Anonymous,* 74 Misc. 2d 99, 345 N.Y.S.2d 430 and the editors' "Notes," *Family Law: Cases and Materials,* 2d ed., ed. Judith Areen, 878–884.

20. The difference may stem from the fact that the unwed father pitted his will against an unwed mother, while the sperm donor transferred his sperm to a married couple, which involved another man. Many people are hostile to women who procreate without legal ties to a man.

21. Rebecca Mead, "Eggs for Sale," *The New Yorker* (August 9, 1999), 56–65, 58.

22. The description in this paragraph is drawn from Patricia M. McShane, "In Vitro Fertilization, GIFT and Related Technologies—Hope in a Test Tube, in *Embryos, Ethics, and Women's Rights: Exploring the New Reproductive Technologies,* ed. Elaine Hoffman Baruch, Amadeo F. D'Adamo, Jr., and Joni Seager (New York and London: The Haworth Press, 1988), 31–46, and Mead, "Eggs for Sale," 56.

23. McShane, "In Vitro Fertilization, GIFT and Related Technologies," 34–38.

24. Curie-Cohen, Luttrell, and Shapiro, "Current Practice of Artificial Insemination" (1979), 589.

25. My impression is that gay fathers face prejudice (and sometimes violence) because of their gay relationship, but that gay fathers gain some sympathy as men raising a child without a woman's help. Lesbian mothers, however, provoke the scorn so often directed at women who forego the company of men. For a powerful fictional rendition of the fear and violence that women, not necessarily lesbians, who live apart from men generate, see Toni Morrison, *Paradise* (New York: Knopf, 1998).

26. Carol Sanger, "Separating from Children," *Columbia Law Review* 96, no. 2 (March 1996): 375–517.

27. Hollinger, "From Coitus to Commerce," reviews many considerations concerning anonymity and discusses the differences between anonymity in adoption and in gamete donation.

28. Strathern, *Reproducing the Future,* 135.

29. Strathern, *Reproducing the Future,* chap. 6, "Partners and Consumers," 128.

A sense of how complex the question of whether we should attribute any social significance (and legal rights or responsibilities) to genetic parenthood can be gained from reading the on-going debate between John Eekelaar and Brenda Almond. See, for example, John Eekelaar, "Parenthood, Social Engineering, and Rights," in *Constituting Families: A Study in Governments,* ed. E. Morgan and G. Douglas (Stuttgart: Franz Steiner Verlag, 1993), and Brenda Almond, "Family Relationships and Reproductive Technology," in *Having and Raising Children,* ed. Uma Narayan and Julia J. Bartkowiak (University Park: Pennsylvania State University Press, 1999), originally published in *The Family in the Age of Biotechnology,* ed. Carole Ulanowsky (Avebury: Ashgate Publishing, 1995).

30. The absence of consideration of the child's perspective in most legal and medical discussions of AID and egg donation is stunning and deeply disturbing. A notable exception are the writings of Barbara Bennett Woodhouse, who argues for child-centered analyses of family law issues. See "Out of Children's Needs, Children's Rights: The Child's Voice in Defining the Family," *Brigham Young University Journal of Public Law* 8 (1994), and "Hatching the Egg: A Child-Centered Perspective on Parents' Rights," *Cardozo Law Review* 14 (1993), among other articles.

It is possible that an adult who seeks the identity of the donor may then feel rejected if the donor refuses to meet him or her. But while access to the information seems to me to be a right of the individual created by the transferred gamete, I do not see why that right would extend to a face-to-face meeting or social relationship if the donor objects.

31. Patricia Williams speaks of the significance of transgenerational history in "On Being the Object of Property," *The Alchemy of Race and Rights* (Cambridge, Mass.: Harvard University Press, 1991).

32. Neil Leighton, "The Family: Whose Construct Is It Anyway?" in *The Family in the Age of Biotechnology,* ed. Carole Ulanowsky (Avebury: Ashgate Publishing, 1995), 91–104, 103. Although I agree with Leighton on the need for a specific narrative of origin, the continuation of this passage uses misleading language about gamete donation: "The pretense that the bioengineered child is the natural child of the pseudo parents presents an experience of family on unsure ground and undermines the essential attributes of intimate human relationships—those of integrity, trust, and openness." I also urge openness, but would note that the child is not "bioengineered," that children conceived by means other than heterosexual intercourse are "natural," and that to call social parents "pseudo" parents is gravely misguided.

33. One of the best contemporary reflections on the relationship between the

norms of family life and of political life is Barbara Kingsolver's *The Poisonwood Bible* (New York: HarperCollins, 1998).

34. The Sperm Bank of California limits donations to ten pregnancies and encourages donors to permit release of identifying information to an adult conceived with their sperm if the adult requests it. Susan V. Seligson, "Seeds of Doubt," *The Atlantic Monthly* 75, no. 3 (March 1995), 28–31.

35. An article in *People* magazine reflected the entry of discussion of reproductive technology and new family forms into mainstream popular culture. The family of Martha Gaines and Margaret Mooney includes their son, conceived with the sperm of a gay friend, and their daughter, conceived with sperm donated by a married friend of the family. A "family photo" in *People* included Martha and Margaret and their children, along with the married donor, his wife and their two children. *People* 53, no. 19 (May 15, 2000), 68–75.

36. Barbara Yngvesson discusses the ways in which children available for adoption appear as "commodities" even when the processes are legal and respectful to the children as well as the adults. Barbara Yngvesson, "Un Niño de Cualquier Color: Race and Nation in Intercountry Adoption," in Jane Jenson and Boaventura de Sousa Santos, eds., *Globalizing Institutions: Case Studies in Regulation and Innovation* (Aldershot: Ashgate Press, 2000).

37. Strathern, *Reproducing the Future*, 130.

38. Strathern, *Reproducing the Future*, 37.

39. Strathern, *Reproducing the Future*, 35.

40. Excellent discussions of the issues raised here are found in Margaret Jane Radin, "Market Inalienability," *Harvard Law Review* 100, no. 8 (June 1987): 1849–1937, and Christine Overall, *Ethics and Human Reproduction* and *Human Reproduction*.

41. Donna Dickenson, *Property, Women & Politics: Subjects or Objects?* (New Brunswick, N.J.: Rutgers University Press, 1997), 158.

42. Daniels and Taylor, "Secrecy and Ownership in Donor Insemination," 1993; Bartha M. Knoppers and Sonia LeBris, "Recent Advances in Medically Assisted Conception: Legal, Ethical, and Social Issues," *American Journal of Law and Medicine* 17, no. 4 (1991): 329–361, 349–352, contains information on most European countries.

On New Zealand, see Ken R. Daniels, "Assisted Human Reproduction in New Zealand: The Contribution of Ethics," *Eubios Journal of Asian and International Bioethics* 8 (1998): 79–81. While I support every child's right to specific information about her or his origin, when I discussed the adoption provisions of the Indian Child Welfare Act in chapter 2, I argued that basing membership in a group *solely* on the basis of blood was unwise. New Zealand's policy, which responded to the insistence of the Maori for information about genetic heritage, challenges this view, and further reading and thought are called for to evaluate these positions.

43. George A. Annas, "Artificial Insemination: Beyond the Best Interests of the Donor," *The Hastings Center Report* 4 (1979), 14–15; David J. Roy, "AID: An Overview of Ethical Issues," in *Human Artificial Insemination and Semen Preservation,* ed. Georges David and Wendel S. Price (New York: Plenum Press, 1980), 499–511.

44. Daniels and Taylor, "Secrecy and Ownership in Donor Insemination," 1993, discuss some psychologists' arguments against secrecy and anonymity and provide a useful bibliography. Robert D. Nachtigall, "Secrecy: An Unresolved Issue in the Practice of Donor Insemination," *American Journal of Obstetrics and Gynecology* 168, no. 6 (1993), calls for research to redress the paucity of information we have about how anonymity and secrecy affect members of families formed by gamete donation.

Philosopher James Lindemann Nelson worries that "we frustrate, by our efforts, something [children] have a right to expect" when we knowingly create a child that will not have a social relationship with one of its genetic parents. This initial intention by the adults involved gives rise to different ethical issues than those that arise when children lose contact with a genetic parent because of divorce, death, or abandonment. Quoted in Seligson, "Seeds of Doubt," 31.

George Annas reiterated his early call for an end to anonymous donation (see preceding note) in "The Shadowlands—Secrets, Lies, and Assisted Reproduction," *The New England Journal of Medicine* 339, no. 13 (September 24, 1998): 935–939.

45. Monica Konrad, "Ova Donation and Symbols of Substance: Some Variations on the Theme of Sex, Gender and the Partible Body," *Journal of the Royal Anthropological Institute* 4, no. 4 (December 1998): 643. Konrad sees anonymity as an integral part of these narratives of assistance, although the notion of enabling someone else to parent could, I think, endure without the condition of anonymity.

46. Mark V. Sauer, "Exploitation or a Woman's Right?" *British Medical Journal* 314, no. 7091 (May 10, 1997): 1403. See also Kolata, "Price Soars for Eggs," *New York Times,* February 25, 1998, p. A1.

47. Georges David and Jacques Lansac, "The Organization of the Centers for the Study and Preservation of Semen in France," in *Human Artificial Insemination and Semen Preservation,* ed. Georges David and Wendel S. Price (New York: Plenum Press, 1980), 15–26, 20. See also Dominique Le Lannou, Bernard Lobel, and Yves Chambon, "Sperm Banks and Donor Recruitment in France," and Patrick Huerre, "Psychological Aspects of

Semen Donation," in David and Price, eds., *Human Artificial Insemination,* 89–94; 461–465. Huerre reported that when donations could not
keep up with the increasing demand, causing some recipients to have to
wait a year for insemination, the centers developed a policy of asking potential recipients to recruit donors (whose semen would not be given to
them, but to others).

48. Ian Craft, "An 'Inconvenience Allowance' Would Solve the Egg Shortage," *British Medical Journal* 314, no. 7091 (May 10, 1997): 1400, argues in
favor of an "inconvenience allowance," and Martin H. Johnson, "The
Culture of Unpaid and Voluntary Egg Donation Should be Strengthened," *British Medical Journal* 314, no. 7091 (May 10, 1997): 1401, argues for
unpaid donation. See also Donna Dickenson, *Property, Women & Politics: Subjects or Objects?* (New Brunswick, N.J.: Rutgers University Press,
1997), for a discussion of the assumptions reflected in England's laws governing gamete donation.

49. Hawley Fogg-Davis, "'She Works Hard for the Money?': Addressing Employment Discrimination in Paid Egg Donation," paper presented at the
Annual Meeting of the American Political Science Association, Washing-
ton, D.C., September 2000. Fogg-Davis argues against attributing any
race to a gamete in "Navigating Race in Gamete Donation," unpublished
paper presented at the Young Scholars Program, Cornell University's
Program in Ethics and Public Life, April 15, 2000.

50. For example, some Jewish recipients might wish to procreate in collabo-
ration with a Jewish donor as a way of affirming the will of the Jewish
people to survive in the wake of the Holocaust, and some Native Americans might seek donors from their tribe for similar reasons.

51. Anita Allen expresses this view in "Does a Child Have a Right to a Certain
Identity," in *Recht, Gerechtigkeit und der Staat* (Law, Justice, and the
State), ed. Mikael M. Karlsson, Ólafur Páll Jónsson, and Eyja Margrét
Brynjarsdóttir (Berlin: Duncker & Humbolt, 1993).

52. There is also a question of whether donors should be able to choose the
recipients, or to specify characteristics (particularly race and religion) of
the recipients. Some donors may wish to contribute genetic material only
to the creation of a child who will be raised with a particular racial or religious identity; for example, the daughter of Holocaust survivors may
wish to donate eggs only to a Jewish couple. I would not prevent donors
from arranging to donate to a specific couple, or prohibit reproductive
clinics from maintaining lists of donors who would give only to people
with particular characteristics, although it is troubling to attribute racial
or religious identity to a gamete.

53. Strathern, *Reproducing the Future,* 34, 31–32. Like Strathern, political the-

orist Michael Sandel and legal theorist Janet Dolgin have observed this same tension between thinking about family relationships as given "by nature" and family relationships as the result of choice. And both worry that legislatures and courts in the United States have leaned too far in the direction of accepting choice as the basis of family relationships, risking the loss of norms of natural obligation, mutuality or reciprocity, and permanence. Michael Sandel, *Liberalism and the Limits of Justice* (Cambridge: Cambridge University Press, 1982) and *Democracy's Discontent* (Cambridge, Mass.: Harvard University Press, 1996), and Janet L. Dolgin, *Defining the Family: Law, Technology, and Reproduction in an Uneasy Age* (New York: New York University Press, 1997).

54. See John Wallach, "Liberalism, Communitarians, and the Tasks of Political Theory," *Political Theory* 15, no. 4 (November 1987): 518–611; Milton C. Regan, Jr., *Family Law and the Pursuit of Intimacy* (New York: New York University Press, 1993).

55. See Jennifer Nedelsky, "Reconceiving Autonomy: Sources, Thoughts and Possibilities," *Yale Journal of Law and Feminism* 1, no 1. (1989): 7–36, and "Law, Boundaries, and the Bounded Self," *Representations* 30 (1990): 162–189. See Ronald Dworkin's argument for moral autonomy in *Life's Dominion: An Argument about Abortion, Euthanasia, and Individual Freedom* (New York: Knopf, 1993). On liberal visions that abjure highly individualistic understandings of the person, see Nancy L. Rosenblum, *Another Liberalism* (Cambridge: Harvard University Press, 1987), and Nancy L. Rosenblum, ed., *Liberalism and the Moral Life* (Cambridge: Harvard University Press, 1989).

56. There might be exceptions to this general rule if revealing information might put someone else's safety in jeopardy.

4. "Surrogate" Motherhood

1. The depiction of events that follows is drawn from the court cases: *In re Baby "M,"* 217 N.J. Super. 374, 525 A.2d 1128 (Superior Court, Chancery Division, 1987); reversed on appeal, *In the Matter of Baby M,* 537 A.2d 1227 (N.J. 1988); and Bonnie Steinbock, "Surrogate Motherhood as Prenatal Adoption," in *Surrogate Motherhood: Politics and Privacy,* ed. Larry Gostin (Bloomington: Indiana University Press, 1990), 123–124. Excerpts from the Supreme Court decision are found in Gostin, ed., 253–260.

2. Joan Heifetz Hollinger, "From Coitus to Commerce: Legal and Social Consequences of Noncoital Reproduction," *University of Michigan Journal of Law Reform* 18 (Summer 1985): 865–932, provides an excellent discussion that compares surrogacy to gamete donation and adoption. Christine Overall, *Ethics and Human Reproduction* (Boston: Allen & Un-

win, 1987) and *Human Reproduction: Principles, Practices, Policies* (Toronto: Oxford University Press, 1993), discusses both gamete donation and surrogacy in useful ways.

3. On women's autonomy see Lori Andrews, *Between Strangers: Surrogate Mothers, Expectant Fathers, and Brave New Babies* (New York: Harper & Row, 1989); Avi Katz, "Surrogate Motherhood and the Baby-Selling Laws," *Columbia Journal of Law and Social Problems* 20, no. 1 (1986); Note, "Baby-Sitting Consideration: Surrogate Mother's Right to 'Rent her Womb' for a Fee," *Gonzaga Law Review* 18 (1983); Carmel Shalev, *Birth Power: The Case for Surrogacy* (New Haven: Yale University Press, 1989); Marjorie Maguire Shultz, "Reproductive Technology and Intent-based Parenthood: An Opportunity for Gender Neutrality," *Wisconsin Law Review* 1990, no. 2 (1990): 297–398.

   On commissioning parents' "right to procreate" see John Lawrence Hill, "The Case for Enforcement of the Surrogate Contract," *Politics and the Life Sciences* 8, no. 2 (1990): 147–160; John Robertson, "Procreative Liberty and the Control of Contraception, Pregnancy and Childbirth," *Virginia Law Review* 69 (1983): 405–462, "Embryos, Families and Procreative Liberty: The Legal Structures of the New Reproduction," *Southern California Law Review* 59 (1989): 942–1041, and *Children of Choice: Freedom and the New Reproductive Technologies* (Princeton: Princeton University Press, 1994); and Shalev, *Birth Power.*

4. See, for example, Katharine T. Bartlett, "Re-Expressing Parenthood," *Yale Law Journal* 98 (1988): 293–340; Carole Pateman, *The Sexual Contract* (Stanford: Stanford University Press, 1988), ch. 7; Barbara Katz Rothman, *Recreating Motherhood: Ideology and Technology in Patriarchal Society* (New York: Norton, 1989); Susan M. Okin, "A Critique of Pregnancy Contracts," *Politics and the Life Sciences* 8, no. 2 (February 1990): 205–210; and Martha A. Field, *Surrogate Motherhood: The Legal and Human Issues* (Cambridge, Mass.: Harvard University Press, 1988), and "The Case against Enforcement of Surrogacy Contracts," *Politics and the Life Sciences* 8, no. 2 (February 1990): 199–204.

5. On the importance of taking account of social facts see H. N. Hirsch, *A Theory of Liberty: The Constitution and Minorities* (New York: Routledge, 1992).

6. See, e.g., *Hoyt v. Florida* 368 U.S. 57 (1961), which held that Florida's automatic exemption of women from jury duty because they might have dependent children at home was not unconstitutionally over-broad. See generally Deborah L. Rhode, *Justice and Gender* (Cambridge: Harvard University Press, 1989), 29–50.

7. Marjorie Maguire Shultz, "Reproductive Technology and Intention-

based Parenthood: An Opportunity for Gender Neutrality," *Wisconsin Law Review* 1990, no. 2 (1990): 297–398, 304.

8. Shultz, "Reproductive Technology and Intention-based Parenthood," 344.
9. Shalev, *Birth Power*, 11–12, 96.
10. Avi Katz, "Surrogate Motherhood and the Baby-selling Laws," *Columbia Journal of Law and Social Problems* 20, no. 1 (1986): 1–52, 21.
11. Shalev, *Birth Power*, 103.
12. See, e.g., Andrews, *Between Strangers*, 252–272; Shalev, *Birth Power*, 144; and Hill, "The Case for Enforcement of the Surrogate Contract," 157–59. In his decision in Orange County (California) Superior Court, Judge Richard N. Parslow awarded custody to the commissioning parents and "proposed that all parties to any surrogate agreement undergo psychiatric evaluation, that all agree from the start that the surrogate mother would have no custody rights, that she have previous experience with successful childbirth and that a surrogate be used only in cases where the genetic mother is unable to give birth." *New York Times*, Metropolitan ed., 23 October 1990, p. A14.
13. Andrea E. Stumpf, "Redefining Motherhood: A Legal Matrix for New Reproductive Technologies," *Yale Law Journal* 96, no. 1 (1986): 187–208, 195.
14. Shultz, "Reproductive Technology and Intention-based Parenthood," 398.
15. Shalev, *Birth Power*, 121.
16. Quoted in Andrews, *Between Strangers*, 92, 223.
17. Kathryn Kish Sklar, "Why Were Most Politically Active Women Opposed to the ERA in the 1920s?" in *Rights of Passage: The Past and Future of the ERA*, ed. Joan Hoff-Wilson (Bloomington: Indiana University Press, 1986), 25–35.
18. Lucinda Finley, "Transcending Equality Theory: A Way Out of the Maternity and the Workplace Debate," *Columbia University Law Review* 86 (1986): 1118–82. On the Family and Medical Leave Act, which established a right to parental leave for both men and women, see Eva Feder Kittay, *Love's Labor* (New York: Routledge, 1998).
19. Lisa Newton, quoted in Andrews, *Between Strangers*, 267. Judge Parslow said that Anna Johnson had served as a "home" for the embryo she carried, "much as a foster parent stands in for a parent who is not able to care for a child." *New York Times*, October 23, 1990, National ed., p. A14.
20. Shalev, *Birth Power*, 157, 94.
21. Andrews, *Between Strangers*, 259.
22. Margaret Jane Radin, "Market Inalienability," *Harvard Law Review* 100, no. 8 (June 1987): 1849–1937.

23. The debate over whether prostitution should be decriminalized finds feminists on both sides of the issue, sometimes for reasons akin to those which divide them with respect to contract pregnancy. See discussions in Alison Jaggar, "Prostitution," in *The Philosophy of Sex: Contemporary Readings*, ed. A. Soble (Totowa, N.J.: Rowman & Littlefield, 1980).

24. Sharyn L. Roach Anleu, "Reinforcing Gender Norms: Commercial and Altruistic Surrogacy," *Acta Sociologica* 33 (1990): 63–74, and Janice G. Raymond, "Reproductive Gifts and Gift Giving: The Altruistic Woman," *Hastings Center Report* (Nov./Dec. 1990): 7–11, both criticize gift surrogacy on the ground that it reinforces gender stereotypes of women as altruistic conduits for fulfilling others' needs. Anleu, but not Raymond, would allow commercial surrogacy. Uma Narayan, "Rethinking Parental Claims in the Light of Surrogacy and Custody," in *Having and Raising Children: Unconventional Families, Hard Choices, and the Social Good*, ed. Uma Narayan and Julia J. Bartkowiak (University Park: Pennsylvania State University Press, 1999) would allow both gift and commercial surrogacy but would not enforce pregnancy contracts.

25. A few writers propose legalizing commissioned adoption or creating a market in babies, but they are in a minority, and they arrived at their views from considering issues other than contract pregnancy. Richard Posner declares that the objections to the sale of babies for adoption are unpersuasive. Even the poor might do better in a free baby market than under present adoption law because people who did not meet adoption agencies' requirements might, "in a free market with low prices, be able to adopt children, just as poor people are able to buy color television sets." *Economic Analysis of Law*, 3d ed. (Boston: Little Brown, 1986), 141–42. See also Elizabeth Landes and Richard A. Posner, "The Economics of the Baby Shortage," *Journal of Legal Studies* 7 (1978): 323; but see Posner, "Mischaracterized Views," letter, *Judicature* 69, no. 6 (Nov./Dec. 1986): 321, where he says he "did not advocate a free market in babies." Cited in Margaret Jane Radin, "Market Inalienability," *Harvard Law Review* 100, no. 8 (June 1987): 1850, 1863.

26. Radin, "Market Inalienability," 133.

27. *New York Times*, August 12, 1990, Metropolitan ed., p. A1.

28. Heléna Ragoné, "Of Likeness and Difference: How Race Is Being Transfigured by Gestational Surrogacy," in *Ideologies and Technologies of Motherhood: Race, Class, Sexuality, Nationalism*, ed. Heléna Ragoné and France Winddance Twine (New York and London: Routledge, 2000), 56–75, 57.

29. *New York Times*, October 23, 1990, National ed., p. A14. Judge Parslow makes a false distinction between gestational mothers who have a genetic relationship to the fetus they bear and those who do not. The absence of

a genetic relationship should make no more legal difference to a gestational mother's custodial rights than it does to her experience of pregnancy. A gestational mother undergoes all the extensive hormonal and physiological changes of pregnancy, and her social experience as a pregnant woman will be the same whether she has a genetic tie to the fetus or not. From her perspective, the distinction between "full surrogacy" (in which she donates an ovum) and "partial surrogacy" (in which she bears no genetic relationship to the fetus) may very well be slight or immaterial.

30. Iris Marion Young, "Pregnant Embodiment: Subjectivity and Alienation," in *"Throwing Like a Girl" and Other Essays in Feminist Philosophy and Social Theory* (Bloomington: Indiana University Press, 1990), 167.

31. Gwendolyn Brooks, "The Mother," *Norton Anthology of American Literature*, 3d ed., vol. 2 (New York: Norton, 1989), 2505.

32. Barbara Johnson, *A World of Difference* (Baltimore: Johns Hopkins University Press, 1987), 190.

33. Adrienne Rich, *Of Woman Born: Motherhood as Experience and as Institution* (New York: Norton; Bantam ed., 1976), 47.

34. Young, *"Throwing Like a Girl,"* 167.

35. Carole Pateman, *The Sexual Contract* (Stanford: University of California Press, 1988), 216.

36. Elizabeth Anderson, "Is Women's Labor a Commodity?" *Philosophy and Public Affairs* 1990: 71–92, 75, 82, 81, 92. In recommending the prohibition of payment under any circumstances, Anderson assumes the existence and desirability of mother-fetus bonding; I do not assume that such a bond always develops. When a gestational mother does experience a strong tie with the child she is carrying, however, law and social practice should recognize and protect that bond.

37. Ragoné, "Of Likeness and Difference," 72.

38. Both studies are reported in Mary Briody Mahowald, *Genes, Women, Equality* (New York: Oxford University Press, 2000), 127–142. The original publications were J. G. Thornton, H. M. McNamara, and I. A. Mantague, "Would You Rather Be a 'Birth' or a 'Genetic' Mother? If So, How Much?" *Journal of Medical Ethics* 20 (1994): 87, and Amy J. Ravin, Mary B. Mahowald, and Carol B. Stocking, "Genes or Gestation? Attitudes of Women and Men about Biologic Ties to Children," *Journal of Women's Health* 6, no. 6 (1997): 1–9.

39. 5 Cal. 4th 84; 85 P2d 776 (1993) at 781.

40. Narayan, "Rethinking Parental Claims in the Light of Surrogacy and Custody," in *Having and Raising Children*, 65–86, similarly advocates a custody hearing in such cases.

41. Shultz, "Reproductive Technology and Intention-based Parenthood," 377–78, 364.

42. Shultz, "Reproductive Technology and Intention-based Parenthood," 384.

43. Even if one accepts my argument that a woman's contract to relinquish all custodial claims should not be enforced against her will, the question of how to deal with the custodial claims of the commissioning parent(s) is enormously difficult. One could argue that these claims should be adjudicated on a case-by-case basis, but that would not serve the goal of stabilizing the child's situation as quickly as possible, nor would it give more weight to an actual physical relationship and nurturance than to intentionality alone. Yet the claims of the commissioning parents are real and certainly stronger than those of a biological father who "unintentionally" becomes a parent through unprotected intercourse (and who can claim paternal rights and responsibilities in many jurisdictions). Society might do well to develop forms of acknowledging the existence of "intentional" and biological, as well as nurturing, custodial parents.

    On the need to avoid disruption in a family see Karen Czapanskiy, "Interdependencies, Families, and Children, *Santa Clara Law Review* 39 (1999): 957–1035.

44. Robert D. Goldstein, *Mother-love and Abortion: A Legal Interpretation* (Berkeley: University of California Press, 1988). I do not believe all women experience "mother-love" during pregnancy, and I disagree strongly with Goldstein's assumption that "mother-love" must continue to privilege a mother's relationship to her child over the father's after birth.

45. Ferdinand Schoeman. "Rights of Children, Rights of Parents, and the Moral Basis of the Family," *Ethics* 91, no. 1 (1990), 35.

46. Goldstein, *Mother-love and Abortion*, 35, 65, x.

47. Kenneth Karst, "The Freedom of Intimate Association," *Yale Law Journal* 89, no. 4 (1980): 624–93.

48. When the intended parents are both males, of course, one contributes sperm and neither carries the fetus.

49. Joan Hollinger argues that imposed visitation rights for the noncustodial genetic parent may be sufficiently disruptive to the child that the law should hold that pregnancy contracts are enforceable, and that a surrogate who changes her mind has no ground on which to claim visitation. I share Hollinger's concern that the child not bear the burden of adults' mistakes. In order to recognize the multiplicity of significant relationships involved, I propose a hearing in cases where a surrogate and the intentional parents disagree about custody. A court might deny visitation to a blameless genetic parent on the ground that doing so is best for the child. I would not regard it as an undesirable consequence if these proce-

dures discouraged surrogacy. Hollinger, "From Coitus to Commerce," 865–932.

50. Dorothy E. Roberts, "The Genetic Tie," *University of Chicago Law Review* 62 (1995): 209–273, 257–264, gives several examples of courts denying custody claims to parents who had different racial features than their child. Maureen T. Reddy, *Crossing the Color Line: Race, Parenting and Culture* (New Brunswick: Rutgers University Press, 1997), recounts her experience as a white mother of a biracial child who is regarded by society as black.

51. Anna Johnson, who sometimes described herself as "African-American" and sometimes as mixed black-white (the media referred to her as a black woman), was impregnated with a pre-embryo created by in vitro fertilization from Mark Calvert's sperm and Crispina Calvert's egg. Crispina, age thirty-four, had lost her uterus to cancer but still had functioning ovaries. When she was seven and a half months pregnant, Anna Johnson filed a lawsuit asking for custody on the grounds that the Calverts had neglected her during the pregnancy and failed to make payments, and that she had developed a bond with the fetus. She told reporters that she hoped at least to get joint custody and visitation rights. Anita L. Allen, "The Black Surrogate Mother," *Harvard Blackletter Journal* 8 (1991): 17–31, 19 note 17.

52. Jeremy Rifkin and Andrew Kimbrell, "Put a Stop to Surrogate Parenting Now," *USA Today*, August 20, 1990, p. A8, quoted in Allen, "The Black Surrogate Mother," 30.

5. Lesbian Co-Mothers, Sperm Donors, and Fathers

1. *In the matter of Alison D. v. Virginia M.*, 77 N.Y.2d 651, 572 N. E.2d 27, 569 N.Y.S.2d 586 (1991).

2. *In the Matter of a Proceeding for Paternity Under Article 5 of the Family Court Act Thomas S. v. Robin Y.*, 157 Misc. 2d 858, 599 N.Y.S. 2d 377 (April 13, 1993); *In re Thomas S. v. Robin Y.*, Supreme Court, Appellate Division, 209 A.D. 2d 298, 618 N.Y.S. 2d 356 (November 17, 1994); *Matter of Thomas S. v. Robin Y.*, Court of Appeals of New York, 86 N.Y. 2d 779, 655 N. E. 2d 708, 631 N.Y.S. 2d 611 (July 26, 1995).

3. *Alison D. v. Virginia M.*, at 654. For an account of a nonbiological co-mother's commitment to remaining a parent to her daughter after she and the biological co-mother separated, see Toni Tortorilla, "On a Creative Edge," in *Politics of the Heart: A Lesbian Parenting Anthology*, ed. Sandra Pollack and Jeanne Vaughn (Ithaca, N.Y.: Firebrand Books, 1987), 168–174.

4. Oregon Rev. Statutes §109.19 [1] (1985, amended 1988) (1989), quoted in *Alison D. v. Virginia M.*, at 657.

5. *Alison D. v. Virginia M.,* at 662.
6. Jane Levine, David Chambers, and Martha Minow, *Brief for Amici Curiae,* Eleven Concerned Academics, Court of Appeals, State of New York, Index No. 000692–88 (1990), p. 5.
7. *Thomas S. v. Robin Y.,* 599 N.Y.S. 2d 377 (Family Court, 1993).
8. *Thomas S. v. Robin Y.,* 618 N.Y.S. 2d 356 (Appellate Division, 1994), 362 and 363.
9. *Thomas S. v. Robin Y.,* 631 N.Y.S. 2d 611 (Court of Appeals, 1995).
10. John A. Robertson, *Children of Choice: Freedom and the New Reproductive Technologies* (Princeton: Princeton University Press, 1994), 104–105. This proprietary view informs Robertson's understanding of a number of issues that arise from new reproductive technologies. For example, he argues that posthumous procreation with frozen sperm, with the offspring having rights of inheritance from the sperm donor, is acceptable if it was clearly the intent of the deceased that someone should use his genetic material for this purpose. He also holds that a person may prohibit the use of his or her genetic material in procreation; he views the right *not* to procreate as a corollary of the right to procreate.

    Robertson's emphasis on an individual's relationship to his or her genetic material leads him to conflate the work of social reproduction (which involves the rearing of a child over many years) and biological procreation (which brings together sperm and egg): "In a sense, reproduction is always genetic. . . . Thus, a woman who has provided the egg that is carried by another has reproduced, even if she has not gestated and does not rear resulting offspring" (*Children of Choice,* 22). I would say that she has donated materials used in procreation, not that she has "reproduced." Barbara Katz Rothman discusses this distinction between procreative and reproductive activity in *Recreating Motherhood: Ideology and Technology in a Patriarchal Society* (New York: Norton, 1989).
11. Brief for Petitioner-Appellant, at 28, quoted in Fred A. Bernstein, "This Child Does Have Two Mothers . . . and a Sperm Donor with Visitation," *New York University Review of Law and Social Change* 22 (1996): 1–58, 30.
12. The issue, said the court, was whether it could "cut off the parental rights of a . . . biological father" without complying with due process procedures of New York's Social Services Law; *Thomas S. v. Robin Y.,* 618 N.Y.S. 2d, at 358, citing N.Y. Social Service Law, sec. 384.
13. Marjorie Maguire Shultz, "Reproductive Technology and Intention-based Parenthood: An Opportunity for Gender Neutrality," *Wisconsin Law Review* 1990, no. 2 (1990): 297–398, 300, 302–303.
14. Robertson, *Children of Choice,* 143, 125.
15. Robertson, *Children of Choice,* 135.
16. Robertson, *Children of Choice,* 127.

17. Martha Albertson Fineman, *The Illusion of Equality* (Chicago: University of Chicago Press, 1991); Katharine Bartlett, "Re-Expressing Parenthood," *Yale Law Journal* 98 (1988): 293 and "Rethinking Parenthood as an Exclusive Status: The Need for Legal Alternatives when the Premise of the Nuclear Family Has Failed," *Virginia Law Review* 17 (1984): 879.

18. *Alison D. v. Virginia M.*, Judge Kaye dissenting, at 662.

19. Bartlett, "Rethinking Parenthood as an Exclusive Status," 946–947.

20. Nancy Polikoff, "This Child Does Have Two Mothers: Redefining Parenthood to Meet the Needs of Children in Lesbian-Mother and Other Nontraditional Families," *Georgetown Law Journal* 78 (1990): 464.

21. Polikoff, "This Child Does Have Two Mothers," 542. Massachusetts recently adopted a "de facto parent" rule in a case involving a visitation claim by a former partner in a same-sex couple, basically reflecting the "functional" approach to parental rights. *E.N.O. v. L.M.M.*, 429 Mass. 824, 711 N. E. 2d 886 (Mass. 1999). Thanks to Milton C. Regan, Jr., for this reference.

22. Bernstein, "This Child Does Have Two Mothers . . . and a Sperm Donor," 30.

23. *Thomas S. v. Robin Y.*, 618 N.Y.S. 2d 356 (Appellate Division, 1994), 362.

24. Bernstein, "This Child Does Have Two Mothers . . . and a Sperm Donor"; Brad Sears, "Winning Arguments/Losing Themselves: The (Dys)functional Approach in *Thomas S. v. Robin Y.*, *Harvard Civil Rights-Civil Liberties Law Review* 29 (1994): 559–580; Kate Harrison, "Fresh or Frozen: Lesbian Mothers, Sperm Donors, and Limited Fathers," in *Mothers in Law: Feminist Theory and the Legal Regulation of Motherhood*, ed. Martha A. Fineman and Isabel Karpin (New York: Columbia University Press), 1995.

25. *Alison D. v. Virginia M.*, Judge Kaye dissenting, at 660, quoting *Matter of Bennett v. Jeffreys*, 40 NY2d 543, 546.

26. *Alison D. v. Virginia M.*, Judge Kaye dissenting.

27. *Thomas S. v. Robin Y.*, 618 N.Y.S. 2d 356 (Appellate Division, 1994), 367, 368.

28. *Thomas S. v. Robin Y.*, 618 N.Y.S. 2d 356 (Appellate Division, 1994), 367.

29. Barbara Bennett Woodhouse, "Hatching the Egg: A Child-centered Perspective on Parents' Rights," *Cardozo Law Review* 14 (May 1993): 1756, 1754–1755.

30. Woodhouse, "Hatching the Egg," 1864.

31. Woodhouse, "Hatching the Egg," 1864.

32. Harrison, "Fresh or Frozen," 187.

33. Woodhouse, "Hatching the Egg," 1815.

34. See, for example, Philip Gambone, "The Kid I Already Have: On Considering Fathering a Child with a Lesbian," in *Sister and Brother: Lesbians*

and *Gay Men Write About Their Lives Together,* ed. Joan Nestle and John Preston (New York: HarperSanFrancisco, 1994), 251–264; see also Kate Hill, "Mothers by Insemination: Interviews," Sandra Pollack, "Two Moms, Two Kids: An Interview," and Carolyn Kott Washburne, "Happy Birthday from Your Other Mom," all in *Politics of the Heart: A Lesbian Parenting Anthology,* ed. Sandra Pollack and Jeanne Vaughn (Ithaca, N.Y.: Firebrand Books, 1987), 111–119, 120–1244, and 142–145, respectively.

35. See, for example, the difficult issues raised by the dispute in *Troxel v. Granville,* 120 S. Ct. 2054 (2000).

36. Bartlett, "Rethinking Parenthood as an Exclusive Status"; Bernstein, "This Child Does Have Two Mothers . . . and a Sperm Donor"; Sears, "Winning Arguments/Losing Themselves"; Harrison, "Fresh or Frozen."

37. Harrison, "Fresh or Frozen," 192.

38. Harrison, "Fresh or Frozen," 191, 190.

39. Harrison, "Fresh or Frozen," 191, 190.

40. Katharine Bartlett, Brad Sears, and Fred Bernstein all argue that a child's interest in maintaining relationships with important adults justifies creating nonexclusive parenting status or visitation rights for "limited" parents. The majority on the Court of Appeals that granted Thomas's right to petition for an order of filiation made it clear that at most Thomas had a claim to visitation, not custody; they might have preferred to declare Thomas a limited parent rather than Ry's legal "father," had such a category existed.

41. Harrison, "Fresh or Frozen," 199.

42. One of the most thoughtful writers on the tension between the child's need to maintain relationships and to have parents whose authority may properly be exercised to exclude other adults is Karen Czapanskiy, "Interdependencies, Families, and Children," *Santa Clara Law Review* 39 (1999): 957–1035, and "Child Support and Visitation: Rethinking the Connections," *Rutgers Law Journal* 20 (Spring 1989): 619–665.

43. Woodhouse, "Hatching the Egg," 1811.

44. Martha Gaines, personal communication, October 9, 2000.

Epilogue

1. Naomi Cahn, "The Moral Complexities of Family Law," *Stanford Law Review* 50 (November 1997): 225–271, 225. Hendrik Hartog noted this clash in various debates in constitutional law: "Either family rights became the individualistic, libertarian rights of individuals within a family, or they were equated with the property rights of a patriarchal head of household." Hendrik Hartog, "The Constitution of Aspiration and 'the Rights that Belong to Us All,' " *The Journal of American History* 74, no. 3

(December 1987): 1027. On the tension between individual and family see also Jean Bethke Elshtain, "The New Eugenics and Feminist Questions," in *Politics and the Human Body*, ed. Jean Bethke Elshtain and Timothy J. Cloyd (Nashville: Vanderbilt University Press, 1995).

2. See, for example, Virginia Held, *Feminist Morality: Transforming Culture, Society, and Politics* (Chicago: University of Chicago Press, 1993), and Joan Tronto, *Moral Boundaries: A Political Argument for an Ethic of Care* (New York: Routledge, 1993).

3. Nancy Hirschmann, *Rethinking Obligation: A Feminist Method for Political Theory* (Ithaca: Cornell University Press, 1992).

4. John Stuart Mill, *The Subjection of Women* [1869], ed. Susan Moller Okin (Indianapolis: Hackett, 1988).

5. *A Call to Civil Society: Why Democracy Needs Moral Truth* (New York: Institute for American Values, 1998), signed by many prominent academics, public intellectuals, community activists, and government officials: Enola Aird, John Atlas, David Blankenhorn, Don Browning, Senator Dan Coats, John DiIulio, Jr., Don Eberly, Jean Bethke Elshtain (chair), Francis Fukuyama, William Galston, Clair Gaudiani, Robert George, Mary Ann Glendon, Ray Hammond, Sylvia Ann Hewlett, Thomas Kohler, Senator Joseph Lieberman, Glenn Loury, Richard Mouw, Margaret Steinfels, Cornel West, Roger Williams, James Q. Wilson, Daniel Yankelovich.

6. Anita Garey, *Weaving Work and Motherhood* (Philadelphia: Temple University Press, 1999).

7. Hannah Arendt eloquently praises the value of leading a public life in *The Human Condition* (Chicago: University of Chicago Press, 1958).

8. Milton C. Regan, Jr., *Alone Together: Law and the Meanings of Marriage* (New York: Oxford University Press, 1999), 24. See also Annete C. Baier, "The Need for More than Justice," in *Science, Morality & Feminist Theory*, ed. Marsha Hanen and Kai Nielsen (1987), 59: "[Individuality] is not something a person has, and which she then chooses relationships to suit, but something that develops out of a series of dependencies and interdependencies, and responses to them."

9. Regan, Jr., *Alone Together*, 12.

10. On the obligations of care, and on the need to think of the provision of care as a public responsibility, see Tronto, *Moral Boundaries;* Mona Harrington, *Care and Equality* (New York: Knopf, 1999); Eva Feder Kittay, *Love's Labor* (New York: Routledge, 1999). On care for the disabled, and the new issues concerning people with disabilities created by reproductive technologies, see Adrienne Asch and Michelle Fine, "Shared Dreams: A Left Perspective on Disability Rights and Reproductive Rights," *Radical America* 18, no. 4 (1984): 51–58, and other works by them.

11. William Julius Wilson, *The Truly Disadvantaged: The Inner City, the Underclass, and Public Policy* (Chicago: University of Chicago Press, 1987).
12. On the obligation of society and government to provide care see Robert Goodin, *Protecting the Vulnerable: A Reanalysis of Our Social Responsibilities* (Chicago: University of Chicago Press, 1985).

Selected Bibliography

Allen, Anita. "Does a Child Have a Right to a Certain Identity?" In *Recht, Gerechtigkeit und der Staat* (Law, Justice, and the State). Edited by Mikael M. Karlsson, Ólafur Páll Jónsson, and Eyja Margarét Brynjarsdóttir. Berlin: Duncker & Humbolt, 1993.

Anderson, Elizabeth S. "Is Women's Labor a Commodity?" *Philosophy and Public Affairs* 19 (Winter 1990): 71–92.

Andrews, Lori. *Between Strangers: Surrogate Mothers, Expectant Fathers, and Brave New Babies.* New York: Harper & Row, 1989.

Annas, George A. "The Shadowlands—Secrets, Lies, and Assisted Reproduction." *The New England Journal of Medicine* 339, no. 13 (September 24, 1998): 935–939.

Asch, Adrienne, and Michelle Fine, eds. *Women with Disabilities: Essays in Psychology, Policy and Politics.* Philadelphia: Temple University Press, 1988.

Banks, R. Richard. "The Color of Desire: Fulfilling Adoptive Parents' Racial Preferences Through Discriminatory State Action." *Yale Law Journal* 107 (1998): 875–964.

Baran, A., and R. Pannor. "Open Adoption." In *The Psychology of Adoption.* Edited by D. M. Brodzinsky and M. Schechter. New York: Oxford University Press, 1990.

Bartholet, Elizabeth. "Where Do Black Children Belong? The Politics of Race Matching in Adoption." *University of Pennsylvania Law Review* 139 (1991): 1163–1256.

———. *Family Bonds: Adoption and the Politics of Parenting.* Boston: Houghton Mifflin Company, 1993.

Bartlett, Katharine T. "Re-Expressing Parenthood." *Yale Law Journal* 98, no. 2 (December 1988): 293–340.

Baruch, Elaine Hoffman, Amodio F. D'Adamo, Jr., and Joni Seager, eds. *Embryos, Ethics and Women's Rights: Exploring the New Reproductive Technologies.* New York: Haworth Press, 1988.

Bates, Douglas J. *Gift Children: A Story of Race, Family, and Adoption in Divided America.* New York: Ticknor and Fields, 1993.

Becker, Mary. "The Rights of Unwed Parents: Feminist Approaches." *Social Service Review* 63 (December 1989): 496–518.

Bernstein, Fred. "This Child Does Have Two Mothers . . . and a Sperm Donor with Visitation." *New York University Review of Law and Social Change* 22 (1996): 1–58.

Billingsley, Andrew. *Climbing Jacob's Ladder: The Enduring Legacy of African-American Families.* New York: Simon and Schuster, 1992.

Boling, Patricia, ed. *Expecting Trouble: Surrogacy, Fetal Abuse and New Reproductive Technologies.* Boulder: Westview, 1995.

Bowen, James S. "Cultural Convergences and Divergences: The Nexus between Putative Afro-American Family Values and the Best Interests of the Child." *Journal of Family Law* 26, no. 3 (1987–88): 487–544.

Callahan, Joan C., ed. *Reproduction, Ethics, and the Law.* Bloomington: Indiana University Press, 1995.

Carp, E. Wayne. *Family Matters: Secrecy and Disclosure in the History of Adoption.* Cambridge, Mass.: Harvard University Press, 1998.

Cahn, Naomi. "The Moral Complexities of Family Law." *Stanford Law Review* 50 (November 1997): 225–271.

Cahn, Naomi, and Jana Singer. "Adoption, Identity, and the Constitution: The Case for Opening Closed Records." *University of Pennsylvania Journal of Constitutional Law* 1 (December 1999): 150–194.

Collins, Patricia Hill. *Black Feminist Thought.* Boston: Unwin Hyman, 1990.

Czapanskiy, Karen. "Interdependencies, Families, and Children." *Santa Clara Law Review* 39 (1999): 957–1035.

Damico, Alfonso J. "Surrogate Motherhood: Contract, Gender and Liberal Politics." In *Public Policy and the Public Good.* Edited by Ethan Fishman. Westview, Conn.: Greenwood Press, 1991.

Daniels, Cynthia R. *At Women's Expense: State Power and the Politics of Fetal Rights.* Cambridge: Harvard University Press, 1993.

Daniels, Ken, and Karyn Taylor. "Secrecy and Ownership in Donor Insemination." *Politics and the Life Sciences* 12 no. 2 (August 1993): 155–170, 156.

David, Georges, and Wendel S. Price, eds. *Human Artificial Insemination and Semen Preservation.* New York: Plenum Press, 1980.

Davis, Peggy Cooper. *Neglected Stories: The Constitution and Family Values*. New York: Hill and Wang, 1997.

Dickenson, Donna. *Property, Women, and Politics: Subjects or Objects?* New Brunswick, N.J.: Rutgers University Press, 1997.

Dolgin, Janet L. *Defining the Family: Law, Technology, and Reproduction in an Uneasy Age*. New York: New York University Press, 1997.

Dowd, Nancy E. *Redefining Fatherhood*. New York: New York University Press, 2000.

Elshtain, Jean Bethke, ed. *The Family in Political Thought*. Amherst: University of Massachusetts Press, 1982.

———— and Timothy J. Cloyd, eds. *Politics and the Human Body*. Nashville: Vanderbilt University Press, 1995.

Erickson, Nancy S. "The Feminist Dilemma Over Unwed Parents' Custody Rights: The Mother's Rights Must Take Priority." *Journal of Law and Inequality* 2 (1984): 447–472.

Etzioni, Amitai, ed. *New Communitarian Thinking: Persons, Virtues, Institutions and Communities*. Charlottesville: University Press of Virginia, 1995.

Field, Martha A. *Surrogate Motherhood: The Legal and Human Issues*. Cambridge, Mass.: Harvard University Press, 1988.

Fineman, Martha Albertson. *The Illusion of Equality: The Rhetoric and Reality of Divorce Reform*. Chicago: University of Chicago Press, 1991.

———— and Isabel Karpin, eds. *Mothers in Law: Feminist Theory and the Legal Regulation of Motherhood*. New York: Columbia University Press, 1995.

Fogg-Davis, Hawley. *The Ethics of Transracial Adoption*. Ithaca: Cornell University Press, in press.

Galston, William. *Liberal Purposes: Goods, Virtues and Diversity in the Liberal State*. Cambridge: Cambridge University Press, 1991.

Glendon, Mary Ann. *Rights Talk*. New York: Basic Books, 1991.

Goldsmith, Donna. "Individual vs. Collective Rights: The Indian Child Welfare Act." *Harvard Women's Law Journal* 13 (1990).

Goldstein, Leslie Friedman, ed. *Feminist Jurisprudence*. Lanham, Md: Rowman & Littlefield, 1992.

Goldstein, Robert D. *Mother-love and Abortion: A Legal Interpretation*. Berkeley: University of California Press, 1988.

Goodin, Robert. *Protecting the Vulnerable: A Reanalysis of Our Social Responsibilities*. Chicago: University of Chicago Press, 1985.

Gostin, Larry, ed. *Surrogate Motherhood: Politics and Privacy*. Bloomington: Indiana University Press, 1990.

Grossberg, Michael. *Governing the Hearth: Law and the Family in Nineteenth-Century America*. Chapel Hill: University of North Carolina Press, 1985.

Hanigsberg, Julia E., and Sara Ruddick, eds. *Mother Troubles: Rethinking Contemporary Maternal Dilemmas*. Boston: Beacon Press, 1999.

Harrington, Mona. *Care and Equality.* New York: Knopf, 1999.

Harrison, Kate. "Fresh or Frozen: Lesbian Mothers, Sperm Donors, and Limited Fathers." In *Mothers in Law: Feminist Theory and the Legal Regulation of Motherhood.* Edited by Martha A. Fineman and Isabel Karpin. New York: Columbia University Press, 1995.

Hartog, Hendrik. *Man and Wife in America: A History.* Cambridge: Harvard University Press, 2000.

Hearst, Alice. "Domesticating Reason: Children, Families, and Good Citizenship." In *Governing Childhood.* Edited by A. McGillivray. Aldershot: Dartmouth Publishing, 1997.

―――. "The Indian Child Welfare Act." Unpublished paper, Smith College, Northampton, Mass. (1996).

Held, Virginia. *Feminist Morality: Transforming Culture, Society, and Politics.* Chicago: University of Chicago Press, 1993.

Hill, John Lawrence. "The Case for Enforcement of the Surrogate Contract." *Politics and the Life Sciences* 8, no. 2 (February): 147–60.

Hirschmann, Nancy. *Rethinking Obligation: A Feminist Method for Political Theory.* Ithaca: Cornell University Press, 1992.

Hollinger, Joan Heifetz, ed. *Adoption Law and Practice.* New York: Matthew Bender, 1998, Suppl. 2000.

―――. "Adoption and Aspiration: The Uniform Adoption Act, the DeBoer-Schmidt Case, and the American Quest for the Ideal Family." *Duke Journal of Gender and Law Policy* 2 (1995): 15–40.

―――. "From Coitus to Commerce: Legal and Social Consequences of Noncoital Reproduction." *University of Michigan Journal of Law Reform* 18 (Summer 1985): 865–932.

Howe, Ruth-Arlene. "Transracial Adoption (TRA): Old Prejudices and Discrimination Float Under a New Halo." *The Boston University Public Law Journal* 6, no. 2 (Winter 1997): 409–472.

―――. "Adoption Practice, Issues, and Laws, 1958–1983." *Family Law Quarterly* 17 (1983).

Indian Child Welfare Act: Hearings on S. 1214 Before the Senate Select Committee on Indian Affairs, 95th Cong., 1st Sess. (1977); *Indian Child Welfare Program: Hearings Before the Senate Committee on Interior and Insular Affairs,* 93rd Cong., 2nd Sess. (1974).

Karst, Kenneth. 1980. "The Freedom of Intimate Association." *Yale Law Journal* 89, no. 4 (March): 624–93.

Kennedy, Randall. "Orphans of Separatism: The Painful Politics of Transracial Adoption." *The American Prospect* 17 (Spring 1994): 38–46.

―――. "How Are We Doing with *Loving?*: Race, Law, and Intermarriage," *Boston University Law Review* 77 (October 1997): 815–822.

Kittay, Eva Feder. *Love's Labor.* New York: Routledge, 1999.

Knoppers, Bartha M., and Sonia Lebris. "Recent Advances in Medically Assisted Conception: Legal, Ethical, and Social Issues." *American Journal of Law and Medicine* 17, no. 4 (1991): 329–361, 349–352.

Lifton, Betty Jean. *Journey of the Adopted Self: A Quest for Wholeness.* New York: Basic Books, 1994.

Macedo, Stephen, and Iris Marion Young. NOMOS XLIV: *Child, Family, and State.* New York: New York University Press, in press.

Mahowald, Mary Briody. *Genes, Women, Equality.* New York: Oxford University Press, 2000.

Martin, Emily. *The Woman in the Body: A Cultural Analysis of Reproduction.* Boston: Beacon Press, 1987.

Michie, Helena, and Naomi Cahn. *Confinements: Fertility and Infertility in Contemporary Culture.* New Brunswick, N. J. Rutgers University Press, 1997.

Minow, Martha. "'Forming under Everything that Grows': Toward a History of Family Law." *Wisconsin Law Review* 1985, no. 4 (1985): 819–898.

———. *Not Only for Myself: Identity, Politics, and the Law.* New York: The New Press, 1997.

——— and Mary Lyndon Shanley. "Relational Rights and Responsibilities: Revisioning the Family in Political Theory and Law." *Hypatia* 11, no. 1 (Winter 1996): 4–30.

Narayan, Uma, and Julia J. Bartkowiak, eds. *Having and Raising Children: Unconventional Families, Hard Choices, and the Social Good.* University Park: Pennsylvania State University Press, 1999.

Nedelsky, Jennifer. "Law, Boundaries, and the Bounded Self." *Representations* 30 (1990): 162–189.

Okin, Susan Moller. *Justice, Gender, and the Family.* New York: Basic Books, 1989.

Overall, Christine. *Ethics and Human Reproduction.* Boston: Allen & Unwin, 1987.

———. *Human Reproduction: Principles, Practices, Policies.* Toronto: Oxford University Press, 1993.

Pateman, Carole. *The Sexual Contract.* Stanford: Stanford University Press, 1988.

Perry, Twila L. "The Transracial Adoption Controversy: An Analysis of Discourse and Subordination." *New York University Review of Law & Social Change* 21 (1993–94): 33–108.

———. "Transracial and International Adoption: Mothers, Hierarchy, Race, and Feminist Legal Theory." *Yale Journal of Law and Feminism* 10 (1998): 101–164.

Pertman, Adam. *Adoption Nation: How the Adoption Revolution Is Transforming America.* New York: Basic Books, 2000.

Polikoff, Nancy. "This Child Does Have Two Mothers: Redefining Parenthood to Meet the Needs of Children in Lesbian-mother and other Nontraditional Families." *Georgetown Law Review* 78, no. 3 (1990): 459–575.

Radin, Margaret Jane. "Market Inalienability." *Harvard Law Review* 100, no. 8 (June 1987): 1849–1937.

Raymond, Janice G. "Reproductive Gifts and Gift Giving: The Altruistic Woman." *Hastings Center Report* 20, no. 6 (1990): 7–11.

Regan, Milton C., Jr. *Alone Together: Law and the Meaning of Marriage.* New York: Oxford University Press, 1999.

———. *Family Law and the Pursuit of Intimacy.* New York: New York University Press, 1988.

Rich, Adrienne. *Of Woman Born: Motherhood as Experience and as Institution.* New York: Norton; Bantam Ed., 1976.

Roberts, Dorothy E. "The Genetic Tie." *University of Chicago Law Review* 62 (1995): 209–273.

———. *Killing the Black Body: Race, Reproduction, and the Meaning of Liberty.* New York: Pantheon, 1997.

Robertson, John. "Embryos, Families and Procreative Liberty: The Legal Structures of the New Reproduction." *Southern California Law Review* 59 (1989): 942–1041.

———. *Children of Choice: Freedom and the New Reproductive Technologies.* Princeton: Princeton University Press, 1994.

Rosenblum, Nancy, ed. *Liberalism and the Moral Life.* Cambridge: Harvard University Press, 1989.

Rothman, Barbara Katz. *Recreating Motherhood: Ideology and Technology in a Patriarchal Society.* New York: Norton, 1989.

Rodham, Hillary. "Children under the Law." *Harvard Educational Review* 43, no. 4 (November 1973): 487–514.

Sandel, Michael. *Liberalism and the Limits of Justice.* Cambridge: Cambridge University Press, 1982.

Schneider, David M. *American Kinship: A Cultural Account.* Chicago: University of Chicago Press, 1968.

Schoeman, Ferdinand. "Rights of Children, Rights of Parents, and the Moral Basis of the Family." *Ethics* 91, no. 1 (October 1980): 6–19.

Shalev, Carmel. *Birth Power: The Case for Surrogacy.* New Haven: Yale University Press, 1989.

Shanley, Mary Lyndon. *Feminism, Marriage and the Law in Victorian England.* Princeton: Princeton University Press, 1989.

Shultz, Marjorie Maguire. "Reproductive Technology and Intention-based Parenthood: An Opportunity for Gender Neutrality." *Wisconsin Law Review* 1990, no. 2 (1990): 297–398.

Smith, Janet Farell. "Analyzing Ethical Conflict in the Transracial Adoption Debate: Three Conflicts Involving Community." *Hypatia* 11, no. 2 (Spring 1996): 1–33.

———. "Parenting and Property." In *Mothering: Essays in Feminist Theory.* Edited by Joyce Treblicot. Totowa, N.J.: Rowman and Allenheld, 1983.

Solinger, Rickie. *Wake Up Little Susie: Single Pregnancy and Race Before Roe v. Wade.* New York: Routledge, 1992.

Spelman, Elizabeth V. *Fruits of Sorrow: Framing Our Attention to Suffering.* Boston: Beacon Press, 1997.

Stack, Carol. *All Our Kin.* New York: Harper and Row, 1974.

Stanworth, Michelle. *Reproductive Technologies.* Cambridge: Polity Press, 1987.

Strathern, Marilyn. *Reproducing the Future: Essays on Anthropology, Kinship and the New Reproductive Technologies.* New York: Routledge, 1992.

Strober, Myra H., and Sanford M. Dornbusch, eds. *Feminism, Children, and the New Families.* New York: Guilford Press, 1988.

Sweeney, Maureen A. "Between Sorrow and Happy Endings: A New Paradigm of Adoption." *Yale Journal of Law and Feminism* 2, no. 2 (Spring 1990): 329–369.

Thorne, Barriie, and Marilyn Yalom, eds. *Rethinking the Family.* Rev. ed. Boston: Northeastern University Press, 1992.

Tronto, Joan C. *Moral Boundaries: A Political Argument for an Ethic of Care.* New York: Routledge, 1993.

Ulanowsky, Carole, ed. *The Family in the Age of Biotechnology.* Avebury: Ashgate Publishing, 1995.

Wadia-Ellis, Susan, ed. *The Adoption Reader: Birth Mothers, Adoptive Mothers, and Adopted Daughters Tell their Stories.* Seattle: Seal Press, 1995.

Williams, Patricia. *The Alchemy of Race and Rights.* Cambridge: Harvard University Press, 1991.

Woodhouse, Barbara Bennett. "Hatching the Egg: A Child-Centered Perspective in Parents' Rights." *Cardozo Law Review* 14 (1993): 1747.

———. "Out of Children's Needs, Children's Rights: The Child's Voice in Defining the Family." *Brigham Young University Journal of Public Law* 8 (1994): 321.

Yngvesson, Barbara. "Negotiating Motherhood: Identity and Difference in 'Open' Adoptions." *Law & Society Review* 31, no. 1 (1997): 31–80.

———. "Un Niño de Cualquier Color: Race and Nation in Intercountry Adoption." In *Globalizing Institutions: Case Studies in Regulation and Innovation.* Edited by Jane Jensen and Boaventura de Sousa Santos. Aldershot: Ashgate Press, 2000.

Yngvesson, Barbara, and Maureen Mahoney. " 'As One Should, Ought, and Wants to Be': Belonging and Authenticity in Identity Narratives." *Theory, Culture and Society* 17, no. 6 (December 2000).

Young, Iris. "Pregnant Embodiment: Subjectivity and Alienation." In *"Throwing Like a Girl" and Other Essays in Feminist Philosophy and Social Theory.* Bloomington: Indiana University Press, 1990.

Zainaldin, Jamil S. "The Emergence of a Modern American Family Law: Child Custody, Adoption, and the Courts, 1796–1851." *Northwestern University Law Review* 73 (1979): 1038–89.

Acknowledgments

*M*any friends and colleagues have helped me with their knowledge of the issues I discuss in this book. Some shared their academic or professional expertise, others shared their experiences of one or another aspect of family life with great openness and generosity. Many did both. To all of them I am deeply grateful.

Two people have encouraged and sustained this work throughout its long journey from my first ruminations on ethics and family policy to publication. Mona Harrington discussed this book with me at every step of the way. She read the entire manuscript several times, first in pieces as articles and convention papers, then in its entirety as a book. There could be no better intellectual companion. At one point when I nearly abandoned the project due to family illness she refused to hear of it. That the book exists at all is due to her unflagging confidence and encouragement, her incisive intellect, and her concrete editorial help. Nearly a decade ago over lunch Martha Minow helped me outline a book on "the contractual family" that I never wrote, but whose ideas led to the present volume. We subsequently coauthored an article that developed some of the ideas about individualism and family relationship that are found here. Most of all, Martha repeatedly assured me that I did not need a law degree in order to write about law, while graciously explaining legal points that I didn't understand.

Naomi Cahn, Fred Chromey, Ann Congleton, Hendrik Hartog, Joan Hollinger, Milton C. Regan, Jr., Jill Schneiderman, Vicky Spelman and Patricia Wallace read and gave me detailed comments on large portions of the manuscript, a labor for which I am deeply grateful.

Martha Ackelsberg, Prema Agrawal, Anita Allen, Elizabeth Bennett, Joan Callahan, Diane Churchill, Graciela Di Marco, Stephen Ellmann, Nancy Erickson, Hawley Fogg-Davis, Leslie Goldstein, Sarah Barringer Gordon, Luke Harris, Alice Hearst, Virginia Held, Morris Kaplan, Mary Fainsod Katzenstein, Walter Keady, Steve Macedo, Nan Bauer Maglin, Arthur Martin, Kate Meyer, Uma Narayan, Susan Okin, Carole Pateman, Joan Posner, Dorothy Roberts, Carol Sanger, Arlene Saxonhouse, Beatriz Schmukler, Joseph Singer, Janet Farrell Smith, Karen Stolley, Joan Tronto, John Wallach, and Barbara Yngvesson commented on parts of the book, and I am deeply grateful to each of them. Diane Blair, who died just before I completed this book, sustained my work with her conviction that ideas *do* matter in political life, her generosity of spirit, and her irrepressible wit.

Vassar College has provided a community of scholars and friends which I value immeasurably. Space does not permit me to mention all who have enriched my life and thought, but among them are Elizabeth Arlyck, Ralph Arlyck, Miriam Cohen, Elizabeth Daniels, Janet Gray, Michael Hanagan, Diane Harriford, Eileen Leonard, Peter Leonard, Deborah Moore, Daniel Peck, Wilfrid Rumble, Peter Stillman, Blanca Uribe, and Adelaide Villmoare. My colleagues in the Department of Political Science are truly without peer, and I value greatly the friendship and intellectual companionship of each of them. Librarians Lucinda Dubinski, Barbara Durniak, Flora Grabowska, Kathleen Kurosman, Shirley Maul, and Kappa Waugh have been unfailingly generous and helpful.

Several former Vassar students who have become friends and colleagues have contributed to this work through conversations and comments on my written work. I am particularly indebted to Martha Gaines, Kim Glickman, Matthew Kavanagh, and Rachel Simmons, who commented on drafts of some chapters, and to Camille Carey,

Sara Luther, Susan Reed, and Jodi Sandfort, who shared their insights about families with me. My Exploring Transfer students, in the most stimulating classes I have been privileged to teach, contributed greatly to my understanding of the complexities of family lives. Mark Hoffman provided excellent assistance as I prepared the manuscript for publication.

I enjoyed the hospitality and intellectual companionship of several friends while working on this book. Ann Congleton and Frank Hutchins, and Mona Harrington and Paul Gagnon often opened their homes to me while I was doing research. Clara Bargellini and Gabriel Cámara and their family gave richly of their friendship and thoughts while I wrote parts of this manuscript in Tepoztlán, Mexico.

Deborah Chasman was a superb editor, whose encouragement and excellent advice helped me first imagine the shape of this book and later to bring the project to completion. I was very fortunate to have the benefit of her intellect and skill, and that of her assistants, Edna Chiang and Julie Hassel.

Irene Bastian provided much-appreciated practical help as well as friendship.

I have been blessed in my family relationships: Sheppard Shanley read the entire manuscript, and his constant support and love immeasurably enrich my life. Nancy Chromey and Tina Chromey have sustained me with their love and friendship not only during this project but throughout the time we have been family to one another. Doris and Stanley Osgood have accompanied me in every undertaking of my life.

My husband, Fred Chromey, has helped me to live fully and think well for thirty years; I cannot find words to express what those gifts have meant to me. He and our children, Kate and Anthony, have greatly deepened my understanding of and appreciation for family life. Our life together is the source of my greatest joy and satisfaction.

I began work on this book while a Fellow at the Center for Human Values at Princeton University, and I am grateful to Amy Gutmann, Director of the Center, and my colleagues there, Kristen Monroe and Daniel Batson, for their support and encouragement. I am indebted to the members of the 1990 Mellon Faculty Center at Vassar College who helped me think about contract pregnancy, and to members of the

Women's Studies Program at Smith College who invited me and Kathleen Sands to lead an intensive two-day faculty seminar about our work in 1997. A fellowship from the National Endowment for the Humanities in 1996–97 provided invaluable time for research.

Chapter 1 is a revised and expanded version of "Toward New Understandings of Adoption: Individuals and Relationships in Transracial and Open Adoption," delivered as the NOMOS lecture at the Annual Meeting of the American Society for Legal and Political Philosophy, 1999 (forthcoming in *NOMOS* 64: *Child, Family and State,* ed. Stephen Macedo and Iris Marion Young, New York University Press). Portions of Chapter 2 originally appeared in "Fathers' Rights, Mothers' Wrongs?" in *Hypatia* 10, no. 1 (Winter 1995): 74–103 and in "Unwed Fathers' Rights, Adoption, and Sex Equality: Gender-neutrality and the Perpetuation of Patriarchy," *Columbia Law Review* 95, no. 1 (Winter 1995): 201–244. Parts of Chapter 4 were published in "'Surrogate Motherhood' and Women's Freedom: A Critique of Contracts for Human Reproduction," *Signs: Journal of Women in Culture and Society* 18, no. 3 (Spring 1993). I first developed some of the ideas in Chapter 5 in "Lesbian Families: Dilemmas in Grounding Legal Recognition of Parenthood," in Julia E. Hanigsberg and Sara Ruddick, eds., *Mother Troubles: Rethinking Contemporary Maternal Dilemmas* (Boston: Beacon Press, 1999), 178–207.

I am indebted to every one of these individuals, institutions, and publications. Needless to say, none of them bears responsibility for any mistakes I may have made despite their best efforts to save me from error.

Index